"Without a doubt it is one of the most exciting books I have ever read."
—Robert Schuller, author and pastor,
The Crystal Cathedral, Garden Grove, California

"Inspired insights into his personality, . . . how he perceived himself, what really were the dimensions of the Son of Man, his everyday thought life. This "interview" with Jesus will provide your mind with great thoughts and ideas, your heart with renewed compassion, and your soul with fire. It is a book that has been blessed by the Spirit."
—Reid Carpenter, president,
Council of Leadership Foundations

"Once in a while a book comes along that really changes the way you look at a topic you thought you knew. In this book, Andrew Hodges brings a fresh perspective to the person of Jesus. After reading it, you'll understand Jesus in a whole new way."
—Denny Rydberg, president,
Young Life

"Next to the Bible, it's the most important book I've ever read, for it unveils the heart of the most extraordinary man who ever lived far better than the fifty years of sermons I've heard."
—Mike McManus, syndicated religion and ethics columnist

"Seldom has the Incarnation been so intriguingly portrayed. Seldom has the Incarnation been port___ ___ ___ personal terms. A ___nse of intimacy pervades the pages ___ ___tional experience of forgiveness, hea___ ___ made possible in identifying with Je___

—___ ___tianity

"Now we have a thinking Christian—a psychiatrist, no less—who isn't afraid to contemplate the experience of Jesus the man. . . . Only a modern day Gnostic, denying that Jesus is both God and man, will fear to read and applaud this book."

—Bruce Lockerbie, chairman,
PAIDEIA, Inc., Stony Brook, New York

"A fascinating book about the mind of Christ. . . . I highly recommend it to any serious Christian."

—Bruce Larson, author and pastor

"Surprising, challenging, informative, inspirational, and, most of all, extremely theological. . . . The book should inspire readers to grow in their Christian lives and gain strength and direction from God's word, just as Jesus did."

—*CBA Marketplace*

"[Dr. Hodges's] efforts in this volume are fascinating and profoundly interesting. . . ."

—R.C. Sproul, President,
Ligonier Ministries, Orlando, Florida

"This book charms us with mind- and faith-stretching ideas, . . . a helpful new and fresh look at the Incarnation. We won't use it as a basis for a new theology, but the one we already have will be enriched, challenged, and deepened."

—Jay Kesler, chancellor,
Taylor University, Upland, Indiana

"Warm. Loving. Sensitive. Reverent. Delightful. But dangerous—your Jesus will never be the same to you after reading it."

—Curtis B. Moyes, pastor,
Covina, California

"Fascinating writing using a sanctified imagination. . . . I only wish I had written . . . it myself."

—The late Jamie Buckingham, speaker, editor, and author

"Impressive. Hodges has used his imagination and biblical knowledge in a lucid and compelling 'interview' with Jesus."

—Ray Anderson, Professor of Theology and Ministry,
Fuller Seminary, Pasadena, California

"This Bible-based book will be a blessing to untold thousands of people in years to come."

—Landrum P. Leavell, president (retired),
New Orleans Baptist Seminary, New Orleans, Louisiana

"Scripturally based yet so insightful the reading seems inspired. This book will fulfill a special ministry in enabling people to recognize in the example of Christ's humanness their own potential."

—Grace Ketterman, psychiatrist and author

"I was deeply moved by this thoughtful, honest look at the problems Jesus must have had to wrestle with as he came to terms with the fact that he was indeed God on earth veiled in human flesh."

—Victor L. Walter, former Chairman of Practical Theology,
Trinity Divinity School, Deerfield, Illinois

"Dr. Hodges has done a fantastic job in speculating about what Jesus might have said and done during those silent years of His life and work."

—The late Grady Wilson, associate to Billy Graham

". . . A salutary reminder of the humanness of Jesus. We forget that the earliest Christological heresy was the denial, not of Jesus' deity, but of his humanity."

—David K. Lowery, professor (N. T. Literature and Exegesis),
Dallas Theological Seminary, Dallas, Texas

". . . I have learned more about Jesus from Dr. Hodges's depth of perspective as a psychiatrist than from most theologians. . . . It will become a classic Christian book."

—Altus Newell, pastor and former president,
International Theological Seminary, Ruschlikon, Switzerland

A PSYCHIATRIST LOOKS AT CHRIST'S HUMANITY

JESUS:
An Interview Across Time

ANDREW G. HODGES, M.D.

Kregel
Publications

Jesus: An Interview Across Time: A Psychiatrist Looks at Christ's Humanity

© 1986, 2003 by Andrew G. Hodges, M.D.
Second edition

Published by Kregel Publications, a division of Kregel, Inc., P.O. Box 2607, Grand Rapids, MI 49501.

Cover design: John M. Lucas

Library of Congress Cataloging-in-Publication Data
Hodges, Andrew G.
Jesus: an interview across time: a psychiatrist looks at Christ's humanity / by Andrew G. Hodges.
    p. cm.
Originally published: Birmingham, Ala.: Village House Publishers, © 1986.
Includes bibliographical references and index.
1. Jesus Christ—Humanity. 2. Jesus Christ—Psychology. 3. Imaginary conversations. I. Title.
BT218.H63   2003   232.9'03—dc22   2003018318

ISBN 0-8254-2790-8

Printed in the United States of America

2 3 4 5 6 / 09 08 07 06 05

CONTENTS

FOREWORD

BY MICHAEL J. MCMANUS

IMAGINE THAT YOU WERE GIVEN THE opportunity to interview Jesus, the most remarkable human being of all time. What would you ask? What would he say? That is the premise of this book by Andrew G. Hodges, a practicing psychiatrist in Birmingham, Alabama, a man accustomed to interviewing people about their lives, motives, hopes and fears, and dreams.

Originally published in 1986, the book is timeless. The questions are those you or I might ask; the answers are given as if Jesus were sitting beside us, chatting leisurely on a hill in modern Galilee. Thus, he can cite C. S. Lewis or Sigmund Freud as well as give his first impressions of Peter. The answers are hypothetical, of course, a creative interpretation based on Dr. Hodges's idea of what Jesus was like as a person. He gives us an idea of who the man might have been.

Dr. Hodges believes the humanity of Jesus has been neglected. He has creatively fashioned a format in which Jesus answers intimate questions about the details of his life, including some that are not recorded in the Gospels. For example, what would Mary have told Jesus the child about the Incarnation?

> Mother never told me directly who I was as a child. . . . She let my father tell me.
>
> *Joseph?*
>
> No, my father.

You mean your father in heaven! How did he tell you?

My father revealed who I was at just the right time. He was asking for enormous trust and faith from some very special people in order to carry out his plan. . . .

Why didn't God just come out and tell you who you were by coming to see you himself?

That would have changed everything that made my life important. Then I wouldn't really have been human like you. I would know nothing about trusting him, about living by faith. How could I teach you about faith if I hadn't experienced it myself?

Hodges believes that moment of final understanding could have come as the twelve-year-old Jesus questioned the theologians in the temple about the coming Messiah. Thus, Jesus was not omniscient (he veiled his omniscience in his unconscious) but a person whose understanding of his role grew gradually. Certainly, this is plausible. Jesus was able to confirm His growing conviction about Himself by hearing the scribes and Pharisees confirm details about His life that were predicted by Scripture. However, Hodges imagines that as a boy, Jesus was teased for being illegitimate and got into fights.

You told your followers to turn the other cheek.

I did, and I meant it. Always, always try to do that first, but that approach won't work every time. The Scriptures also say, "Love is not easily angered." They don't say that love is never angered. Again, Scripture says, "Love always protects." That includes one's self, as well as one's family and neighbors.

Dr. Hodges assumes that the Father first spoke directly to confirm Jesus' beliefs at his baptism.

The story also draws on those indications in the Gospels of Jesus' rich sense of humor. He imagines the disciples with Jesus around a campfire, laughing at Peter's impersonation of a Pharisee. Jesus is asked whether it is lawful to heal on the Sabbath, so he turns to the man with the withered hand and says, "Let me answer that brilliant, penetrating question in this way: You are healed."

Did you ever wonder what Jesus wrote in the dirt when the adulteress was brought before him, the words that made all of the Pharisees who wanted to stone the woman melt away?

Hodges's Jesus explains: "In the dirt, next to the girl, I began writing the names of each of the Pharisees and a particular sin of which he was ashamed. For example, I wrote, 'Jacob bar Shanda—stealing, age fifteen. Joshua bar Samuel—lying, age thirteen.' Some of them had sinned sexually earlier in their lives, and next to their names I would write the name of the person with whom they had sinned. I hadn't said anything to the Pharisees until I had finished the first six names. I pointed out each name and looked at each man directly. I said, 'The law regarding adultery says that if this woman is found guilty, she is to be stoned to death. He who is without sin, let him cast the first stone.'"

Nearly two billion people claim some identification with Jesus. No other man has had such an influence. It was Jesus who inspired reformers to educate the masses so that they could read the Bible. He caused millions to open hospitals to heal the sick, to seek justice, to open universities to train preachers, to write constitutions guaranteeing freedom of speech, press and religion, to create magnificent art and sculpture. His words have inspired millions to transform their lives from great sin into great service for others.

When we ask who this man was, no one has answered the question better than Dr. Hodges.

MICHAEL J. McMANUS has written a nationally syndicated column, "Ethics & Religion," since 1981. He is a former TIME correspondent, TV producer, and the author of six books, including *Marriage Savers: Helping Your Friends and Family Avoid Divorce* and *50 Practical Ways to Take Your Kids Back from the World*. With his wife, Harriet, McManus heads Marriage Savers, a nonprofit group based in Potomac, Maryland. His marriage-saving work has been featured in reports over network and public television, in news magazines, and newspapers.

PREFACE

IN THE INTRODUCTION TO HER BOOK about the life of Christ, *The Man Born to Be King,* Dorothy Sayers said that it is impossible for an author to do justice dramatically to the story of Jesus Christ, for such is the greatness of his character. One man: human and divine. Yet in the same book, Miss Sayers felt that an author should try to tell the story if one was as honest as he or she knew how to be. Miss Sayers insists that the artist must present the divine Christ as really becoming a man. Specifically, one test that she insisted upon was that theology must meet the demands of drama:

> There is no more searching test of a theology than to submit it to dramatic handling; nothing so glaringly exposes inconsistencies in a character, a story, or a philosophy as to put it on stage and allow it to speak for itself. . . . As I once made a character say in another context, "Right in art is right in practice"; and I can only affirm that at no point have I yet found artistic truth and theological truth at variance.*

Unquestionably, then, according to Miss Sayers's definition of living with the pressures of human existence, I think the Scriptures give evidence that Jesus led, from beginning to end, the most dramatic life that a human being has ever lived. "Tempted in all things as we are," as the epistle to the Hebrews reveals (4:15 NASB). Thus, according to Miss Sayers, since I have written a story about this unique One, I have

---

* Dorothy Sayers, *The Man Born to Be King* (Grand Rapids: Eerdmans, 1943), 3.

attempted the impossible. Although I surely haven't gotten it exactly right, the book is as right as I can make it.

Some will raise questions: Is this work valid? Is it scriptural? Is it consistent with church history? Even those who espouse the doctrine of "fully man, fully God" regarding Christ are not in agreement here as to how the two natures interface. Some people in the church take the position that at times Christ operated out of his human identity and at times out of his divine identity, including his complete omniscience, vacillating at will. The most important and last major church council on this subject (Chalcedon, 451) declared that Christ was "fully God and fully man," two natures, human and divine, in one person; two natures united without mixture or division, confusion or separation. While claiming to be in agreement with Chalcedon, this position of alternation functionally denies Christ's complete humanity.

To help clarify the issue, at any given point when Christ the man is allegedly using his omniscience, ask the question, "Is he now fully human?" Those who assume the alternated natures forget the major victory won at Chalcedon by those who insisted that Christ's humanity was as complete as his deity. Better a formulation that leaves Christ fully functional as a man and, at the same time, retains his deity. Yet there is this dilemma: How did he maintain his deity and become one of us? Above all, we must be most careful with his deity, but we must be equally as zealous to guard his humanity because eternal life rests on it. The Scriptures are crystal clear that only by becoming human could he remove the curse of death on humanity (Heb. 2:14).

In this light, it is crucial to understand the battle that has gone on in the church for the last two hundred years. The church has suffered significant damage within its own ranks from detractors who have repeatedly attacked Christ's full deity because of his humanity. "If indeed he was human, he couldn't have been fully divine," they contend. These thinkers have shaped many of our seminaries and, hence, our pulpits. Never has a clearer answer regarding Christ's humanity been needed from those who maintain his deity. Yet deity is omniscient, omnipotent, and infinite; humanity is finite and ignorant; never the twain shall meet. Or will they?

The last thirty years have witnessed a tremendous expansion in the awareness of the horizons of the human subliminal mind, although this is not yet fully appreciated.* Now, very possibly, we are near the answer to our theological dilemma.

A human being—little, limited humankind—is far more gifted and glorious than anything we have imagined! For a human possesses a subliminal mind that has observed and recorded in remarkable detail every moment of his life, beyond anything a computer or video-camera can do, a subliminal mind that has come to striking individual (separate from the conscious) conclusions based on its observations.

In essence, man has a vast mind, processing incoming information simultaneously on two tracks, conscious and unconscious, with the subliminal track possessing, for the most part, by far the greater abilities. To communicate its observations, this great subliminal mind, as it were, secretly guides a person's ideas, embedding distinct symbolic messages in the conscious communication unbeknownst to him or her consciously. The conscious mind speaks literally; the unconscious mind speaks symbolically. For example, a patient in therapy might consciously feel she is ready to stop but repeatedly talk about people with unfinished business. This is a way to communicate unconscious awareness of the need for further work.

To put it more simply, a person can communicate two separate messages at one time with the same words. Hence, educated or uneducated, every person possesses a brilliant unconscious observer beyond his or her wildest dreams—as the unconscious mind has repeatedly proven to be far more perceptive than our conscious mind.

The psychoanalyst who primarily discovered the vast perceptual ability of this unconscious mind said in amazement as he viewed clearly the unconscious of a patient during a case presentation, "It's like being in the room with an almost omniscient being."**

Now it is, in one sense, only one short step to the Incarnation. By analogy, of course, but a very impressive analogy. If man himself possesses

---

* Andrew G. Hodges, *The Deeper Intelligence* (Nashville: Nelson, 1994).
** From a seminar with Robert Langs, M.D., New York City, 1985.

an "almost omniscient" nature, both knowing and not knowing simultaneously, is it not conceivable that Jesus the man could have possessed Jesus the God at the same time?

Now with our present understanding of the human mind, what once seemed beyond belief is fully possible. Could not the divine Christ have chosen to truly become one of us in such a unique way that maintains the integrity of both natures as well as the unity of one person? Would not the existence of two distinct but united natures and, hence, two distinct but united minds, similar to the way our own conscious and unconscious minds interface, meet fully the stringent criterion of Chalcedon—two natures united without mixture or division, confusion or separation? The theologian J. O. Buswell thought so, interestingly choosing the exact analogy of the conscious and unconscious mind as a picture of the Incarnation. Buswell states,

> It has been shown that there is no contradiction in the statement that the Son [in his human nature], at the time of the Olivet discourse, did not know the day and the hour of his second coming [divine nature], and yet he [in his person] retained, in the Incarnation, all the attributes of his eternal deity [divine nature], including his omniscience [divine nature]. There is no contradiction, I say, because it is a fact that even in human psychology there are different levels of consciousness. It is not a contradiction to say that a person may know something that he does not know. In one sense of the word, he knows it, in the sense of the power of recall. In another sense he does not know it—he does not hold it in his active consciousness. Prior to the Incarnation the eternal second Person [divine nature] of the Trinity chose when he [divine nature] became flesh, to operate in a normal horizon so that he [human nature] might literally have common human experience. Thus, though omniscient, he [divine nature] chose not to have in his active consciousness [human nature] at this time, the knowledge of the day and hour of his return [divine nature].*

---

* J. O. Buswell, *A Systematic Theology of the Christian Religion* (Grand Rapids: Zondervan, 1962–63), 2:406. Brackets used within the quotation are the author's interpretation.

Now we can understand how Christ could have been tempted in all things as a man, and, at the same time, was actively Lord of the universe.

The implications for Christians viewing the Incarnation in this way are significant. While some may initially feel that Christ's veiling his omniscience detracts from him, further reflection reveals that this position would actually make things more difficult for him: for example, not to know consciously which event or temptation was coming next.

Ultimately this makes his life and great accomplishment, the Atonement, much more dramatic and far greater. He then would in truth "wear our shoes." Thus, the crucifixion becomes not just an event endured by a superman, but unquestionably the greatest deed in human history. Furthermore, if Jesus limited his access to his own omniscience and had to learn about himself (as Luke in his gospel makes plain) and his Father just as we do, this exalts the Scriptures even further. Our Lord studied them too. If indeed Jesus Christ himself submitted to the necessity of studying the Scriptures and to their authority, how much more should we?

Even further, what dignity our Lord brings to us as humans if he really chose to step within our boundaries and live life as it should be lived. What compassion for us. What courage he offers us as he himself faced the very worst possible human conditions and rose above them, yet never once denied the pain. In essence, how loved we would be if he truly became one of us and one with us—as loved as the son was by the father. We could love one another in the same way. The beloved could then take the message around the world to the ignorant, the pagan, the poor, the crippled, the homeless, the sick, the prisoners, the rebels, and the outsiders.

As I have pondered the subject of Christ's humanity and deity, I am reminded of a friend who once said, with great feeling, that the crucifixion would have meaning to him only if he knew that Christ thought of him when he hung on the cross. Before I understood what I now know about the human mind, I wondered how it could be possible for a man to think of every individual in the world in one afternoon, particularly a man who was engulfed by unspeakable pain. As a physician I had seen many people in great pain. In those moments they could think of little else but the pain. Yet I realized that my friend was saying something profound, seeking in reverent anguish personal recognition from a personal God at the moment of crucifixion.

Now, some years later, I understand. I believe that Christ the man, in his human conscious mind, was engulfed by pain and suffering. Simultaneously, in his divine unconscious mind, Christ the all-knowing God thought of every single person for whom he was making this sacrifice. In pain on the cross, he thought of you and me, and I am convinced that he will tell us that one day, face to face.

INTRODUCTION

J OHN, THE ONE CALLED "THE BAPTIST," held me under the water for a long time, until my whole body was in pain from the lack of oxygen. John wanted me to feel that pain—it was so much like death—to let me know that he understood what this was costing me, that one day I would lie in a grave. Finally, he brought me up out of the water. I was gasping for air, and he just stood there with his hand on me. It was a strong hand. After several seconds I caught my breath, and then it happened. I heard my father's voice for the first time: "This is my beloved son in whom I am well pleased." I can still hear that rich, majestic voice. Heaven had opened. The door was no longer shut. I had heard my own father's voice at last. I had waited thirty years, and the impact on me was startling. All those years of preparation, of making sure, of waiting, of living on his written words, of keeping the faith—it had been validated firsthand. For days afterward his voice kept coming back to me: "This is my beloved son." It was all I could think about.

It was such an overpowering experience that I wanted to be alone to savor it. I almost had to be alone to contain it. Before I went out into the world, I also wanted as intense an awareness of him as possible. I knew from experience that the way to heighten my sense of him was to be totally alone with him and to fast. I had to go over with him what I was to do and what I was to say. That knowledge could come only by waiting before him. I felt that my father was saying, "Before you go out into the world, go over my words one more time. Live on them. Fast for forty days to test yourself."

So I did. He led me every step of the way. For forty days I wanted almost continually to eat. But I didn't.

Was this fast an encouraging time for you?

Fasting is a lot like seeing in the dark. At first, everything is black, and all you can think about is pain and food. After a while, you begin to "see" things, to perceive things that you couldn't at first.

What became clearer for you?

Everything depended on me. Salvation by me—and me alone. No one else could please God ultimately. No matter how hard they had tried, they had all failed and always would. But I would please him. He had promised—I was his son.

His spirit was there in a new way. It was even more alive. You know how someone's personality can affect you when they are right there beside you, talking. You can feel their spirit, their energy. I couldn't see him, but I could feel him. His words had never been more alive. I was completely one with him, and now I knew that my words would be his words. Everything I would say would have just as much authority as if he said it. Even better yet, he would be saying it through me when I spoke. At this particular time in the wilderness I was exuberant. God had never been closer. He was right there beside me.

I had just finished the forty-day fast when Satan surprised me. As I was starting back to town, I came around a boulder, and suddenly a man appeared. He was a little on the short side, had a winsome smile, and seemed to be exceptionally gentle and kind. After a few minutes with him, I decided that he was perhaps the most striking person I had ever met. He radiated warmth. We began talking, and it was obvious that he knew what I had been doing. As time went on, I began to think that this was perhaps one of my father's ways of revealing himself to me. After all, God had just spoken to me for the first time, and in the Old Testament angels had often appeared to various men.

I halfheartedly wondered if this was a trick, but he was the kind of person who dispelled doubt and put you at ease. Besides, I hadn't talked to another human being for forty days. We both laughed when he said, "I don't suppose you are hungry?" He volunteered, "I have been in heaven with your father, and I have come to talk to you. God wants you to use your power. He doesn't want you to suffer any longer. Go ahead. Use the power he's given you. You are hungry." In an encouraging way, he said, "If you are the son of God, turn those stones into bread." Things were really moving fast for me at this point. Was God, my father, pushing me to trust him more?

Had something like this actually happened at the temptation of Jesus—the Son of God, the Holy One, God Incarnate, the worker of miracles? Was he truly tested? Did he actually become a man with all of man's limitations?

I wondered how Christ himself would answer these questions if he spoke to us about it. I went over the record of his life again. As I did so as a psychiatrist specializing in the study of indirect verbal messages, the Scriptures astounded me, not only by their direct communications, but also by their consistently clear, indirect, encoded messages. Thus, I came to the conclusion that the Scriptures give many hidden clues to Christ's human development and the so-called "missing years."

The Scriptures themselves support the idea that there is much more in them about Christ than we realize. As Psalm 40 states prophetically about the Messiah, "Lo, in the volume of the book it is written of me" (v. 7).

Knowing that our Lord himself had studied the Old Testament Scriptures, and continuing to be amazed at the vastness of the Scriptures myself, I looked at the Gospel accounts of Jesus' life afresh. The personality of Jesus emerged in a new way, a personality that continually surprised me as I was freed from my preconceptions. How complex this man was. Demanding, but humble; tender when I expected anger; angry when I expected tenderness; almost always doing the unexpected. The courage . . . the authority . . . the brilliance. He predated by two thousand years what, in my opinion, remains the most important discovery in my field. He understood clearly the workings of the unconscious mind.

As I looked at the man and understood the context in which he lived out his life, I stood in awe. As a psychiatrist I have spent numerous hours listening to human beings. I have interviewed more than one person who thought he or she was the Messiah. This man Jesus reminded me of none of those. As Christ's personality became clearer to me, and as I listened to his powerful words speaking across the centuries, I could almost hear his answers to my questions echoing in my mind. That is how the story begins.

Much of the book is speculation, however biblically based, and obviously it is colored by my own personality, as any author's book would be. Therefore, I would admonish you to read the Scriptures, to separate fact from fiction, to "check it out."

Imagine that Jesus of Nazareth, Son of God, Son of Man, is telling his story. The One of whom it was said, "All the armies that ever marched, all the navies that ever sailed, all the parliaments that ever sat, all the kings that ever reigned, put together, have not affected the life of man on this earth as much as that one solitary life."

He is the one on whom our calendar is hinged, the one whom the demagogues and dictators of planet Earth have not been able to banish, the one who has promised to return "in power and great glory."

Imagine that this man has agreed to talk about how he came to his unique position in history, how he came to realize for himself who he really was, and what his thirty-three years on this earth were like.

CHAPTER ONE

Preparation and Revelation

In the Beginning

God does not seem to be very popular these days.

Oh? I never had any trouble finding a great many people who were interested in God. In fact, I found people who would endure great hardships, walk miles, go without food, and actually knock your door down to learn about God if you presented him as he is. If God is not very popular today, it is not his fault. It is the people who tell his story. They are using the wrong version.

Which version is that?

The boring version.

I have always wondered how a story about someone who claims to be God and who acts like God could be boring. Your story is about healing the sick, raising the dead, walking on water, taking on the establishment, allowing himself to be murdered, and finally, coming back from the dead, returning to power, and spreading your people to every culture. How could that be boring?

People who have lost the story's power in their own lives tell it over and over, until it is as stale as they are. It is easy to forget that this story is by the same creator who brings you the Grand Canyon, the Alps, Niagara Falls, and the Atlantic and Pacific Oceans, as well as the entire human race!

Let's get to your story. As I was reading about you recently, I came across the time you were speaking to a crowd, and you told them, "I am the Light of the world." It made me wonder. Did an angel dramatically appear to you one day with an orchestra and bright lights and say, "You are God's son," or did you always know who you were?

Neither. An angel did appear to my mother without the orchestra, but I never heard my father's voice aloud or saw an angel until I was thirty. Of course, on the night of my birth some very special things happened. There was a very bright star in the East. Angels told some shepherds in Bethlehem about me. Wise men began a journey from the East to honor me with precious gifts. But it was a long time before I knew about those events and my unique relationship with God, although my mother and father knew.

Then how did you find out that you were the chosen one, the Messiah? Did your mother tell you?

My mother would say such things as, "You are a very special child. One day when you get older, you will realize you were sent to serve God in a special way." But a lot of Jewish mothers say those things. As a young boy, I remember asking her, "How did you decide to name me Jesus?" She, as if joking, always gave me the same answer: "An angel came down from heaven and gave us your name."

Which he did.

Exactly. But Mother never told me directly who I was as a child. Think about it. You are a mother, and you are going to tell your child that he is not altogether your son, but is God's only son—and that he has been appointed, despite all his humble surroundings, to be the

Messiah, the savior of the world! That's an unbelievable story to tell your child.

You've given birth to the most important person who's ever lived. How do you tell your son that fact without all the neighbors finding out and thinking you're a heretic or insane? Your mother could have been killed for telling what she knew to be true.

She would have been killed. So my mother did a very smart thing. She let my father tell me.

Joseph?

No, my father.

You mean your father in heaven! How did he tell you?

My father revealed who I was at just the right time. He was asking for enormous trust and faith from some very special people in order to carry out his plan. He made sure that none of us were alone in this plan by making it a "family matter." He first disclosed my coming to the prophets who came before me. Then, when the time was approaching, he told my mother and her cousin Elizabeth, older by many years, what was going to happen. He said that each of them would have a unique son.

The circumstances were amazingly similar. Both women were childless. Both were told by angels that they would bear children miraculously. First Elizabeth, who was so old that she was postmenopausal, was informed that she would bring forth a child. Then six months later my mother Mary, while still a virgin, was told that she was to have a baby without any help from a man.

I had never realized the striking similarities.

Both women were to have sons. Angels told both what to name their sons. Both were told what their sons would do. Even the sons had much in common, for they were long awaited and prophesied. Together these two men would turn the world toward God. One was a great prophet who would go before the other, serving him by announcing to the world that a great light had come into its midst. That prophet was my cousin, John, known as the Baptist.

And the other was the Messiah, the savior of the world. That's you?

Yes.

Why do you think it was such a sensitive thing to do to keep it all in the family?

It's difficult to believe that you're a miracle or part of one. My father knew that doubts could come to all of us. Could this really be true? When the doubts came, all we had to do was look at our own family, people we could immediately trust, and there were the miracles confirming the story. He also mentioned us in the Scriptures so that everyone could know who we were. In fact, that's how my father told me who I was. He left me written messages in the Scriptures that he confirmed to me with "circumstances."

Why didn't God just come out and tell you who you were by coming to see you himself?

That would have changed everything that made my life important. Then I wouldn't really have been human like you. I would know nothing about trusting him, about living by faith. How could I teach you about faith if I hadn't experienced it myself?

Still, the Scriptures seem a strange way for God to communicate, particularly with his only son.

On the contrary, the Scriptures were a brilliant idea. My father was a genius in finding a way to communicate with all people everywhere over thousands of years. A book was the only way to communicate to people without a radio or television. It was unforgettable, unchanging, and yet still alive—just as he was. He created that communication form so that a person could always check on what he had just said.

To communicate in a way that is fresh moment after moment to whoever listens and then to confirm a message with fulfilled prophecy—that's an astounding idea! He foretold the future in Scripture, and it came to pass just as he predicted. I found myself in the middle of the Psalms and elsewhere in Scripture.

Why did you trust his words?

Because they were true and because I realized ultimately they were my father's words. It would have been harder not to believe them. All around me was the history Scripture talked about. I could see Jacob's well, Solomon's partially rebuilt temple, Jerusalem with her huge walls and gates, the same roads that King David had walked. David's city was there, Bethlehem, where I was born. The Jordan River my people crossed to get into the promised land—the very land in which I lived—was evident. Despite what some of your modern thinkers say, I think my ancestors were intelligent enough to recognize a miracle when it occurred. Moses, who wrote the first books of the Bible, was basically an honest man and an accurate reporter.

The reputations of many good men rest on these words. Besides Moses, look at who else wrote part of this book: Joshua, who replaced Moses; Samuel, the prophet who anointed David; David the shepherd king; his son Solomon; prophets such as Isaiah and Jeremiah. All of these men were contributors to the Old Testament, which was the only part of the Scriptures that I had in my day. After I came along, I was quoted accurately in what is known as the New Testament by three of my disciples: Matthew, Peter, and John, along with a physician by the name of Luke.* Later, "on their own," Peter wrote two more books

---

* Because the book of Mark contains so much personal information about him, Peter is considered the disciple who provided most of the information and material for the book. It was written by a younger disciple of Christ, John Mark, who was not in the original twelve. Peter is thought to have been John Mark's mentor, and the book of Mark is commonly considered Peter's gospel.

[1 Peter and 2 Peter], and John wrote four more [1, 2, and 3 John and Revelation], and a man named Paul wrote about thirteen books. Their writings constitute most of the New Testament. You have the word of some honest men on how things happened, besides having my father's word. Another reason these words seemed so authentic was that they never covered up for their "heroes"—they reported everything just as it happened. Noah drank too much at times. Moses, David, and Paul were murderers. Abraham slept with his wife's servant. Jacob was a swindler.

Did you ever consider that these words might just be myths?

I considered it, but accurate, fulfilled prophecies destroy myths. They become facts. Facts are very convincing, particularly when you happen to be one of them.

When you read the prophecies about the Messiah—prophecies which had been there for centuries—did you begin to realize that you were the one who fit all those descriptions, particularly when you were told where the Messiah would be born—Bethlehem—where he would come from—Galilee—and which of the twelve tribes of Israel he would come from—Judah?

At first it was the furthest thing from my mind. Remember, my mother became pregnant with me during her engagement and then left town to go and tell her cousin Elizabeth. When she finally returned to Nazareth to be married, she was about three months pregnant. Nazareth was no different from any other small town. It didn't take the neighbors long to start the rumors flying. They continued my entire life.

Why do you think God arranged the circumstances in such a way that your mother and Joseph would have to endure such great suffering?

First of all, he was making a clear statement that I was virgin born, and, characteristically, he went to a great deal of trouble to make things very plain. What people thought initially about my mother was not his first concern.

Why do you think he chose Mary to be your mother?

Because of her faith and her courage. Imagine the courage it took for her to wait three months at her cousin's house. All that time she was not married, and realized that each passing day would only make the rumors about her "illegitimate child" worse. Really, she didn't know if she was to be married at all, because she didn't know what her fiancé Joseph would think about the situation. And, too, the angel Gabriel had promised her only a son. He hadn't promised her a husband!

Why do you think Mary stayed at Elizabeth's so long, then? Why didn't she return to Nazareth sooner and take care of business?

She wanted to be present at the birth of John. That was enormously comforting to her. I'm sure there were other reasons besides that one that led my mother to wait three months, but whatever they were, you can be sure she felt it was God's will. She was a woman of real faith. You know, God always pushes us to increase our faith. At the same time, in the middle of our trials, he repeatedly encourages us. At that time, my mother's cousin Elizabeth paid her the supreme compliment. She said,

> You are favored by God above all women, and your child is destined for God's mightiest praise. What an honor this is that the mother of my Lord should visit me. When you came in and greeted me, the instant I heard your voice, my baby moved in me for joy! You believed that God would do what he said; that is why he has given you this wonderful blessing.[1]

That's a great tribute.

By causing my mother to wait three months after she was pregnant to get married, my father was teaching me from the beginning of my life through the tough circumstances of my birth that I was to be identified with the sinners and unfortunates of the world. How many people have been born into circumstances that they would have liked to change? I can identify with the poor, the illegitimate, the crippled, and those with the "different colored" skin. How many people because of their sin have gotten themselves into circumstances filled with suffering which they later sincerely regretted having done? Although I was sinless, I was to be one with all of them in all of their pain. More than that, from the first second in my mother's womb, my father was making known to me my role in this world. I was to be abused so that my people could be free. I was to be illegitimate so that they might be legitimate. My father was preparing me to learn how to take suffering. When I got older I heard the taunts of some of my peers: "He doesn't know who his father is. He doesn't know who his father is."

That must have hurt.

I also caught the ridicule of the adults. Between my house and the synagogue were the town gate, where the businessmen gathered, and the market, where much of the wine was drunk by the idlers lounging around. Occasionally as I walked to the synagogue, I would hear the snide comments of some of the men gathered at the gate, but the men at what you would call the "bar" were the worst. They made up a song about me in which they would guess who my father was and name five or six despicable characters. It became a game each day to add another name to the list, and then they would sing the same chorus and finally all of them would laugh. Every day there was that thought: "I'm a bastard." That's who they were telling me I was.

It got so bad that my half-brothers became ashamed of me and harassed me, too. One of them, James, was later to write a New Testament book in which he addressed hypocrisy and true religion as opposed to false religion. He had a great deal to say about the true test of brotherly love, about looking past what people appeared to be on the surface. He had even more to say about how vicious the tongue can be and how hard a person must work to control it. After all was said and done, my brother learned well. He never forgot how he had treated me and how human beings deceive themselves.

Another one of my brothers who harassed me was Jude, who also later wrote a New Testament book. As you might have guessed, Jude wrote about heretics and those who lack faith.

It's amazing to me how many people mentioned in the New Testament Scriptures were once declared enemies of yours. They included people from all walks of life—the Pharisees, Nicodemus, the corrupt tax collectors, Zacchaeus and Matthew, the prostitute, Mary Magdalene, and the self-righteous Paul. Down through the ages in the history of the Christian church, the story is the same—Augustine had been a pagan womanizer. John Newton, the preacher and songwriter who wrote "Amazing Grace," had been a hardened slave-trader. But you and your father specialized in winning these kinds of people over to your side.

If you're a follower of mine, you were once my enemy.

The Early Years

Years later, didn't the Pharisees use that rumor about your illegitimacy and accuse you of being illegitimate when you said that you were God?

They did. But it didn't bother me nearly as much as before. When you're a little boy ten years old, you know how much you love your mother—particularly if you've got a good one, and I had one of the best. They were calling her names, and I was crushed. More than anything else, I wanted to be devoted to God and to serve him—for a true Jew there is no higher calling—but I felt like the worst sinner. Then I had the horrible thought that my mother must have been ashamed of me when I was born.

How did you handle your suffering?

I went to God. I didn't want to talk to my mother or my father Joseph about it right then. I wondered why God would allow this humiliation. Could he help me? Would he help me? I knew that David as a young shepherd boy alone tending his sheep had developed an enormous sensitivity to God and had written many of the psalms. I thought that if David could find help from God, I could too. So many times, on the verge of tears, I prayed to him and I read his Scriptures, particularly the psalms.

You mean at first you read the Scriptures to find comfort and not to find out about the Messiah?

I rather "accidentally" found out who I was. There was a lot of talk about the Messiah because we were an oppressed people. God had promised us a deliverer. As a Jew I was interested in the Messiah and longed for him, but I didn't see how he particularly related to me.

What did you read in this holy book that helped you?

One of my two favorite characters in the Old Testament was Joseph. As a young boy, he was betrayed by his older brothers and eventually sold into slavery in a foreign land, Egypt. Totally alone except for God, Joseph spent many years as a slave, suffering one setback after another. But he always remained faithful to Jehovah God. God didn't forget about him, and one day, overnight, God made him second in command to the Pharaoh in Egypt—one of the most powerful kingdoms of that time. It was an absolute miracle—a foreigner becoming prime minister. There, Joseph reigned for many years until his death.

I thought many times about Joseph, and I knew he must have been close to my age when he was kidnapped. I knew how alone he must have felt, how desperately he needed God and clung to him and held on for years. Somehow, if Joseph could do it, I could.

So through this "old book," Joseph became a very real person to you?

There are all kinds of real people in the book just waiting to meet people in similar circumstances. My second favorite character was

David. Around the age of twelve, David became a national hero. This young shepherd boy challenged the giant Goliath, leader of Israel's enemy, face to face. Goliath was terrorizing Israel. Not one Israeli would stand up to him. Goliath was ten feet tall and would come down in the valley between the two enemy camps every day and dare anyone from Israel to fight him.

When David arrived on the scene to bring food to his older brothers, he couldn't believe anyone was talking this way to Israel when the Lord Almighty was their God. To David, Goliath was spitting in God's face! David became incensed and volunteered on the spot to fight Goliath in the name of Jehovah.

No one wanted him to go out, but David insisted. He took his slingshot, stopped at a brook, picked up five stones, and went after the huge warrior who was adorned in full armor. In the name of Jehovah, David charged him, dodged the profane giant's spear, and hit him directly between the eyes with his first and only shot, knocking him unconscious. With the giant's own sword he then cut off Goliath's head and carried it around all day. He was fearless! This happened right after God promised David that one day he would be the king of Israel. But God made David wait about eighteen years to be king. During the latter part of those years, he lived in a barren wilderness, sleeping in caves as he ran from King Saul, who didn't want David to be king. As he was pursued, David had opportunities to kill King Saul and to assume his throne, but he chose not to. He was waiting for God to give it to him.

What I began to see from the stories of Joseph and David was that "great men" suffer, many of them when they are young. It was the suffering that enabled God to come to the rescue, and that's how they came to love him. What God was going to do for me I didn't know, but I knew he would help me. By the way, David's writings in the Psalms touched me as much as the story of David's life.

Could you give me an example?

One night I had come to my lowest point. I didn't think I could take the drunkards singing that song about me one more time. My zeal for God had burned hot within me. Now I felt utterly despised. My very presence was a stumbling block to those around me. I was convinced that I was a terrible sinner to deserve such a birth. As a sign of my mourning, I began to wear sackcloth, but that seemed only to make things worse by leading to more ridicule.

How could you feel guilty if you were God?

Just because I was God didn't mean that I couldn't come to the wrong conclusions as I grew up. I had to learn too. I had a sensitive conscience, and I felt as if I had done something terribly wrong. You can imagine the relief I experienced when I read Psalm 69. There was a perfect description of me:

> Shame covers my face. I am a stranger to my brothers, an alien to my own mother's sons. . . . When I weep and fast, I must endure scorn; when I put on sackcloth, people make sport of me. Those who sit at the gate mock me, and I am the song of the drunkards.[2]

David had been through the same thing I had. I didn't know at the time that Psalm 69 was a prophecy, but I knew God wanted me to read that particular psalm on that particular night. You have to experience God's use of the Scriptures in that way to see how sensitive he is. That night when I was ten years old, I began to understand that he knew everything about me, even though it took me years to appreciate just how well. Later on, I discovered that many experiences I was to have in the future had already been written in the Scriptures so that I would know who I was. My father was communicating with me and preparing me. Already, I was learning how to suffer.

I learned something else from the experience. Sometimes you have to wrestle to find out which Scriptures are messages from God to you for a particular time. When I was ten, Psalm 23 wasn't as comforting as Psalm 69, which went straight to my heart.

Life in the Family

I can't believe your mother and father watched you suffer at such a young age and never told you who you were.

They didn't know it was going on until my brothers started giving me trouble. Of course they had known that I would hear rumors about my birth. They understood to a significant degree that, for some reason, my real father must have wanted me to face ridicule at an early age. As my mother later told me, when I was a very young child of four or five, she and Joseph had talked about how they were going to handle it when I found out about my birth. Joseph in particular anticipated that I probably wouldn't find out in the kindest of ways, and he debated over whether they should say to me: "Something might come up about your birth." Yet, both my mother and father had experienced comparable pain because of the circumstances. They both understood that God intended that they suffer this pain.

They didn't understand entirely the purpose of this pain, which they were learning how to handle so that they could teach me. They did understand in some way that God was telling them through the turmoil that surrounded my early life that my life was not going to be easy. The rumors about their marriage, the long journey they had had to make when my mother was eight and one-half months pregnant, the threat on my life by Herod when I was only one year old, and the sudden trip to live in a foreign land for two years: all of these things made them realize that God had his hand in these events.

Joseph reminded my mother that the old man Simeon had confirmed when I was eight days old that I would go through much suffering. Simeon blessed them but also told Mary: "A sword shall pierce your soul, for this child shall be rejected by many in Israel, and this to their undoing. But he will be the greatest joy of many others."[3]

My mother preferred to cling to the words of her cousin, Elizabeth, and to the words of the angel who told her she was pregnant with her son, "He shall be very great, and shall be called the Son of God. And the Lord God shall give him the throne of his ancestor, David. And he shall reign over Israel forever; his kingdom shall never end!"[4]

She had to cling to these words emotionally to get through her pregnancy. She had been upset by what Simeon had said and wanted to push it out of her mind. She didn't want her son to suffer.

Both had a great respect for God's timing and sovereignty, a real sense of "God is setting the stage." They believed strongly that he should be the one to tell me who I was. After all, he was my father, and he had been able to communicate with them. Because of this, Joseph decided that they would say nothing directly to me about my birth during my early years. Instead, he and my mother would continue to let God provide the circumstances, and they would be available to me whenever I needed them.

When did you realize there was more in the Scriptures about you, and that you were the Messiah?

In reading the Scriptures I had come across the prophecies that the Messiah would be born in the City of David, Bethlehem, that he would be from Galilee, and that he would come out of the tribe of Judah. It was interesting to me that the Messiah and I would be born in the same place, from the same tribe, and the "same neighborhood." I thought it was nothing more than coincidence. A short time later I came across another prophecy that stated that the Messiah would come out of Egypt. That struck me as strange: An Israelite to be born in Bethlehem and from Galilee? How could he also be from Egypt?

A week later—you'll see how God, the master director, blends in circumstances—my mother was sorting out the contents of an old trunk and there on the floor was a little cloth I had never seen before with an Egyptian design on it. I asked her, "Where did we get this?" and she said, "In Egypt."

"In Egypt!" I stammered. She told me that she and my father had not wanted to frighten me, but just after I was born was a dangerous time for Jewish boys. Herod, the Roman Governor, had heard that the Messiah had been born and was executing all male children two years old and younger. She and Joseph had moved to Egypt to be safe for a couple of years.

Then I remembered something—huge faces of stone, rising from the ground, so overwhelming that they were frightening. I could see them in my mind just standing there surrounded by a barren land. Was it a dream? It seemed so real. Where had I seen them, those faces?

My mother saw my mind had wandered, and asked what I was thinking. I told her what was coming to mind and she said, "Those are the Great Pyramids of Egypt. We walked right by them on our journey. You saw them. You were fascinated by them and kept pointing to them. I remember passing by them again as we were leaving Egypt, and your father and I talked about how much you had grown between the time we arrived in Egypt and when we left. You had just turned one on the first occasion that we saw them. When we left Egypt, you were nearly three years old."

Your mother didn't tell you any more?

Not at that time. She seemed to be waiting for me. I didn't ask, but I surely did ask God! He seemed to be leading me, and I wanted to find out from him. Next, I came across a prophecy in the seventh chapter of Isaiah that said the Messiah would be born of a virgin. The whole issue of my birth was on my mind and that caught my attention. I had already figured out that I was born less than nine months after my parents married. Naturally, I was hoping for an explanation. Reading that Scripture was the first time I had the thought that I might be the Messiah. I was almost embarrassed.

It seemed preposterous, but I kept reading. Certain memories began to come back. Years before, when John the Baptist's mother and father had been visiting us, I remembered their whispering, thinking I was asleep in the next room:

"Does he know how he got here yet?"

"I wouldn't have believed it either if John's birth hadn't been so miraculous."

"Those gifts. Have you shown them to him yet?"

"No, Joseph thinks we should wait for the right time."

What gifts? What were they talking about? Who were the three wealthy men in their beautiful robes with their caravan, who just happened to be passing by Bethlehem the night I was born, the ones my parents kept mentioning from time to time? Why would they stop and speak to a poor Jewish family?

What did you think about the Messiah as you read these prophecies?

The more I read, two things became clear. First, there was more in the Scriptures about the Messiah than people realized. Second, he was to be a great deal more important than the Jews were aware. They naturally wanted immediate deliverance from the Romans, but the Scriptures spoke of the Messiah as being the savior to the whole world and reigning over it. Something else puzzled me—something which everyone seemed to ignore. Not only was the Messiah to reign, but also to suffer. It was as if the Scriptures were talking about two men.

Another ignored prophecy was that he would be a plain man, and not striking in appearance—somewhat homely and certainly not handsome. I had no problem fitting that role and, once again, this was God's pattern. He always seemed to choose seemingly insignificant men for great tasks.

It occurred to me that God, if he operated the way he usually did, would fool everybody when he picked the Messiah, just as he did when he chose David to be the king of Israel. The prophet Samuel had gone with instructions from God to go to the house of Jesse, David's father, where God would select one of Jesse's sons to be the next king of Israel. After the seventh and final brother had been presented, Samuel, almost in desperation, asked, "Are you sure there is not another son?"

They were all taken aback and told him, "Well, there is our little brother who is out in the fields with the sheep—he is very dirty and smells bad. All he does is play his harp. But if you really want to see him we can go get him."

His family forgot about him, but God didn't.

As you know, that little neglected shepherd boy became the greatest warrior and king in Israel's history. Just the mention of his name put the fear of Almighty God into Israel's enemies.

You often referred to yourself as the good shepherd. Did you identify strongly with David?

More than that, David's story was my story. It was a message to me from my father. The Scriptures made a close connection between David and the Messiah. They would both come from the same tribe, Judah. The Messiah would be a direct descendant of David. As the Scriptures said, "I will not lie unto David. His seed shall endure for ever."[5]

David was just a shepherd, and I was just a carpenter. Both of us were common laborers. Looking back, God was saying to me: "Often when I am talking about David, I am talking about you."

You seemed to have comprehended a great deal for a young boy.

Remember, the Bible was our "television." These biblical characters were very real and I "went to school" every day from age five on to learn the Scriptures. School was demanding.

So you were coming more and more to the realization that you were the Messiah?

It came slowly, very slowly. It was an almost unbelievable thought, but I kept coming across these prophecies such as in Psalm 72, which said that the son of David who will reign as king will have gifts brought to him by men from far away. Did that explain those gifts? My mother had said those wealthy men who visited me had been from foreign lands. Then there was another story in the Scriptures that intrigued me. David's son, Solomon, who succeeded him as king, had become world famous. Great rulers in other lands came long distances to bring gifts because of his greatness. Was God saying to me in another way, "Just so you don't miss it, I am repeating myself"? "The true king of Israel, the son of David, will have gifts brought to him from far away lands."[6]

As I began to hear the messages and to see what no one else had seen, it frightened me. I asked myself, "Do I understand what I think I do?" Once again, there was the prophecy about the Messiah in Isaiah: "The Spirit of the Lord will rest on him, the spirit of wisdom and understanding, the spirit of counsel and strength, the spirit of knowledge and the fear of the Lord."[7]

I thought that was the reason I understood so much. He had given me special understanding.

It was his wisdom, his understanding. So Solomon was a picture of you, too?

God was saying it directly and indirectly to make it clear. "Don't be surprised; I intended for you to have great understanding."

It seems strange that your father communicates in a hidden, indirect form. Didn't that bother you? Some people say you can read things into the Bible that aren't there.

Don't you see that the two levels of communication tend to validate each other and serve as a checkpoint? We all communicate indirectly every day. My father is a genius at indirect communication, but he always starts out directly so that there is no doubt about the indirect messages: "In the beginning, I created the heavens and the earth." That's direct. Certainly, a human follower of mine has to be very careful about what he or she is reading into the Scriptures on both levels. The indirect only confirms the direct. It never contradicts.

The greater danger is that antagonists of mine seek to deny the truth of both the direct and the indirect words of Scripture. That even goes back to Satan in the garden of Eden. After my father had specifically told Adam and Eve not to eat the fruit of one particular tree, Satan approached them, saying, "Did God really say not to eat the fruit of that tree?" That was a direct lie and an attack on the truth.

What else happened as you read the Scriptures?

As I was in the process of discovering who I was, there was something else going on inside me. I began to love God, his counsel and his ways. He actually "became" my father. He comforted me many times with the Scriptures, particularly the Psalms. He loved me with these words; he taught me with them. When I was suffering tremendous abuse he lifted me above it with the Scriptures. I learned not to retaliate but to turn the other cheek, and from that I gained great respect from my fellowmen.

I was growing "in wisdom and in stature, and in favor with God and man." Because I had said nothing when the taunts were hurled my way, the "good" men in town, after watching how I handled what I was going through, silenced the songs at the bar and the town gate. More than ever I had a zeal to do what God wanted. If it meant being a carpenter like my father Joseph, a teacher, or the Messiah, I would do whatever he wanted.

Then, shortly before my thirteenth birthday, which was right after Passover . . .

Wait. Passover is in the spring. I thought your birthday was in December.

To undercut a pagan Roman celebration and to draw attention to me, fourth-century Christians set the date of my birth. But I was born in the spring.

As I was saying, at twelve, I came across a well-known prophecy pointing out that immediately before the Messiah came there would be a forerunner, "a voice crying in the wilderness."

I rested comfortably in that, knowing that a prophet would appear prior to the Messiah's coming to announce to the world who the Messiah was. It didn't depend on just one person who thought that he himself was the Messiah.

Did you know much about John the Baptist at that point?

One evening a short time later, my parents spoke to me alone and told me that they had something important to tell me. They thought I was now old enough to know about my cousin, John, since I would soon legally be a man and since I would soon attend my first Passover in Jerusalem. They told me how an angel had appeared to John's father, Zacharias, telling him that he and his wife, Elizabeth, were miraculously going to have a child in their old age. This son would be the prophet who would precede the Messiah and announce to the world his coming. When they finished, they asked me not to tell anyone.

That's as close as they ever came to telling you directly who you were?

What they had told me made my head spin. It was another piece of the puzzle. The forerunner of the Messiah was alive, and that meant the Messiah was alive or soon would be. Now I had a chance to go to the temple in Jerusalem where all the scholars were. I had a great many questions. I knew that if I were the Messiah, confirmation would come in some way through the Scriptures and scholars. I couldn't wait to get there.

Journey to the Temple

So you journeyed to Jerusalem. That was the Passover the Scriptures talk about when you spent the whole week asking the scribes questions.

God's timing is superb. I was on the threshold of Jewish adulthood. My bar mitzvah was not far away, if everything went well. As all devout Jewish boys, I had to appear before the teachers of the Law in Jerusalem before I could be declared a man. There I would be examined regarding the Law and the Scriptures to determine whether I had come to a true understanding of God. Also, quite naturally, I began to wonder what was expected of one when he was "a man." Jerusalem was a seven-day journey, and I had a great deal to think about. During the entire journey there, one part of me was thinking, "This is preposterous; you're just a boy from Nazareth. Look at you—just one among thousands going to the holy city—and you think you could be the chosen one, above all these people?" At the same time, it was my first

Passover, and I looked forward to seeing Jerusalem, where David had reigned, the city everyone always talked about—Jerusalem, the heart of Judaism, the heart of our nation, the site of the temple where God met his people.

Several times on that journey one of my parents would tell me, "This is the same road you rode on twelve years ago, on that donkey when you were growing in your mother's womb." Little did I understand at that time that I would ride down this same road on yet another donkey on a day that would eventually come to be known as Palm Sunday.

We walked for seven long days with thousands of other Jews. We sang with them over and over again the "Pilgrim Psalms." Those are the fifteen psalms that come immediately after colossal Psalm 119, the longest psalm in the Scriptures, the psalm that exalts like no other the fact that the Scriptures are the very words of God. Time after time in the Pilgrim Psalms, the people cry out for deliverance. Finally, in Psalm 132 comes the promise: "The Lord swore an oath to David, a sure oath that he will not revoke: One of your own descendents I will place on your throne . . . for ever and ever."[8] On this, the first trip to Jerusalem that I could remember, I was faced again and again with God's great promise to David.

As his promise resounded through the crowds in the Psalms, the thought went through my mind, "Was it possible that in this caravan of Jews, hundreds of years after the promise of a Messiah, God was now fulfilling his words to David?" Every time I heard that promise sung, it seemed to get louder and louder. So much was going on inside me.

My mother and father had told me that when the hills around Jerusalem first came into view, the people would immediately begin singing Psalm 121, and they did: "I will lift up mine eyes unto the hills, from whence cometh my help. My help cometh from the Lord, which made heaven and earth."[9]

I felt as if I walked back through history. Finally I was seeing Jerusalem. It was the most striking city in the entire world, a city built on layered mountains. Although Nazareth was to the north, to get into

Jerusalem we had to wind around the highest mountain in the region, the Mount of Olives, to enter Jerusalem from the south. Because the mountain was so high, the view of Jerusalem from that direction was completely blocked until you were almost upon it. As we came toward the top of the Mount of Olives, around a west bend there for the first time we saw Jerusalem. The first thing I could see on the west side of the city was Mount Zion, the Zion of the prophets. Sitting on top of it was Herod's palace—the site where David's palace had previously stood.

In my view of the rest of Jerusalem, everything to the east was blocked by the Mount of Olives. After our first glimpse of the city had momentarily disappeared I was overcome by a burst of indescribable reverence and anticipation as we sang the Pilgrim Psalms while climbing that last hill. Suddenly the whole city came into view. At the top of the magnificent tiered city on the right, three hundred and fifty feet away, directly across from Mount Zion on Mount Moriah I saw it— the temple, the house of the living God. Finally, I had seen it with my own eyes. With the pilgrims, I immediately began singing Psalm 122, "I was glad when they said unto me, Let us go unto the house of the Lord."[10]

That psalm ended with, "O Jerusalem, may there be peace within your walls and prosperity in your palaces. This I ask for the sake of all my brothers and my friends who live here."[11]

Were those my words? Was I to bring peace to my people? Was I the prince of peace? Indeed, as I was to discover later, Psalm 122 was telling me I was, and Psalm 22 was telling me how I was going to do it.

What happened then?

As we walked down the Jerusalem side of the Mount of Olives, we were surrounded by flowers and the lush green canopy of trees that nature provided. There were orchards everywhere. Olive and fig trees mingled with pine and cypress. The cool shade after our long dusty walk was a striking contrast. God had left a reminder of the garden of Eden right outside his city. We made one more descent, then went across the Kidron Valley and up to Jerusalem, three hundred feet from point to point, but three times as long by ground.

Descent and ascent, that's how you get into my father's city. It's still that way. That's the road every believer must take, descent from pride and ascent to glory. This was even more evident as I continued to be taken aback by a tiered masterpiece in front of me that kept rising, one level upon another, until it reached its crescendo in the golden-domed temple. I couldn't wait to get there. I had a strange indescribable feeling that I was heading toward my goal.

Once inside the city, the most common route to the temple was via a huge bridge from Mount Zion to Mount Moriah overlooking the Tyropoeon Valley. The bridge was mounted in places on columns of massive stone, some individual columns forty feet in length, with the valley two hundred and twenty-five feet below. It was three hundred and fifty feet across the fifty-foot-wide bridge to the Royal Port, the most magnificent entrance to the temple at the southwestern corner. There we walked through a striking triple colonnade arranged in four rows of forty pillars each with the central aisle being about fifty feet wide with gigantic white columns one hundred feet high on either side. The two outside aisles were thirty feet wide, with the outside pillar being fifty feet high. This colonnade ran the entire length just inside the southern wall of the temple proper and formed a "porch" along the edge of the first and outermost temple courtyard. There were smaller porches along the other three walls of the temple square, all forming natural classrooms in which I was to spend the next week with the rabbis and, in later years, where I was to teach.

The view of the city and of the temple had been unbelievable from the Mount of Olives, but now, as I went through that entrance and saw everything up close, my heart was in my throat. I had never seen the cities of the world, but surely there was nothing like this, so condensed and yet so awesome. With my parents, I walked all the way through those forty columns, until we ran into the eastern wall where another porch, seven hundred and fifty feet long, started. At that corner it was four hundred and fifty feet from the top of the temple wall to the Kidron Valley below. One day an evil angel in disguise would urge me to jump from that spot. After we reached this corner, we walked out into the temple courtyard, the Court of the Gentiles. It was huge—six hundred and fifty yards in length. About three hundred feet away, in broad daylight, running almost the entire length of the opposite wall from the Royal Porch, stood the temple. It was surrounded by several terraces. Everything seemed to get higher and bigger and more condensed. It was so massive it was frightening. I hadn't yet even seen the inside of the temple itself. Now I knew why everyone talked about Jerusalem and the temple.

The name of the first courtyard had an obvious meaning. Gentiles, properly respectful, could go no further. Inside the courtyard, as one came near the temple, was an exquisitely ornamented marble screen about five feet high with warnings in both Latin and Greek that any Gentile who went beyond this point could be killed. It was as though God was saying to these Gentiles, "You can get a good look at some of my glory, but there's a great barrier between us." He would say the same thing inside the temple to the Jews. At the time, I didn't know I would be the one who would eliminate both barriers.

Scattered about the courtyard were many large heavy tables with moneychangers. The temple had nine gates. By far the most magnificent was the one generally entered for worship, the Eastern or Beautiful Gate. It had massive double doors that took twenty men to open and close.

The inside of the temple consisted of three courts, each higher than the previous one, concluding with the Holy of Holies at the far end, to the west. The first was the Court of Women, two hundred feet long by two hundred feet wide, so named because, except for sacrificial reasons, women could go no further. On another day yet to come, Judas Iscariot would hurl thirty pieces of silver—blood money—at the Pharisees in this same room. From the Court of Women inside the temple, the next court was westward up fifteen steps and quite shallow—about seventeen feet—but extremely wide, running the entire two hundred-foot width. On this very narrow courtyard, the priests performed their sacrificial duties on a great altar of unhewn stone, forty-eight feet long and fifteen feet high.

You are rather precise about the size of things in your descriptions.

Remember I was the son of a carpenter. Behind the altar area was the Court of Priests, over two hundred fifty feet long by two hundred feet wide. Altogether, at one time this colossal temple inside was twice the size of the Colosseum at Rome. In the center of the back or western wall, up another series of steps fourteen feet high, stood the sanctuary itself, which contained the holy places. It was made from marble block roughly seventy feet high, covered with gold, and had a massive veil in front. Behind that veil was the Holy Place, and behind that was the Holy of Holies—a room entered only by the high priest and only once each year on Yom Kippur, the Day of Atonement. During Passover, the chief priest went only into the Holy Place to offer incense on the golden altar, and at that moment all the people would fall silent.

Finally, one hundred twenty priests with long silver trumpets gathered facing the people on the steps leading up to the altars, along with fifteen Levites who faced the sanctuary. The priests and Levites would sing the song of the day, always in three sections, each one followed by three trumpet blasts. The people then began bringing their sacrifices to the altar. It became so crowded during Passover that as many as five hundred priests were needed to handle this part of the worship.*

I can still remember those huge terraced courts, the gleaming white columns, the trumpets blaring, thousands of worshipers singing in unison. But what stood out for me were all those sacrifices of young, unblemished animals—rams and oxen. I had never seen so much blood. I thought, "Surely God has required the shedding of much blood."

The Discovery

Was this the week you discovered who you were?

I stayed in the temple through the entire week and then a few days longer, joining the gatherings of the rabbis and scribes. I was surrounded

---

* Alfred Edersheim, *The Temple* (Grand Rapids: Eerdmans, 1975), 170.

by the greatest minds in Israel. On the one hand, a whole new world was opening up for me, stretching my mind to see things I never had before. On the other hand, many times my own answers to questions amazed them—and me. When I realized that often I saw further than they did, I again thought of that promise to the Messiah in Isaiah, "The Spirit of the Lord will rest on him—the Spirit of wisdom and of understanding."[12]

Was there much talk about the Messiah among these men?

Everybody, including the scholars, talked about the Messiah. For over six hundred years, Israel had been under the heel of the four biggest boots the world had seen up to that time. Four great empires ruled the world from 600 B.C. All had come to power just as the prophet Daniel had said in about 500 B.C. that they would: Nebuchadnezzar and the Babylonians, Cyrus the Great and the Medo-Persians, Alexander the Great and the Greeks, and the Romans. It was startling foresight for a Jewish eunuch in a foreign culture.

Let me tell you how accurate Daniel was with his prophecies. In 332 B.C., when Alexander the Great marched into Jerusalem, Jewish scholars met him at the city gate with the Scriptures and said, "We've known you were coming for two hundred years."[13] They showed him the Scriptures and he was so impressed that he knelt in Jerusalem and worshiped "the gods" and left the city unharmed.

For six hundred years the people of Israel had awaited the Messiah and for deliverance from one master after another. All the prophets of the Old Testament talked about the Messiah. The last one, Malachi, prophesied four hundred years before my coming. Then there were four hundred years of silence from God.

Your people endured six hundred years of waiting, including four hundred years of silence. That's almost beyond comprehension.

In all this time, the cry in Israel for their Messiah got louder and louder. I told you my father was a good director. He was making them wait, building their anxiety, highlighting the Scriptures.

An heir of David, the great warrior king, was coming who would be even greater than he.[14] Israel's longing for the Messiah grew directly in proportion to this oppression. The stage was being set; the Messiah was to come in the fullness of time when the whole world cried out for him.[15] Pagan Rome was beginning to crack at the seams, soon to be tried and found wanting by the world, just as the previous world empires had failed to bring peace and happiness.

For the Jews, Passover was a natural time to think about deliverance. Passover looked back to when God had led his people out of Egypt across the Red Sea after four hundred years of captivity. From the time of the Passover when I was twelve, it was nearing the moment when another silent period of four hundred years—from the time of the last prophet, Malachi—would be broken by my cousin, John. But until then, it was a time of high anxiety that built with each succeeding Passover. It was a time for dreaming and hoping for the deliverer.

History records that you shocked the scribes with some of your questions and answers.

I asked them if it were not true as the prophet Isaiah had written, that the Messiah was to deliver the whole world. They acknowledged that prophecy, but seemed to downplay it. I asked them, "You say the Messiah is to reign, yet Isaiah says he is to be meek and mild. He will be broken as a reed and will not utter a word. Isaiah also says that by his wounds he will heal his people. Will he suffer as well as reign?" Just like the common people, most of the scholars wanted a hero and an immediate deliverer. They, too, ignored those prophecies that stood out so clearly about the Messiah's suffering.

In a way, it was natural because they had been oppressed so long that all they could see was a David. Israel had seen Nebuchadnezzar, Cyrus the Great, Alexander the Great, and Julius Caesar. The nation wanted its own mighty conqueror. I spent all my life confronting the misconception that the Messiah would come first as the warrior hero, even though one day he would be more than that. Now I was beginning to realize how my father had prepared me to understand the Messiah's role and suffering through what I had already suffered up to this point in my life.

During that Passover I investigated all the prophecies I thought were messianic. I asked the rabbis how we would know someone was the Messiah. They talked about his being from the house of David, the tribe of Judah, and they discussed his birth in Bethlehem, the city of David. They knew he would have some connection with Egypt and with Galilee, but more often than not, a scribe would try to explain away that fact because most expected him to come from Jerusalem. After all, that was God's city. They did agree that there would be a forerunner, a prophet to go before the Messiah announcing his presence. I asked them about two Scriptures that I felt were disguised prophecies. One was from Psalms and the other from Isaiah. Both concerned a new king being brought gifts. I wanted to know if those Scriptures could apply to the Messiah and his birth. There was debate, but the two brightest scholars agreed, "Yes, the Scriptures were talking about the Messiah in those verses."

Then I asked them about the Scripture in Jeremiah where the coming of the Lord's king is associated with mothers grieving over the loss of their children.

You were thinking of Herod killing all those children when you were born?

Many were puzzled by my question, but again, one scholar said that this portion of the book of Jeremiah was referring to the Messiah. It did seem to suggest that a grief-causing event for some Jewish mothers was connected with the Messiah's coming. Fleetingly, I thought, "The Messiah's life will be surrounded by suffering, from beginning to end."

Finally, I asked them, "The Scriptures say the Messiah will be a royal king, one who will reign mightily, and yet the Scriptures also say the Messiah will be a plain man about whom there is nothing striking." There were some scribes who had the integrity to say, "I don't know." One scholar said, "The Messiah may indeed be plain in a way, and he may suffer—how we don't yet understand—but he will also be very special. I believe men will come from far away to see him and to bring him gifts. His birth, as the seventh chapter of Isaiah says, will be miraculous for he will be born of a virgin—the Almighty will father a child." Looking straight at me, he said, "You know, ten or twelve years ago, there was even a rumor around Bethlehem that the Messiah had been born. The story is still going around that an angel appeared to some shepherds one night and told them that the Savior had been born.

"They reportedly found him in Bethlehem. About a year later some wise men came on camels from the Far East bearing gifts for this alleged Messiah, inquiring where he might be. They said that the stars had led them to Bethlehem and had indicated a very special birth had taken place in that year. As you know, Herod became so frightened that he murdered all the young Jewish boys, two and under, around Bethlehem.

"No one knows what happened to that little boy, or whether the story was true, but this Messiah could be alive today; and he could even be about your age."

Now it all came together in a hurry—being born in a stable but receiving those expensive gifts, moving to Egypt, which explains the prophecy about grieving mothers. Now I had heard it from someone else. I understood what had happened to my mother. Even though she was a virgin, God had made her pregnant. At that moment I discovered my unique identity. I knew who I was. I was the Messiah!

At that great moment there were no angels, no burning bushes, no blinding lights, and no voices from heaven?

No, but there was all that and more going on inside me. He had taken the holiest book in the world and put me in the center of it. He talked to me through it. Burning bushes last only a moment, but the word of God endures forever.

How did it affect you when you realized who you were?

One thought stuck in my mind. "The Almighty will father a child." He was actually my real father. I was his only son. It seemed incredible! As that thought kept coming back, I became more curious. These men who had studied my father—what else did they know about him? What was he like? What was he trying to do here on this earth?

All the learned minds were there and one man would say, "The Lord is the Lord of justice." Another would say, "The Lord is the Lord of mercy. His mercies extend to the sky." Questions would come up. In a good man, why would God permit suffering? Why is he making us suffer now as a nation? After several more days of questioning, I began to understand what my father was about—his complexity, the mystery of his plan. He intended to preserve justice eternally and yet simultaneously to save his people who would be destroyed by his justice.

You fulfilled over three hundred specific prophecies about the Messiah, yet the scholars, the ones who were supposed to teach the people what to look for in the Messiah, missed your appearance entirely. Why?

They didn't miss it. They chose to deny the truth, to keep it hidden away deep in their unconscious. That initial Passover was my first real association with Pharisees in great numbers, and their corruption was obvious. They had become self-righteous. They had turned Judaism into a religion of little rules that they themselves could keep and thereby exalt themselves. They were much more interested in quoting each other and what "some other brilliant scholars" like themselves had written, than in knowing my father's words.

The Long Walk Home

Apparently you became so engrossed at the temple that you forgot your departure time?

(Jesus burst out laughing when I brought that up. Laughing was some-

thing he did often.) Yes. My mother and father had walked for two days in the caravan back to Nazareth before they discovered I wasn't with them. The women walked together, starting out before the men who would catch up with them by the end of the day. When my mother and father got together at the end of the first day of the journey back, they discovered I was missing. Both felt certain I must be with another family. I was always responsible, being the oldest child. I had never given them any trouble, and after all I was the Messiah; nothing could happen to me. They decided to continue walking for another day. When there was no sight of me by the end of that day, they immediately started back to Jerusalem in panic. This was the Messiah that they had lost.

Similar things had happened before in Israel's history. Visions of the patriarch Joseph's being kidnapped as a boy came to mind. They felt careless. They had taken so much for granted.

The painful journey twelve years before on the same road when my mother had been nearly nine months pregnant with me had been nothing like this. This was a different kind of pain. Never in all she had gone through had my mother been this distraught. The whole way back to Jerusalem my father Joseph tried to reassure her, but his words had little effect. She had been charged with caring for the Messiah, who was also her first-born son, and she had failed. Never had any mother anywhere loved a child more, or felt her responsibility more strongly.

The Scriptures record that they had to walk back to Jerusalem two more long days and it took them another three days of searching in Jerusalem before they found you in the temple. I'm sure they were impressed when they saw you discussing questions with the teachers of the Law, amazing everyone with your understanding. Still, as parents, they must have been upset.

The reason I stayed so long at the temple was that because of Passover, I couldn't really talk with the teachers in the depth that I needed to. I assumed that my parents, particularly since they knew I was soon to be an adult and also knew about my life's work, would know I was in the temple. I assumed they were giving me the time I needed to work things out. They had been so patient before. But I tested them rather severely.

Upon finding me, my father Joseph, as usual, showed extraordinary restraint. Despite his frustration he waited to hear my answer. But my mother couldn't contain herself any longer and immediately scolded me, "Son, . . . Why have you done this to us? Your father and I have been frantic, searching for you everywhere."[16] I told them, "Don't you know I must be about my father's work? Didn't you know you could find me here in my father's house?"[17]

Did they realize you had found out who you were?

It wasn't the first time nor was it the last I was to be misunderstood by my family. They didn't immediately appreciate my discovery. I have often looked back at that moment and thought, "Here you find out you are the Messiah, the savior of the world, God's only son, and the next minute you are an adolescent being disciplined by your parents."

In a way, rightfully so. You were only twelve. Did you ever think that perhaps you were mistaken—that you had jumped to conclusions?

Certainly I wondered. I had a mother and father and relatives who had told me some of the facts but never the whole story. At that point, I was confident they would confirm it.

As we made the long walk home, I also thought of all those other seven-day journeys to Passover in Jerusalem, the hot, tired, dusty but joyous crowds of thousands of Jews singing the Pilgrim Psalms together until they cried out in one voice for the Messiah. It was on the road toward home that I began to think of myself as their leader and I remember saying to myself, "Your Messiah is here. This long, dusty walk is worth it. I know it's hard to believe, but he is here." They were going to be my sheep and I was going to be their shepherd. That was who God made me to be.

For the next eighteen years when I would enter or leave Jerusalem for Passover, I was always comforted by the thought of God's promise that one day the Messiah would enter Jerusalem with the people surrounding him, acclaiming him and proclaiming him king. That was almost more than I could imagine.

Many years would pass before that would happen. I got used to waiting. Palm Sunday was twenty-one years away. Even now, I've been waiting nearly two thousand years to come back in all my glory. God makes us all wait on our blessings, including myself.

On that walk back home, did you tell your mother and father what had happened to you and what you had learned?

Since the caravan had returned a week earlier to Nazareth, we had all our time together on our journey back. After a while, my parents calmed down. At one point when my mother and I were walking alone a little behind my father, I asked her, "Is God my real father?" She looked at me and asked me what I meant. I said, "As in the seventh chapter of Isaiah?" She stopped, looked intently at me and said, "I never knew a man before you were born."

She was a very poised lady. She didn't get flustered easily.

Not after what she had been through. Do you remember how she reacted when the angel Gabriel first told her she was going to have God's child? She was the same then. Calmly and very humbly, as Luke records, she told Gabriel, if that was what God wanted, "be it unto me, according to thy word."[18] She also told God how honored she was. "How I rejoice in God my Savior! For he took notice of his lowly servant girl, and now generation after generation forever shall call me blest of God."[19]

This was from Hannah's song in the Old Testament after she dedicated her young son Samuel to God at the temple. My mother knew the Scriptures, too, and made sure I was reared on them.

Let's get back to her response to you on that road.

We walked along in silence for several minutes and then she asked me, "How did you find out?" I told her about my search and what had prompted it. Of course, she knew about my suffering and the name-calling. She was aware that I had been reading the Scriptures a great deal. I told her what I had found regarding the prophecies. I described all the questions that had come into my mind. I told her what had happened at Passover and asked her about the story the rabbi had heard.

She called ahead to Joseph and told him there was something all three of us needed to talk about. He came back with us. My mother simply said to him, "He knows." She went back over the story I had heard several times—several hundred, probably. Growing up, I would often ask her to tell me the story about how upset and disappointed she was that her new baby, her first baby, was going to be born in a stable—a barn. God had made it such a special night. In the fresh air scented with the sweet smell of newly dried hay, a new baby cuddled next to her with the bright stars visible outside above the partial walls and through the open door. God had thought of everything in that stable.

She said, "But there were some things I had left out of that story. It was the clearest night you can imagine. The sky was all lighted up. There was a new star—the brightest one in the sky and one that we'd never before seen. Everything was so peaceful.

"Suddenly, shepherds were running toward us. They seemed confused, searching. Then the one who first saw you in the manger cried out, 'Here's the baby!' Immediately, they all came over, fell on their knees, and praised God. They didn't even notice your father and me at first. Finally, after they had finished praising God, they looked up and realized that Joseph and I were there. One of them blurted out, 'We know who he is. You won't believe this, but we were in our fields, looking after our sheep, and an angel appeared to us.' I told him I believed in angels. He went on, 'The first thing the angel said was "Fear not." The angel waited for a few seconds until we could become calmer, and then he went on, "for behold I bring you tidings of great joy, which shall be to all people. For unto you is born this day in the city of David a Savior, who is Christ the Lord. And this shall be a sign unto you: ye shall find the babe wrapped in swaddling clothes, lying in a manger.'"[20] At that point, the shepherd stopped and pointed toward your little wrappings, and your crib.

"Another shepherd said, 'That's not all. Right after that, hundreds of angels surrounded us and sang the most beautiful chorus you have ever heard. The words were, "Glory to God in the highest and on earth peace, good will toward men."[21] Then the angels disappeared. We could hardly believe what we had just seen. We had to find him.'

"Another one said, 'We just left our sheep. If God chose to tell us, he would look after our sheep for us tonight while we were gone.'

"Then the tallest shepherd asked me, 'He is the Messiah, isn't he?' He quickly added, 'He is a boy, isn't he?'

"I said, 'Yes, he is a boy, and he is the Messiah.' I told them that an angel had appeared to me, too, before I was married and said that I was going to have a child whose father would be God and who would be the Messiah, the savior of the world. I told them the angel had instructed me what to name him. The shepherds asked what your name would be.

"Then Joseph told the shepherds that an angel visited him in a dream shortly after the angel had spoken to me and that the angel had told him the same thing, including what to name the child—'Jesus,' which means 'Yahweh is salvation.' The shepherds stayed for a while, and I asked them to tell us again the angel's song. They gladly repeated it. They couldn't quit talking about it. Finally, when they saw that I was getting very tired, they left.

"I lay there looking up at the wonderfully clear starlit sky. All those beautiful lights made me think of God's promise to Abraham when he had told Abraham to look at the millions of stars to see how many descendents he would have one day. I thought to myself, 'Three of those stars were for shepherds and the rest of them are for people who will one day be followers of my son. Everybody is going to have his own star one day.'

"Later I lay there with you beside me and told God how right he was for arranging your birth in a stable. You were meant to be born outside, where everyone and all of nature could see you, for he had given you to the whole world. Just before falling asleep, I thanked him for making the night so beautiful, for making it so special by sending the angels and the shepherds."

I'll never forget what Mother said then. "Many times I have suffered because of the circumstances of your birth; the accusations, the slander; but I have always treasured the memory of that night. It has seen me through all the pain."

How did you feel after your mother told you that?

It made me love God more. I saw how well he had taken care of my mother. She continued with the story, saying, "God is so good. He didn't stop there. Eight days later, when we took you to the temple to be circumcised, another significant event occurred. As we were walking into the temple, a very old man named Simeon walked up to us. I'll never forget him. He was such a gentle man, but so alive and so excited. His eyes were filled with tears of joy. He told us that the Lord had promised him—just a humble, devout Jew, who had waited expectantly for the Messiah for years—that he would see the Messiah before he died. Simeon never told us how God had relayed that message, but he did tell us that on this particular morning he had sensed the strongest urge to go to the temple. He knew that the Messiah would be there this day! God had placed it in his heart. He waited and waited for the right baby. When he finally saw you, he immediately knew you were the one.

"He looked at Joseph and then at me even more intensely as I was holding you and said, 'Do you realize that this child is the Messiah?' Your father and I just nodded. Simeon asked if he could hold you and we let him. Then he lifted up his eyes to heaven and said, 'Lord, now I can die content! For I have seen him as you promised me I would. I have seen the Savior you have given to the world. He is the Light that will shine upon the nations, and he will be the glory of your people Israel!'[22] Your father and I stood there in amazement."

She didn't tell me at that time that Simeon had also told her that a sword would pierce my mother's soul, for many in Israel would reject me, but that I would be the greatest joy of others. She saved that for later.

She finished telling me, "As Simeon was talking to us, an old prophetess named Anna came along. She was well over one hundred, and was famous in Jerusalem because she had never left the temple for eighty-four years, ever since she had been widowed. She began thanking the Lord and telling everyone in the temple that now the Messiah was here. By this time a crowd had gathered. As we went through the ceremony with everyone standing around, including Simeon and Anna, I looked around the huge, beautiful temple and thought, 'This is my son's room.'

"There is one other event that you should know about," she said, "the gifts your father sent you when you were born. We haven't shown them to you yet. We have been waiting for this moment. Do you remember the three wealthy men with their caravan who we said visited you? They each brought you a very special gift on that night; however it took a year to get the gift to you. Actually, they came to Bethlehem when you were about a year old, and each brought you a very special gift. Now you should know the whole story.

"The Magi, the three men who brought the gifts, were scholars from the East who had studied the stars and the Scriptures. They told us that they were overwhelmed on the night of your birth by a magnificent star that appeared in the heavens. Never in all their years had they seen a new star appear with such gleaming brilliance. The other stars were as nothing in comparison. This star had a vast tail on it that flooded the heavens with light. It swept across the sky in regal fashion. If ever there was a king's star, this was it, they proclaimed.*

"These three men knew that the Scriptures pointed toward the Messiah being born in Bethlehem. Ours was the only religion that made such a claim of having been promised a Messiah. They knew that if the star were the sign of a king, it was to be the sign of the king

---

* Stars in the ancient East often were associated with the birth of royalty.

of the Jews. They were so impressed with this message from God in the heavens that they began a journey of over two thousand miles. They knew it would take them over a year to find the Messiah.

"You should have seen them when they arrived in Bethlehem with their small caravan. Their servants went through the town inquiring about children who had been born the previous year on the same night that you had. They later told us that you were the only one they found. So one afternoon, suddenly these foreign men with their camels and servants and flowing robes showed up at the house in which we were staying. They were very mannerly as they began inquiring about you.

"After they told us what they had witnessed in the heavens that night, they wondered if we knew anything unusual about you. I could tell what they were thinking, because we weren't exactly overwhelming them with our wealth. Before coming to visit your father and me, they had talked with the Roman governor Herod. Expectation was all over their faces. 'Could this be the one?'

"Joseph told them we saw that same star on that same night. It seemed to stop right above your manger. Incredulous, they asked, 'Manger?' Your father explained to them that he and I were just two ordinary people. But Jehovah God had chosen us to be the earthly parents of his son. And, as Joseph put it, I was really your mother. God had honored us and prepared us by sending angels to tell us of his favor. They were sent not only to us, but also to the parents of your cousin John, who was to be the voice to go before you, crying in the wilderness. Finally he said that God had announced you to the shepherds on the night of your birth. I remember how bold Joseph was.

"Yes, even in the midst of the Magi, with all their splendor, he said to them, 'He is the Messiah. Praise be to God.' He added, 'You know that God our father must have a sense of humor. Last year, he sent shepherds to honor his son. This year he sends wealthy gentlemen like yourselves from far away. I guess he loves everybody.'

"Once the three men realized they were in the right place, they became very somber. Immediately they sent their servants for the gifts they had brought and asked if they could see you. You had been taking a nap and were still asleep when I led them inside our small dwelling.

I'll never forget that moment as they bowed before you. Just as they knelt, you opened your eyes and tears ran down their cheeks. All those miles, all that waiting was worth it when they looked upon your innocence. Then they presented your father and me with three gifts we haven't shown you.

"First, there is a gold box for a king. In that box was some very expensive, sweet-smelling myrrh* that symbolized your humanity. God has identified with his people, and you will continuously be a sweet smell to him." My mother didn't tell me at the time that the myrrh also symbolized my death. She went on, "The last gift in the gold box was frankincense, a picture of the incense used in the Holy of Holies as it drifts up to God, symbolic of the heavenly life you will offer to him. You will be pleasing to him with your life."

Then my mother related the wise men's warning about Herod whom the three of them had naively visited. She told me, "A few days later your father had a dream from God telling us to leave for Egypt immediately to escape the murdering sword of Herod. We obeyed! That was the reason we didn't tell you about the three wise men's coming when they did. We didn't want anyone possibly to suspect that you were the child Herod was looking for that year."

After my mother finished that part of the story, Joseph said they had saved those gifts for me and would give them to me when we got home. I could read between the lines. I knew again why God had given me these two people for parents. Times were very hard in Egypt. But they had been determined not to sell all my gifts unless it was absolutely necessary to save my life, because they were my gifts. My own father had given them to me. Nevertheless, as I was to be their Savior, too, they had to sell most of my frankincense and myrrh to survive in Egypt.

By this time I couldn't believe what I was hearing. I was surprised and overwhelmed again by my father, by how he had kept all these secrets as gifts for me until I could use them—until I understood their true meaning.

---

* Myrrh was a scented gum used for a variety of purposes—perfumes, medicinal ointments, and on burial linens.

My mother continued, "We've waited all these years to tell you these things. But we wanted you to find out first for yourself. We thought you would appreciate it best that way."

You were really close to her, weren't you? Even on the cross you told John, your disciple, to take care of her.

She was very special. She was always open and honest with me. God couldn't have given me a better mother. All the years with the rumors and innuendoes flying, she never fought back, never got even, and never even defended herself. She just waited until the right moment and told me exactly what had happened.

Do you think maybe God wanted you around that kind of person to prepare you for that one day on the cross when you would need not to defend yourself?

My father picked the best possible teachers for me.

What occupied your mind the rest of the way to Nazareth?

I thought about the journey of the Magi. The similarities to our journey were striking. Three of them had left home to find a king in Israel and then made the return journey back having discovered him. There were three of us; Mother, Joseph, and me, making the long trip back to Nazareth after the long journey to Jerusalem where I discovered the king for myself. Every believer must make the same journey of faith in his or her own way that the wise men and I made.

Back Home

What happened when you got home?

When we got back to Nazareth, my parents gave me the gifts my father had sent on the night of my birth. I'll never forget seeing that gold box. I opened it and smelled the fragrant myrrh and frankincense. It was hard to believe that this was mine, but I was learning my new identity. No longer was I just a carpenter's son from Nazareth. Now I was a king. Gold was for kings.

When I thought of gold, I always thought of Solomon, the richest as well as the most brilliant king who ever lived. I thought of the Passover I had just left, when I had amazed the priests and scribes with my wisdom. My father was proclaiming, "See your wisdom. See your gold. You are Solomon; you are the king."

Solomon's father David also came to mind. We both were declared king for the first time at a young age. For both of us the declaration came at the end of someone's journey—in his case, Samuel's, in my case, Mary's and Joseph's. David, I was sure, knew what it felt like to go from being a laborer to being pronounced king overnight. Just as I would, David waited through tremendous sufferings before he sat on his throne. Again my father was saying to me, "See, there you are once more in the Scriptures."

As I stood there holding that box, I could see God's sensitivity. I am sure that David could always remember that oil of anointing on his head, dripping down his face. The taste of it must have stayed with him, just as I would never forget holding that present of gold.

Did Joseph ever say anything more to you about your birth?

At first he simply confirmed my mother's story. Then he told me about his fear, after the wise men had come with their gifts and had related Herod's excessive interest in where this new Messiah was. He told me about the dream he had that night from God telling him to move us to Egypt. It was only a short time afterward that Herod massacred all the young males around Bethlehem.

A few weeks after our return from Passover, Joseph also told me about the doubts he had had about marrying my mother because she was pregnant. These doubts had lingered after the angel appeared to him in the dream and told him that God had given Mary that baby and that he was to marry her. He knew how hard it was to believe something like that could happen, even though it was prophesied in the Scriptures and even though the angel had reminded him in the dream of that prophecy in Isaiah: "Behold, a virgin will be with child and bear a son."[23]

He wanted me to know that it was true: My mother was a virgin until I was born. With great feeling he spoke of how much he revered my mother. When she was all alone at first in her pregnancy with me, and unmarried, he had not believed her story and had wanted to break the engagement. She had never wavered in her faith, and told him to do what he had to do. She said she would understand. In the face of his grief, however, Joseph saw something special in my mother. He couldn't let her be killed, which could have been her fate under Jewish Law. She might have suffered death by stoning for her sin. Joseph was quietly going to find my mother a place to live out of town to have her baby.

When the angel appeared to him and confirmed Mary's story, he had been both relieved and saddened. How alone she was; and he, the man she loved, had walked out on her. How pious he had been, how unbelieving. Then he told me something I should never forget . . . and I didn't. "Son, Jeremiah was right—the heart is deceitfully wicked, particularly when we think we are so pious. That's everybody's heart but yours. Only you will live your life without sin."

After he realized what he had done to Mary, he went back to her, and, although he knew he was supposed to marry her, he feared he had killed her love. He feared that she would marry him out of obedience and necessity; not love. He told her about his dream, and said that he wouldn't blame her if she couldn't forgive him. She just looked at him for a few seconds. To him it seemed like an eternity. She said, "Oh, Joseph," and put her arms around his neck. My father said one more thing to me that day, with tears in his eyes, "Your mother is a great woman." Those were the kind of parents I had.

What happened next in those "silent years?"

I don't think you could understand how much it affected me when I found out God was my father. He was my father! Not just "my father who art in heaven," but my father. It was like finding out at twelve that I was adopted, but that my natural father happened to be God! All the way home, it kept going through my mind: "He is my real father, and he has been communicating with me all along."

What else did you find out about yourself as you began to go back over the Scriptures after your discovery of your messianic identity?

Immediately there was confirmation from God about my birth. Two of the first characters in the Bible were pictures of me. Abraham's son, Isaac, was born miraculously when Abraham was one hundred years of age and his wife, Sarah, was ninety—a biological impossibility just as my birth was. Moses, if you recall, was almost murdered right after he was born because, just as it was in my case, the monarch was killing all young Hebrew males. But God intervened miraculously and protected Moses, who eventually became the leader of Israel.

The Scriptures which had awed me before were now almost overwhelming me. They took me even further. They strongly hinted that Moses, who had had a unique beginning to his life, too, probably didn't find out who his real mother and father were until he was older. He may not even have discovered it until he was twelve or thirteen and on the verge of his official manhood.

Moses' parents were in the same situation as my parents. They could have been killed had their secret been revealed. After all, they had tricked the Pharaoh who was killing Jewish male infants just as my parents had outsmarted the ruler Herod some years later. Good judgment would have demanded caution. If Moses' parents had told him everything too early in his life, it most likely would have gotten back to Pharaoh, and Moses, the great liberator and leader of the exodus, would have been killed.

Through God's amazing actions, Moses was saved and had come to live in Pharaoh's own household. Moses probably grew up thinking that he didn't know his real parents, that he was just a Hebrew baby who had been abandoned by some couple in order to save his life. The Hebrew people who were helping to rear him were just some people whose daughter happened to be nearby, whose mother was still nursing because she had just lost a baby. Imagine how Moses must have felt, how relieved he must have been, when, as a young man the day came when his Hebrew "caretakers" told him, "We are really your mother and father."

Now I understood the prophecy I had always wondered about: why God had wanted the Messiah to live in Egypt for a period of time. That was the land where Israel's deliverers came from—Joseph, Moses, and now me. It was another sign that I was the great deliverer, the second Moses. We both made the same journey to deliver our people. The Scriptures were so sensitive to me. They were my father's way of saying, "It happened just as your mother and father Joseph, said; I planned it that way."

David, Satan, and Death

Besides Joseph and Moses, were there other Old Testament characters whose life mirrored yours?

David continued to have special meaning for me. David himself was promised by God that one of his descendants would sit on his throne and rule Israel forever. The Messiah was always referred to as a Son of David and was to be born in the City of David, Bethlehem. The Jews loved Moses and Abraham, but David was special. He was Israel's greatest king and greatest warrior. He was a tremendous poet whose writing influenced Jews daily. I was to wear his shoes.

David's relationship with your father has always been of special interest to me. God called him "a man after my own heart." David was the only man he ever said that about, and yet David committed some horrible sins. He had an affair with another man's wife, got her pregnant, and then murdered the man and took his wife. How could God feel so good about David?

David never denied who he was. He fully admitted to what he had done. I paid for David's sins, and that stripped them all away. Under that hardened crust of sin, my father found a heart that wouldn't quit beating for him. It takes a great man to repent.

It reminds me of something C. S. Lewis said that it takes a good man to repent, and we're all bad men.

I believe the three most difficult words to speak in the English language are, "I am sorry." But David did that, and that's the type of heart God wants in his people.

What other Scriptures vividly spoke to you about your messiahship?

In the first book, Genesis, the third chapter, the Scriptures speak of a woman who will be given a child who will do battle with the evil one, Satan. Though the child will be injured, he will defeat Satan and deliver his people.

Did you understand all that the passage meant?

Not at the time, but I knew the Scriptures were talking about me and that somehow the Messiah would be hurt. I had already known that from Isaiah. It became more and more evident to me how much Moses, Job, David, Daniel and all the prophets, particularly Isaiah and Jeremiah, were pointing toward a great deliverance. It was as if the Messiah were two separate men—the suffering servant and the great deliverer. I was trying to decide what my "father's work" was that I must be about.

I thought of the gifts my father had meant for me. Strangely, I kept thinking of the myrrh, the gift which had most puzzled me. I couldn't get my mind off that great horrible chapter 53 of Isaiah.

He was wounded for our transgressions, he was bruised for our iniquities: the chastisement of our peace was upon him; and with his stripes we are healed. . . . Therefore, I will divide him a portion with the great, . . . because he hath poured out his soul unto death.[24]

Finally it occurred to me that my father was trying to tell me about a different kind of suffering than I had visualized. I had thought that perhaps through a warrior's suffering I would lead my people to victory. But maybe now he was telling me, "You came into the world to die."

The first time I had that thought, my immediate reaction was, "No. The Scriptures can't mean that. I came to do his will, but they can't mean I came just to die. Dying is insane. Perhaps I will suffer, but not die." Who could do what he was asking? No one could look death in the eye and passively allow it. Most people couldn't even think about death. I could never do that, I thought, even if I were God's son. It seemed too impossible. That's when I asked the question, "Does God give that much courage?" I was going to have to find out the answer to that question if I understood what I thought I did.

As time went by, I finally was able to begin to consider the possibility that I had come into the world to die. But if that were true, I wondered, how would I reign? I continued to search the Scriptures and found more and more clues about him and about me, until one day the Spirit opened my eyes and it all came together. I was to live twice.

This holy book that told me about my early life—my birth, my early years in Egypt, my suffering as a child, and the prophet who would go before me—was indeed now telling me that one day I would be tortured and killed, most likely on a cross. My beard would be pulled out. I would be beaten beyond recognition. My side would be pierced. I was to respond to that persecution without protest. I was to allow myself to be murdered. I was to die for my people in their place as an atonement and then I would be resurrected. Once I saw the plan, I realized how obvious it was. It had been there all along. Atonement is at the heart of Judaism.

Yom Kippur is the Day of Atonement.

Not only were these Old Testament characters a picture of me, but the heart of the Jewish religion was the biggest picture of all—death as atonement for sin. On Yom Kippur a young, unblemished goat was sacrificed symbolically as punishment for the sins of the people. Immediately afterward the idea was repeated, as the priest would lay his hands on a second young goat, symbolically placing the sins of the people on him, and the goat would be sent off into the wilderness to "take away" the sins. That second goat was called the scapegoat. I would become the true scapegoat. I would deliver my people not for some enemy nation like Rome, but from themselves and from God and his justice. Then I was to deliver them to God.

The Scriptures were telling me this not only directly, but indirectly as well. The first Jewish father-son relationship described in the Scriptures was that of Abraham and Isaac. Isaac had been a much-loved and long-awaited son who was born in a miraculous way. To test Abraham's faith, God later asked him to kill his only son. Abraham agreed to do it, even though he hated to carry out this command. But he was prepared to be obedient. At the final moment, God stopped him from going through with it but the message was there. The next time, a father who greatly loved his only son would kill him. I was that son.

Then I thought of Joseph. As far as his father and family were concerned, Joseph was dead. But he "rose from the dead" as prime minister of Egypt to save not only his own family—the future nation of Israel—but also Egypt and much of the pagan world from famine. When Joseph was "resurrected," he became second in command to the Pharaoh. I was second in command to my father. The Scriptures were stunning in their portraits of me.

Even the final miracle four hundred years after Joseph that caused Pharaoh to let the Jews return to Israel was a picture of me. The death of the oldest son in every Egyptian family was the miracle that delivered Israel. I was to be the Passover Lamb. I had even lived in Egypt, as had two other deliverers, Moses and Joseph.

Amazing "coincidences."

I also thought about David running down that hill to meet Goliath, charging him in the name of Jehovah God. If it was my job to die for my people, I wanted to do it charging, not retreating. But I wasn't ready to face Goliath yet. Sometimes I would get that myrrh and take it with me to the top of a hill just outside Nazareth. It was about five hundred feet high, and from it you could see to the west the beautiful Mediterranean Sea, to the east Mount Tabor, to the north the highest mountain in all of Israel, Mount Hermon. I could see a temple to the ancient Canaanite god Baal up there.

One day I would be transfigured on Mount Hermon, but for now I would tell my father that if by my life I could bring that temple down and build his kingdom, I would do it. Then I would take that sweet-smelling myrrh out of my pocket, look at those hills all around me, and recall Psalm 121: "I will lift up mine eyes unto the hills, from whence cometh my help."[25]

That first verse was the pagan's cry—mountain worship, nature worship. But the psalm continues with my father's magnificent answer—help would come not from nature, nor from Baal, nor from the sun or the water, "my help cometh from the Lord, which made heaven and earth."[26]

I would need his help, too. Then I looked to the south of Nazareth where the vast wilderness and plains stretched through the valley of Armageddon, the valley that had impressed Alexander and would impress Napoleon because of its potential as a battleground.* It's ironic, isn't it, that the person who was to have the biggest internal battle in history grew up next to the place where the largest external battle in history will take place. Both battles were in the same land.

I knew little about armageddon then. Whenever I sought my father, he was always there to meet me. Many times I spent hours with him on that particular hill, often early in the morning. That was where I found my courage. So many times, he spoke to me there. I would look all around me and I knew if he could make all this, he could see me home.

---

* Upon viewing the vast plain of Megiddo, which is identified with the future Battle of Armageddon, Napoleon was quoted as saying that all the armies of the world could do battle here.

Did it bother you that your own father would allow you to die?

The closer I came to my death, the more it bothered me. I knew how angry he was. God's wrath had been stored up for centuries because of the sin of humanity, and I had to take it. It was a huge cup of fury. That's why later I asked my disciples whether they thought they could drink from my cup.

It's very hard for us to imagine that God actually took out his rage on you.

Do you find it difficult to accept that my very own father took my life? Remember, I was Isaac and he was Abraham. You must understand justice. His rage is righteous. He has to express it, or justice will be a sham. You see, atonement is really atonement, and God really does punish. At the same time, it hurt him to punish me. It was the hardest thing he ever had to do. He was Abraham having to kill Isaac. His pain was greater than mine, because he had to do the killing. Do you think he's going to let anybody take his pain or mine lightly?

No one can ever imagine the cost of the pain because we love each other more than any two personalities ever have. We voluntarily separated from one another. I "became evil" when the world put all its evil into me. Then he judged me. His whole plan was a catastrophe for both of us. Ultimately, it succeeded because he had the power to bring me back to life.

You asked me if it bothered me. It did. But I was also "Isaac," and if you look at "the script," Isaac went totally willingly. The same thing was true for Isaac's grandson, Joseph. As you know, Joseph suffered for years in a foreign country for the eventual good of his own country before suddenly becoming a hero. All the time he was suffering, Joseph never complained. He trusted God to work it out for good.

Did you ever stop and think, "Can this really be me the Scriptures are talking about?"

It took a long time to get over the difference in who I had been chosen to be and who I was. For twelve years I had been an average

Jewish boy from a rather poor blue-collar family, not at all similar to someone who is to be the leader of the world. All of us were nobodies to start with.

That is the point of the gospel. We are all ordinary people who happen to be sons of the king. One day we all will reign. As far as being surprised to find myself in the Scriptures, I was. All my followers should be equally surprised to find themselves there, too. If you believe in me, repeatedly the Scriptures talk about you. For example, in the book of Hebrews, every one of my followers is called a joint heir.

That's hard to believe.

I know.

So you learned about your death from Scripture. How did you find out about your resurrection?

As I continued to study the Scriptures, what eventually shocked me most was the fact that if I was going to reign over my people and if I was to die for them, it meant only one thing—resurrection.

Did it seem like a preposterous idea to you?

It did and it didn't. It always made sense to me that God could do it. He could do anything. By this time, I had such confidence in the way he was communicating with me through the Scriptures that once I knew I was to die, I knew the answer would be there—resurrection. Moses, Job, David, and the rest of the prophets all looked forward to the resurrection. Never was it more precise than in David's sixteenth psalm, "You will not leave me among the dead; you will not allow your beloved one to rot in the grave."[27]

Jonah gives a perfect picture of death and resurrection. He spent three days in the deep, in the belly of a fish. I would be in the belly of the Earth, before I was resurrected. People find it difficult to believe that story about Jonah, just as they find it hard to believe that I was resurrected, completing the sign of Jonah. If you can't believe that God can save Jonah, can you believe that he would save me?

Creating a large fish and putting him in the part of the ocean where you want him to be is easy. The hard part is making a man. If you can create a person, you can do anything. It's creation that enables you to appreciate the resurrection. It helped me. More than anyone, I had to believe the resurrection. I was the one who was going to be in that grave. Yet initially it was hard to believe in a way, because it was such an incredible story.

It still is.

When I realized my task, one overriding question remained. Why? It was one I asked again many times, even in that garden on the last night I was alive.

Why was it really necessary? Why couldn't God just forgive them and start over with another earth? Why did I have to atone for them, die for them? What was so redeeming about that? Why would he be so pleased with me as an atonement? I was only one person even if I was God's son.

You had all those questions going through your mind?

Naturally I was looking for a way out, and I asked every question you can think of about why suffering is necessary and why pain exists. One day as I was reading the Scriptures I came to Psalm 45:6. That was the key to me. That psalm speaks of the Messiah, and in one place it says, "Your throne, O God, is for ever and ever."

I had my answer. For the first time it struck me: I was God, too! That is why I was so important. It might seem strange that I didn't know that yet, but it was an absolutely astounding realization that never ceased to amaze me. I was God. It was true that God was my father, but I was God also.

Imagine standing around with a group of people at a party. Someone is pointing out the guests and she says, "The tall one, that's Bill. That's John on his right with the pipe. The one next to him with the beard, that's God, and he goes by the name of Jesus."

It was hard to believe that I was to be alone on center stage, the one most important person in all of history! It took me a long time to get over being God. I felt so normal.

But the Scriptures took me further. They told me that I had had a "previous life" with my father even before the earth was created. Listen to this: I had created the earth. You talk about having to have faith. Look what I had to believe! I had to believe I had another life I couldn't remember and in it I was God. This was long before I performed any miracles and had the use of all my father's power.

It was at this profound moment that I began to realize how great an identity I had. My father continued to use the great personalities of the Scriptures to confirm what was happening and had happened in my life. It was like he was saying, "See, it's all really true. Remember Moses, who was in the line of succession to rule Egypt? He gave that up to be a Jew, to identify with his people. That's a picture of you giving up your glory to come to earth to serve your people." One day, because of his sacrifice, Moses would become Israel's great leader.

God's promises to me became obvious. One day, because of my self-denial I would reign over all of Israel. I would first get a foretaste but the second time around, when I returned, I would get it all. My second coming was prophesied directly and indirectly. Indirectly, great Jewish leaders had two distinct periods in their lives with greater recognition in the second part. Abram, childless and unknown, became Abraham, the father of many nations. The conniving Jacob became Israel, so named by God later in life, and the beloved father of the twelve tribes of Israel. Joseph, Moses, and David all had two different times of power in their lives. Then there was Noah, the carpenter, who became the shipbuilder that saved the human race.

Did you begin to experience a new responsibility to act as God at this time?

Until this point, I never really understood that I hadn't sinned. Now I wondered. Could I go the rest of my life without sinning? I was a teenager. I had strong feelings of all kinds. Could I control them?

So you were not too different from us. You had to have faith and you had to wait. Do you think we can identify with you as a man?

I was a man, and my biggest stress was imminent death. The other constant stress I lived under was whether good could overcome evil. Most people throughout history would say that hate is stronger than love. My father's way of love versus Satan's way of hate—that was the test. I was here to prove that love was stronger than any force that opposes it, that a person empowered with love will overcome a person motivated by evil, that "love never fails."

In one second my father and I could have crushed Satan with our omnipotent power, but there was much more at stake here than physical power. We were going to see who had the best heart. My heart of love, my father's heart, was to be tested. Would I give in to the destructive forces that surrounded me or would I be faithful to the truth? The whole plan hinged on the fact that good was never to lose to evil. Could I keep from taking my frustrations out on anyone, including my father, particularly when I was tired?

So this was the real contest. Did you ever wonder if you could make it through your suffering?

Until about five minutes before I gave up my life and died, I had these two sides warring within me. Humanly speaking, what he was asking me to do seemed impossible. I felt the weight of those doubts. On the other hand, I had his word that I would make it. When I wondered if I could carry it out, the strength of his promises sustained me. He was saying to me, "I've 'hand-picked' you for the job. I have been waiting for you for hundreds of years. You are my one and only begotten son. I promise that you will accomplish your mission and the joy that follows will make it more than worth it." Can you get a feeling of what kind of father he was to me?

I think I'm understanding him more.

There's no one who makes you as confident as my father. But I had an internal battle raging that I had to win with his promises, just like you do. Our greatest enemy is ourselves, especially our senses that insist that the material world is all there is. I came to the position in which I never stopped expecting a challenge from myself. That's why I could overcome it. I always expected that part of me would find it very difficult to get into the hidden world, the other world. That's why I worked so hard at it. That's why I got up early every morning to spend time with my father.

Divine Limitations, Divine Rights

The traditional viewpoint has been that you were "fully God and fully man." If you were fully God and omniscient, how could you have been a man?

Even to begin to understand this very delicate area requires enormous sensitivity. I couldn't have been anything like a man if I hadn't had to learn things. I could not have been fully man without voluntarily, in a real way, laying aside—not using—some of my godly powers. Just as I veiled my presence, in my full identity I am omnipresent, I veiled my omnipotence and omniscience. Both my omniscience and my omnipotence were there, but veiled—latent, as far as my human nature was concerned.

But I questioned whether the Messiah would have to learn who he was? Would he be that "ordinary"? To my relief, the Scriptures offered me insight. The seventh chapter of Isaiah, speaks of the virgin-born Messiah who would have to learn right from wrong. The Scriptures report that the Messiah would teach himself many things by his deeds. That's why the gospel reporter, Luke, recorded about me: "And Jesus kept increasing in wisdom and stature, and in favor with God and men."[28]

That's one reason the Scriptures make note of my life at age twelve when I was asking many questions. Scripture can't be wrong. When it says I had to learn—I had to learn. What I learned was that my father was omniscient and that I "had been," too. I learned too that I had had a "past life," and I'm not talking about reincarnation. My father and I had coexisted before the beginning of time.

Progressively I also came to an awareness of my self-denial, of how much I had given up to come to earth. That discovery helped me immeasurably to understand who I was. That's why I was able later to withstand Satan's temptation to entice me to use my power. That's why I was even cautious about performing that first miracle.* It took years to know how knowledgeable I was. That seems contradictory, but there's an exact picture in nature. For instance, recent psychiatric studies show that all human beings are brilliantly perceptive, recording and analyzing in great detail every event of their lives in their subconscious or subliminal minds—yet concealed from their conscious mind. Understand, too, there's no way I could have become fully human without some veiling of my omniscience. Otherwise it would have been impossible to be tempted. Therefore, my life would not have had the worth that it did.

The book of Hebrews underscores why my life as a man had so much value: "Only as a human being could he die and in dying break the power of the devil who had the power of death."[29]

When I quoted Moses to Satan during the temptation in the wilderness, saying, "Man shall not live on bread alone, but on every word that proceeds out of the mouth of God."[30] Do you really think I didn't have to do that? Was my father going to deny me the most precious experience a man can have—walking by faith in his words? The minute I had allowed immediate access to my full omniscience would have been precisely the moment that I wouldn't have needed the Scriptures and I wouldn't have had faith.

---

* At first Jesus seemed to refuse to turn the water to wine and told his mother, "Mine hour is not yet come" (John 2:4).

This chosen self-limitation of becoming a man forced me into a mature, dependent relationship with my father. God never intended for any person to have it any differently. To be tempted in all ways includes humanity's biggest temptation: not believing in God, doubting he's there. The first step in every sin is to think that God's not looking. That's why God was so angry with his people following his great deliverance of them at the Red Sea. They quit believing in him. The same goes for atheists who tell the biggest lie of all: "God's not there."

So your definition of a human being is someone who needs the Scriptures and who has to have faith. That's not very heroic at first glance.

Usually you don't see God or true heroes at first glance. As I looked at my life as a man, it took me some time to realize what I was to be about. Finally, I understood the challenge facing me, and why my death was so important. All of humanity was riding on my ability to be perfect, so they could be free—to do God's will at all times instead of Satan's. Nobody had ever done that before. They had failed at some point. I went back to Psalm 40.

> Sacrifice and offering thou didst not desire; mine ears hast thou opened: burnt offering and sin offering hast thou not required. Then said I, Lo, I come: in the volume of the book it is written of me, I delight to do thy will, O my God: and thy law is within my heart.[31]

Here I was, speaking before I was born. You see why this is my script. I knew I could never give in. I had one purpose—to do his will—always! That was who I was. From that time on, whenever I was tempted to sin, I became increasingly aware of how much depended on me.

Wouldn't some psychoanalysts call you grandiose?

(*He laughed especially heartily here.*) Is God truly grandiose when he says he is God? That's like the person who says, "I can't believe in miracles." Well, what do you say to me when I am walking on the water?

Did knowing about your death and exactly what was going to happen to you make it any easier?

It made it both easier and harder. To be able to say one day, "I am the light of the world,"[32] I had to have the manuscript. I had to know for sure that I was that light. At the same time, I was constantly reminded that I was to die—in the Scriptures, by the temple sacrifices, and particularly through crucifixions I witnessed.

Here I was with a great double-edged discovery. On the one hand I found out that I was the Messiah, the son of the living God, and was myself God. On the other hand, because I was God, I was to die. I was to allow myself to be tortured and murdered. That is shocking for a teenager to grasp, while everything is calling out to life. He comforted me by putting me at the center of the most important book in history and had the world wait thousands of years for my coming.

Some people would say that you were a disturbed person reading yourself into the Scriptures.

Only a disturbed person would want to read himself into the role of the Messiah. I realized how they were to torture me—to beat my face beyond recognition, to flog my back with a whip, to pull my beard, to spit in my face, to mock me, to pierce my hands and feet, and to curse me as I hung on a cross. I had seen crucifixions—people screaming in agony, hanging helplessly with their bones out of joint. I wondered how I was going to handle it. At fourteen, it was an impossible task. I knew I could never do it by myself.

Conversations with the Father

So you don't think you could have obeyed your father and gone willingly to your death at fourteen like you did at thirty-three?

Fortunately, he never asked me to do that. He didn't ask me to go to the cross when I was two years old, either. He never lays on us more than we can bear. Ever. The Scripture said that he, the Messiah, would come in the fullness of time. For his part, that meant that the Messiah would be ready and mature. God was my manager. When I was fourteen, he knew I was still early in my training for the big fight. He was bringing me along.

But, I'll tell you, at that time I wanted to speak to him directly in person more than at any other time in my life. I even wished an angel would bring me a message from him. The only way he communicated with me directly then was through the Scriptures. I listened to them very carefully.

You trained for the fight on those words?

Once again I found out how great those words really are. As G. K. Chesterton put it, when you are reading the Bible you are "thinking God's thoughts after him." There were, of course, some things in there I didn't like. Every time I read Psalm 22 that describes me on the cross, it took my breath away. Read some of it yourself:

> My God, my God, why have you forsaken me? Why do you refuse to help me or even to listen to my groans? . . . I am a worm, not a man, scorned and despised by my own people and by all mankind. Everyone who sees me mocks and sneers and shrugs. "Is this the one who rolled his burden on the Lord?" they laugh. "Is this the one who claims the Lord delights in him? We'll believe it when we see God rescue him!" . . . I am surrounded by fearsome enemies. . . . They come at me with open jaws, like roaring lions attacking their prey. My strength has drained away like water, and all my bones are out of joint. My heart melts like wax; my strength has dried up like sun-baked clay; my tongue sticks to my mouth, for you have laid me in the dust of death. The enemy, this gang of evil men, circles me like a pack of dogs; they have pierced my hands

and feet. I can count every bone in my body. See these men of evil gloat and stare; they divide my clothes among themselves by a toss of the dice."[33]

After I finished that psalm, I would read the next few psalms and then the answer would come. Do you think it's any accident that the most famous psalm and perhaps the most comforting, Psalm 23, comes right after my annihilation is described in Psalm 22?

The Lord is my shepherd; I shall not want. . . . He leadeth me beside the still waters. . . . Yea, though I walk through the valley of the shadow of death, I will fear no evil: for thou art with me.[34]

Can you sense what he was saying to me? He was with me.

Then came Psalm 24, which promised that I would be strong and mighty in battle and that one day I would reign and walk through those mighty gates in Jerusalem.

I thought of the day David had brought the ark into Jerusalem after recapturing it from the Philistines.* Thousands lined the road into Jerusalem surrounding the city gates, and more stood on the city walls above, looking down on David, who danced ahead of the ark. In one voice, as their king came into Jerusalem, these thousands sang Psalm 24: "Lift up your heads, O ye gates; and be ye lift up, ye everlasting doors; and the King of glory shall come in."

Then the people on the wall sang by themselves: "Who is this King of glory?"

---

* The ark was a moderate-sized golden box that contained three items: the tablets on which God had written the Ten Commandments; Aaron's rod, which Moses held when he delivered Israel from the Egyptians; and manna, the bread God had daily provided for his people for forty years. The ark was kept in the Holy of Holies, the forbidden territory where only the High Priest could enter once a year to ask for atonement before God. The ark was a symbol of God's presence. Once David had recaptured the ark and placed it again in the temple, only the High Priest saw it and sprinkled blood on it one time a year on Yom Kippur, the Day of Atonement.

The crowd down below lining the road and following David and the Ark replied, "The Lord strong and mighty, the Lord mighty in battle."

They all sang: "Lift up your heads, O ye gates; even lift them up, ye everlasting doors; and the King of glory shall come in."[35]

Years later I would tingle all over when after a seven-day walk with another crowd, we would sing that same song in the same place as we came into Jerusalem for Passover. Every year I would think of how David must have felt, and then I would know that they were really singing it to me—although they didn't know it at the time. One day I would feel what David had felt. I'll feel it even more the second time I come. When I finished Psalm 24, I read Psalm 25: "Let not my enemies triumph over me."[36]

That was my concern, too. Psalm 27, my favorite, had the answer, "The Lord is my light and my salvation; whom shall I fear? The Lord is the strength of my life; of whom shall I be afraid."[37]

He promised he would be my strength. The end of that psalm says, "Wait on the Lord: be of good courage, and he shall strengthen thine heart: wait, I say, on the Lord."[38]

He was telling me, "Wait. Wait. Have courage, for I will strengthen you. I will prepare you." So I learned to wait like he asked, and then he did what he said he would do.

There really is a tremendous flow to the Psalms.

These words didn't haphazardly fall together. At a glance it may not look like it, but there is a design to every page, and the author knew what he was doing. I can tell you that because I lived off them. That's why I could do what I did. Some people think of the Scriptures as disjointed, sixty-six books by more than thirty different authors. Nevertheless, there are consistent signs in each book bearing the mark of the true author. As we discussed before, there are common themes. They include the men coming out of nowhere to be great—Abraham, Joseph, Moses, David; and the favorite son who always suffered—Isaac, Joseph, Benjamin, David, and the Messiah.

If you stand back just a bit from the Bible, the consistency is over-whelming. The unity of the Scriptures is in itself a miracle. Of course, some people like to stand too close to the Scriptures and argue over apparent contradictions that have nothing to do with the essence of the Bible and that, in truth, are never contradictions. The Bible has a name for people like that. It calls them *fools*.

In Pursuit of an Identity

Let's get back to what went on inside you during those formative years.

There is a process of identity that takes place as you read the Scriptures. Watch how a family creates a child's identity. "Don't tell a story—you're not that kind of boy. Be fair; share your toys—you don't want to be selfish." Or, "Calm down; don't fuss. Everything is going to be all right; you can handle it." That's the way a family builds into a child truthfulness, fairness, and self-control as long as the family is consistent with their words.

My father did the same thing with me through the Scriptures. As I read them over and over, he was saying to me, "You are my only begotten son. I love you so much that I have written about you in the most important book in the world, and I have had the world waiting for you for hundreds of years. Before the foundation of the world, I begat you, shared my power with you, and you and I created this world, the universe. As I love you, you will love them. You—only you—have come to do my will. Mercy and justice will be your passions just as they are mine. So much will they be your passions, you will die for your friends to protect them from the death justice demands. You are like me, slow to anger, and you will not utter a word when they persecute you. You will overcome all fear because I am with you every minute. You and I are one. Your task looks impossible, but I promise you, you will make it because you have my strength. All that I have is yours. You will do it.

"After they murder you, I will resurrect you. I have your glory waiting for you at your place on my right hand where you will reign forever. Many will refuse the forgiveness and justice you bring, and they must live forever with their own justice and without you. For now, you're to turn over to me all judgment for your persecution. I am the father; you are the son."

That's in essence who he was telling me I was. Of course, the process took years, but isn't that how a child develops? A little girl will play house and take care of her dolls for years so that one day she can take care of a real child. A basketball player will practice shooting baskets a thousand times so he can shoot well twenty times in a game. For me, I practiced on those words. I went over and over: "The Lord is the strength of my life; of whom shall I be afraid?"[39] until he was my strength. I read the verse: "I sought the Lord, and he answered me; he delivered me from all my fears."[40]

I sought the Lord continually until I could go into the world as its Messiah, afraid of nothing—not the establishment, not demons, and not storms. A thousand times I meditated upon the verse: "He was led like a lamb to the slaughter . . . so he did not open his mouth."[41]

Because I believed those words, I could face death silently with courage. I read about how I loved to do his will until I did love to do it. The Scriptures taught me who I was.

Some people would call that brainwashing.

There is a difference between brainwashing and coming to believe the truth. You can imagine all day long that you are God; but when the test comes, you'd better be able to perform.

I believed these words until they became a part of me. I learned to keep from getting overwhelmed, to overcome fear, to be patient, and ultimately to check any insult. I learned to do the right thing, and often it was the most obvious thing to do.

When I was first learning how to use the Scriptures, I would find myself in the middle of a difficult situation and would begin to think about my father's words that I had memorized: "The Lord is on my side; I will not fear"[42] and "I am with thee to deliver thee."[43]

It was like having a coach on the field, a teacher with me at all times. Finally, I reached the point that I had literally incorporated and shared his life. It was no longer memorization. I began to think like him until his thoughts and his confidence became mine.

It's a growth process. I was involved in the process for over thirty years.

Even God the man had to grow up to be truly himself. The process you went through reminds me of what your apostle Peter wrote. He said that the primary goal in life was to share God's life, to "participate in the divine nature."[44]

One truth I've learned that has stood out in my mind is that all of life is a search for the father who wants to share his life with us, and he's the best time of all because he has the best personality. He's the most fun. Think about it. This great God wants to share his life, his personality, his power, his peace with you. When I shared his life enough to know that in every situation he absolutely prevailed, then I had his confidence and was ready to be the Savior of the world.

It must have been a strange feeling all those years to walk around with a great secret that no one knew.

Because they didn't know who I was, I got to see people for who they were. They didn't have time to put on their Sunday faces or tell the family, "Get ready. Here comes the preacher."

Often I thought, "You wouldn't treat me like that if you knew who I was." Later on I realized many people would have treated me badly no matter what, and the only thing that would ever stop them was power.

Having this secret identity gave me tremendous hope. When I was mistreated or saw a hopeless situation, I thought, "It won't always be this way. One day I will make things right." I thought a lot about heaven.

Many people, particularly psychiatrists, would say that studying the Scriptures is neurotic—an escape from the real world.

You are who your friends are. There is sufficient evidence for that. Recent psychiatric findings indicate that we are continuously incorporating others all the time, much more than we thought. I fail to see how it hurts to be around God frequently. I used to tell my brothers and sisters when they were growing up, "Make sure you stay close to God." If you are often surrounded by a vindictive, selfish world and want life on a different plane, "a cut above," then God's the place to get it. He's the person from whom to get it.

Of course, all people come to God for mixed reasons. A person will spend a lifetime sorting out his or her good motives, sifting the truth from the bad motives, the lies. That's the Christian process.

Is that why you said that on judgment day you would say to some of your so-called followers, "I never knew you"?[45]

Some people go to church because they want power, because they want to think they are good, because they want to aggrandize themselves. Some churchgoers actually use the church to judge others. Those who do that exclusively are not my true followers.

Some others come to church because they fear losing control of their sexual or aggressive impulses, as the Freudians say, and they feel the need for a sense of control. That's not a bad reason in and of itself, particularly if you become conscious of it. We are constantly identifying and "taking in," and the Scriptures and the church can be a good place to go. Nobody reads the Bible or goes to church for completely pure reasons.

Freudians don't understand that they are really on my side here. Read Jeremiah, the other prophets, and David. In Psalm 139, David did what Charles Spurgeon, the foremost British pastor of the nineteenth century, called his most courageous act. David said to God, "Search me, O God, and know my heart: try me, and know my thoughts: and see if there be any wicked way in me, and lead me in the way everlasting."[46]

David wanted to see his heart. Truly, what courage he had. It's astounding to realize that this "primitive man" from three thousand years ago recognized the unconscious, which Freud "discovered" in 1899. David knew that all human beings have closets in which they are capable of hiding things, closets they can shut so tightly that they don't even know they are there.

The whole human race ought to have shuddered at what Freud discovered. For the most part they ignored it, as did Freud himself. Freud wasn't very much of a "Freudian," and this continues even to the present day with most of his followers, if you understand the current psychiatric literature. Now we can say to a conscious atheist or agnostic, "You don't know all of yourself, and that hidden part of you is no atheist." Read the first chapter of the book of Romans where it speaks of "men who suppress the truth by their wickedness, since what may be known about God is plain to them, because God has made it plain to them."[47]

There ought to be a new commandment that says, "Fear thyself as thou fearest God." We don't honor ourselves enough and recognize our vast complexity. We think we are so simple, but we are made in the image of God.

No Ordinary Man

As you grew into manhood, did it amaze you that events were happening just as the Scriptures said they would?

It completely amazed me. The whole process captured me. From the shocking effect of fulfilled prophecy—"It's really coming true"— to the joy of becoming what I was meant to be—the light of the world. All of it was amazing.

I enjoyed being that light. I had no hidden motivations. I never boasted, though I was tempted. I didn't envy. I was happy when someone received something good. When I was hurt, my first inclination was not to strike back. I didn't get angry as easily as did others. I didn't delight when someone failed.

Some people—many people—would describe themselves just as you have. You often hear people say, "Can you believe people are like that?" They mean vindictive, angry, mean, or whatever, but they don't see those characteristics in themselves.

They should talk to their neighbors. Those who say that really don't believe they have any closets, they think they know all of themselves, but they certainly don't believe their Bibles. Remember that everybody you've ever met is "a criminal" who deserves capital punishment. We have a holy image of people like Daniel and John the Baptist. With all their great deeds, do you think of their hearts as deceitful, too? We can perhaps see it in David, but it is harder to see the deceit in Daniel or the Baptist. Even the "good people" have closets. You will have discovered why I needed to die for Daniel and for John and for all the saints.

As the Scriptures make plain, you alone were the one human being without sin. There was a real difference in you and in all of the other people who have ever lived. When did you first realize that you were different?

I saw it when I was about eight years old. I had come to that age where one begins to become more aware of others, when children really begin to show who they are. It's the age when everybody wants to go first, but it's no longer cute.

The first time I noticed that I was different, I was in the synagogue being taught with all the other children, and I wondered why all of them wanted to be first. I wanted recognition, too, but I didn't have to be first. It seemed to me that everyone was selfish. I didn't pay much attention to that; I just tried to go on being who I was. Some time later, I was aware that my friends' humor that often turned to cruelty bothered me.

It occurred to me one day was that my parents had never disciplined me for intentionally disobeying them. I was unlike all my friends in this. Later on, this awareness was very important when I began to understand why God was asking me to make such a huge sacrifice.

The Scriptures say that you learned obedience by the things you suffered. That almost sounds as if you had to do wrong, suffer the consequences, and learn the right way. It almost suggests that you would have disobeyed at one point.

I learned the cost of obedience my whole life and never more so than on the last day of my life. I had to learn to obey the rules of nature. If I ran too fast and fell down, it hurt. As I was growing up, if I didn't do a job properly, I had to do it over. I might forget to be home at a certain time and have to suffer the consequences, but I never once willfully disobeyed my parents.

Still, I never paid that much attention to my personality, until I was around ten and everyone started condemning me. I thought that I must be like everyone else—sinful and not able to see it. Later, after I realized who I was and that I hadn't sinned, the thing that was most apparent to me was that I didn't hate like the world did. It just wasn't in my nature to retaliate immediately. The first thing that I usually felt when someone was unkind to me was sympathy. I would wonder, "Why is he so upset?" I was no masochist, and sometimes I had to stop people from abusing me.

Did you ever have a fight?

I had one or two. Once when I was about eleven, I was walking home. The persecution about my birth had died down except for a few older boys, who on occasion perpetuated the harassment. This particular day, two older boys kept pushing me off the road every time I came near them. They weren't going to let me by, and finally I had to fight my way home.

Luckily, I was strong since I had been working in the carpentry shop, helping my father Joseph handle the heavy lumber. I got the better of them. Still, I was beaten up pretty well, too. On the way home, I felt like King David who defended himself against a lion and a bear. When Joseph saw me, he just looked at my bruises and the cut beneath my eye and said, "Who won?" I told him, "I did." All he said was, "Good!" My heavenly father would one day ask me not to defend myself in a fight, but until that fight came, he never told me I couldn't stand up for myself. One day in the temple I would stand up for him and clean out the moneychangers.

You told your followers to turn the other cheek.

I did, and I meant it. Always, always try to do that first, but that approach won't work every time. The Scriptures also say, "Love is not easily angered." They don't say that love is never angered. Again, Scripture says, "Love always protects." That includes one's self, as well as one's family and neighbors. I never taught the people that if a criminal wanted their house, wife, or property they should give it to him. I would have been condoning oppression.

Never forget that my father and I will send people to a horrible, everlasting, ongoing death, where the fire never dies. It will be a death row, a cancer ward, and it will last forever. Although the doors to hell will be locked from the inside, and although, even in their misery, people will be unable to leave evil as it draws them like a magnet, nevertheless the doors will be locked from the outside, too. I was no pushover. Neither is my father.

As far as being different from my fellowman, it was plain and simple: I alone could love perfectly because I was free to love. I didn't have "Adam's disease." My personality wasn't cluttered with hatred or competition. I was like my father. He gave me his understanding. I could feel people's pain and share their dreams. I had his compassion, and despite all of humanity's flaws I could see my father's image in every person. Let me quote chapter 13 of 1 Corinthians. You can see the best picture in Scripture of what my father's like and how he begot me in that image.

> Love is patient, love is kind. It does not envy, it does not boast, it is not proud. It is not rude, it is not self-seeking, it is not easily angered, it keeps no record of wrongs. Love does not delight in evil but rejoices with the truth. It always protects, always trusts, always hopes, always perseveres. Love never fails.[48]

My father was letting me teach the world how to live, how to share. He was bringing me to the point as a teacher that I could say, "Heaven and earth shall pass away, but my words shall not pass away."[49]

Then as a true teacher, I was able to live out my words. Through my sacrifice that matched my words, one day we would all be brothers, sacrificing for one another. I would have an everlasting worldwide impact and bring about the greatest society in history. It would last longer than anything any dictator ever planned. This society would last forever because I had come to die for my country. Only my country happened to be the whole world.

The late John Lennon, the former Beatle, wrote a song called, *"Imagine."* He had the right idea, although he didn't understand at all how to make it happen. There's a line in there that goes something like, "Imagine there are no wars. Imagine all the people living life in peace, and the world could be as one."

That sounds like your teaching and your life.

I was going to do that. God had given me that role. For centuries my people had failed God, failed to keep their part of the agreement. Time after time they failed to keep their covenant with God. I was going to fulfill that agreement and provide a new contract that they could keep. I was going to run that race and finish it, even though that last leg was almost unbearable. Can you see why he was such a great father? He loved me, prepared me, sent me, and empowered me.

You get excited when you talk about your father. The Scriptures say that you had more joy than any man who ever lived. The psalmist described it as "gladness above thy fellows."[50]

I had his spirit. With every passing day, I could love more. To be able to love is a wonderful gift. It became more and more difficult to take that away from me, because I was learning the power of forgiveness. If you were hateful to me, you weren't going to make me hateful or make me hate myself. By mistreating me, you couldn't change who I was, and you couldn't make me stop loving. Inside there was more and more peace, and more and more power. I was just like my father.

That's what the Scriptures were doing to me. They were making me his kind of king for his kingdom. That's why I arose early every morning to listen to him. Oftentimes after being alone with my father I would leave with my heart bursting. I had the privilege of bringing mercy to a merciless world.

Who were your models of mercy besides your father?

Both my human parents in the face of suffering were merciful people. I also had many teachers in the Scriptures. Abraham was one— in obedience he offered his son Isaac as a sacrifice not quite understanding why. Joseph forgave his brothers for kidnapping him and selling him into slavery. Moses pleaded for his people's sins, offering his own life. David forgave Saul repeatedly for trying to kill him. Daniel never retaliated when they tried to kill him in a den of lions.

From what you've said so far, you obviously think the Bible is a very effective means of communicating.

The Bible's words are powerful. They've changed the lives of millions of people, including my own. They have made terrible people into better people, made the proud humble, helped the rich to help the poor. To an unfair world they've brought fairness, and they've given hope over and over when all seemed lost. They've affected the destiny of nations. That's always been their legacy; and even this very minute, those words are alive, comforting and teaching millions of people around the world.

At the same time, critics of the Bible say they've brought destruction and division. The Inquisition is always their favorite subject.

Truth itself brings division. There is often a kernel of truth in every error.

The words are fixed. They're the same words to every person. How then does he make them personal?

He is talking to every person. Truth is truth. That helps. What often is overlooked is the enormous flexibility the Scriptures have. On a particular day, at a particular time, my father can get any message in his word through to anyone. Anyone who has ever listened to God consistently will tell you about his unsurpassed sense of timing. It's how he makes it personal.

That's what went on with me during my private years, and it was quite an adventure. The exciting thing was that each day was different. I faced a fresh set of circumstances that forced me to seek him anew. Every day I had to rediscover the secret way to him, and usually it involved a "new" route with an "old" map. One day our possessions might be threatened, and, as head of the household I was concerned. In the midst of that, Psalm 16 would deliver his message: "He guards all that is mine."[51]

One day I might be feeling very insignificant, not understood by anyone, and I would hear Psalm 56: "You have collected all my tears and preserved them in your bottle!"[52]

Every morning I would read a certain portion of the Scriptures. Before I did, I would always pray that he could give me his eyes. More times than I could count, an event would happen that day which would fit exactly the portion of the Scriptures I had read that very morning. It was exactly what a good father would have said to his son if he was guiding him and was truly interested in him. I remember one morning I read in the book of Job, "Acquaint now thyself with him, and be at peace: thereby good shall come unto thee."[53]

I read that on a morning when I had been tempted to get up early and work because my family really needed some extra money. Instead, I prayed. I had always set that time aside. It came to be a holy time for me. On this particular day I had honored my father and had spent time with him instead of going out early to earn money. God fulfilled the promise in Job by sending me some work that required the most skill and was the most costly that I did—a form of engraving. "Coincidentally," the man had his money with him and wanted to pay in advance. As I look back, my father had been saying to me that morning, "You look to me and I will take care of your material needs. You trust me and rest."

I came to see that he knew every step that I would take and he was going ahead of me, anticipating my stresses. Often when I needed to wait, my Scripture reading for the day would be about waiting on him. Many times when I was puzzled, my Scripture that day would be about enduring hard times and trusting him. Sometimes it was something like, "Weeping may endure for a night, but joy cometh in the morning."[54]

When something good happened as far as a material blessing, my verse for that day often would be about how all blessings come from him. It was convincing to see him use these words in so many creative ways. I began to look forward to my Scripture reading because it was guiding me and preparing me for what I needed that day. There was one other reason why my quiet times with him were especially good: I was talking to my father. That made it so real. I never got over the fact that my real father was someone no one could see.

There's a subtle interaction between God and his people that goes on for the whole of a person's life if one looks for it. God's timing is so perfect because he is such an aggressive, powerful God: "Not by might, nor by power, but by my spirit, saith the Lord of hosts."[55] "He shall call upon me, and I will answer him: I will be with him in trouble; I will deliver him, and honor him."[56]

Repeatedly he reminds us, "I will deliver you."

I also learned to seek out his deliverance. When I needed patience, I would find his words telling me to wait joyfully. If I really wanted his encouragement, I knew where to go to hear him tell me that he loved me. I began to see the Scriptures as a huge sanctuary divided into intricate meeting places with God speaking in all the rooms. I could choose what I needed to hear him say that day, as well as be surprised by him.

He's so powerful and the Bible is so magnificent that you can take one verse and build your life on it. Everyone should have his or her favorite verses and build his or her life on them. The Scriptures should be full of places with warm memories for you.

When you look at a Bible it should remind you of your journey, of your stops along the way in the word. They should be stops where you were comforted, just as Abraham and Jacob and all the great saints had geographical places where they had stopped, had heard God's voice and had built altars as reminders of how God had favored them. Over the years when they would pass by those places, they would be blessed by the memory of the day when God spoke to them.

For people today, the Scriptures should be full of "little altars"— places where God has spoken to them. One day you should be able to say about this whole book, "It's mine!" For it is. It was written to you. That's why, ultimately, I could say what I did about those words. They are so real that you can live off of them.

You see the Bible as a great message carrier.

There is more about God in this book than you can ever learn. There are hundreds of conversations, thousands of interactions you can have with him through these messages. If you want him to tell you that he loves you, he will do so anytime you want to hear it. If you need to be reminded of how secure you are, he will do that, too. If you feel tremendously hopeless and need encouragement, come to him. If it's glory you want, then he will tell you how to get it. If you need peace above all else, he will guide you along the way to it. He will give you his peace: "Cast your burden upon the Lord and He will sustain you."[57]

Do you hear that verse when you are under stress?

Haven't you ever experienced the comfort of a friend, of a spouse? Have you never received an unexpected favor from another person? What we crave most when we're hurting is just to be understood, really understood. Don't we want sympathy or empathy? His powerful words are spoken by his Spirit. This book is alive.

If you want his Spirit to speak to you, open it. Learn to hear his voice. He left emotional treasures waiting for us any time we want them if we read the Bible the way he asks us to read it and if we believe in the power of those words.

Faith, then, makes it true?

No, faith honors the truth.

There will be a thousand moments in your life when God will use this book to get personal messages through to you. He constantly tells you who he is and who you are. He tells you how to approach him and what to expect. He instructs you when to wait, how to wait, and how to trust him. Waiting is half the process because it teaches you who God is. Then you take him with you out into the world.

To find a way of reaching all men everywhere for all time requires a genius. The Scriptures are a miracle, and I never cease to be amazed at the beautiful creation with all its varied levels of communication he built into them. They are like a multistory mansion with all kinds of secret rooms and beautiful hidden gardens.

As you describe them, the Scriptures remind me of precious scrolls that an archeologist might find after years of searching in a foreign country.

And after the people in that country have overlooked what was right under their noses. They are like the man who spends his life in poverty with an oil field beneath his feet. The West today is turning to the Eastern philosophy for "truth," while it's hiding right there in the Westerners' own houses in Bibles.

The biggest criticism of the Bible continues to be the accusation that it is dead, that these words are meaningless, or at best, fairy tales.

Until you're born again, they are. When you are born again, you become an archeologist.

I know that one of the objections to the Bible is that it's such an ancient book. How can a book so old have any relevance for my life? That's a question I've heard repeatedly.

There's always a test to find the secrets. Adolescents wonder how that old man, particularly their father, can know anything. To be old, experienced, is exactly the idea. At first glance, one wonders what the Jews running around a small country thousands of years ago have to do with us. How can a poor Jew dying on a dusty hill two thousand years ago really have something to do with the rest of humankind? He couldn't be that important.

On second glance, that one man has everything to do with you. If his life has no significance, yours doesn't either. It won't be long before it's thousands of years from now, and your life will be meaningless. Humankind yearns for the crucifixion and resurrection, for one man to stand up and give all of us significance. Yes, the Scriptures are old, but check them out. Do they in any way sound like men and women today—and answer humanity's basic problems?

With all his glory, it says something to me about your father's character that he would choose seemingly insignificant ways to reveal himself and to change the world. Through one relatively small book—the Bible—and through one person who was insignificant by the world's standards.

Well, I did a few significant things. You should have tasted the wine I made—and my fish.

Like Paul said, God chose the insignificant of the world to confound the wise. The written word and the living word both came into the world seemingly in a small way. The written word was first given to a limited group of people. I was a plain man, a carpenter. Hollywood would have done it differently. My father and I promise you an ending that Hollywood could never touch. I came first in humble circumstances. Later I'll be back with all my glory.

My grandiose father indeed has a restrained side. Treasures of wisdom are hidden and must be sought after. You must work to find them—you will reap what you sow. Understanding also humbles you, teaches you that you were overlooking something. My father constantly teaches his people humility.

Some modern theologians say that since it has been so long since you were on the earth in person, we don't have your exact words or deeds; and, therefore, we can't trust the Bible.

My followers went to a lot of trouble to preserve my works—scribes were exact to an extreme. Above all, with all his power, God was behind the whole thing. If he can make a man, he can write a book.

Think of all the people who have read those holy words—I read them. So did John the Baptist, Paul, and all the apostles. Even the prophets read what Moses wrote in the Bible.

Some people say that they get nothing out of reading the Scriptures.

People say this is a dead book, and yet I learned everything from it. I found out from the Scriptures who I was, how I was conceived, and when I was to "go public." The Scriptures taught me that I would establish my authority by miracles. Indirectly the Scriptures often led me to perform certain miracles when I was in situations similar to those the prophets had known. Elijah raised a child from the dead. He also fed a family for months with a smattering of grain, and I fed five thousand with a few fish. Elijah stopped the rain for three years, and I calmed a raging sea.

The Scriptures gave me an incredible sense that my father knew everything—even before it happened—that he dominated and that I was to dominate. Then I could teach my men that they were to dominate and the Scriptures were to be a big part of that dominion.

So you meant what you said when you told people that you came so that they might have life abundantly.[58]

My father made Adam, the first man, to have dominion over his creation. He wants his children to dominate today, to overcome whatever pain or fear comes their way. To love in the face of hate. To control the situation instead of letting it control you.

Does that mean that believers are to never need therapists and that those who seek them out lack faith?

The Scriptures teach people to seek wisdom and understanding. To love someone is to help them understand themselves, and a therapist who understands the mind and how people block out the truth because of pain can be of great help in helping people face themselves. The Bible is not a complete textbook on psychology. People who claim otherwise are full of false pride and really don't want to look at the human heart.

Take a man like Freud who, despite his many errors, did people an enormous service by telling them to look deeper into themselves, into the closets of the mind. He discovered that in their heart, what he called the unconscious, people have many hidden deviant motivations, universally rebel against authority, and project their faults onto their neighbors.

As when you said that we see a speck in our neighbor's eye but miss a log in our own?[59]

Exactly. When it came to how badly people can deceive themselves, Freud stood side-by-side with the great prophet Jeremiah, who declared, "The heart is deceitful above all things, and desperately wicked: who can know it?"[60]

Freud also discovered the second language of the mind—the symbolic. This encoded language is the key to the heart or the mind. Freud overlooked the fact that I was using the second language long before he heard about it. So were the Scriptures. When I changed water to wine, I was primarily interpreting to the world that I was changing the way they were acceptable to God—before by their good deeds, now by my atonement. The Old Testament story of Abraham almost slaying his son Isaac contains the much more important message that one day the father would have to slay his only son. I grew up understanding the hidden language—it was how I learned through the Scriptures who I was.

Freud also identified the great capacity for denial particularly around the idea of death. Overall he all but preached the need for a savior who would deliver people from sin and death—only he couldn't see it himself. The psychoanalysts who thrive on understanding fail to see the degree to which "death is the shepherd of all mankind."[61]

My father and I will be lords even over the mind. Do you think true psychoanalysis is not my father's? Paul said it, "Christ, in whom are hidden all the treasures of wisdom and knowledge."[62]

The only words of hope for victory over death, the only interpretations to humans that can offer ongoing life, are hidden in me, in my mind. To really live again, one must accept the Freudian diagnosis of who men and women really are. Deep inside where the abscess of sin exists, the heart is selfish, power hungry, ruthless, and lustful. Even "good people" have the disease. The Freudian cure, self-forgiveness, simply doesn't work, because people can't.

There is one answer alone for the deepest level of humanity's guilt, and that is justice based on my atonement. Since a person's primary conflict in life is with my father who made him or her a human being, that person is well aware that deep down God is the One whom he or she has really attacked.

Each person is keenly aware somewhere in his or her heart that until he or she settles with God he or she will be, however subtly, engulfed with guilt. You will hate yourself and won't be able to look God in the eye. Like Freud, you will even deny he has a face. Until you accept the treasure that only I possess—forgiveness—you will never be a free person. You will never have a father in heaven. That's the interpretation I made with my life from the cross. It was the most painful statement in history.

A Role to Play

Did it bother you that your role was spelled out and that in a sense you were playing a part in a play?

There was a slight difference. The nails in this drama were real. It was a very difficult role to play, and the most difficult part of the script was the death scene, which, the more I read it, was unquestionably the clearest part. I knew down to the last detail how I would die. He made sure of that. I went over the Scriptures a thousand times. My face would be beaten beyond recognition. I would have forty lashes on my back. My beard would be pulled out. I would be nailed to a cross with my bones out of joint and with my mouth so dry that all I could taste would be dust.

How did you prepare for that?

He prepared me. There is some preparation in just knowing that you are going to be murdered. I remember that when I was older I used to pull my beard from time to time just to see what it felt like. One day my mother saw me doing it and asked me about it, and I told her, "You know what Isaiah says." She replied, "Don't! I don't want to think about it." Also, there was a slight comfort in knowing that at least none of my bones would be broken.

Since you were the son of God, God incarnate, many people will hold onto the idea that except for that last day, you were a "super human" being above it all. They would say that you knew everything that would happen, that life was so easy for you that all you had to do was to snap your fingers and you could do or have anything you wanted.

The people who think I was "superman" make a mockery of the incarnation. How was I going to teach people how to seek God, how to relate to him when they couldn't see him, and what to expect from him, if I had never had to seek him?

If all I had to do to find God was to open my eyes and see him or snap my fingers and find him there, I would know nothing about faith. If I'd used my omniscience, I would never have had to have an ounce of faith. Everything I taught, I learned firsthand.

What was one of the most difficult situations you had to face during these years?

When I was seventeen, my father Joseph became very sick. He and I were very close. I was his first child and oldest son, and he taught me his trade, carpentry. To watch him work was an education. He was thorough and proud in the right sense. When a piece of furniture left his shop, it had his name on it. Around Nazareth he had quite a reputation for integrity and quality. I noticed the respect other men had for him. He would never think of doing a job just to make money. If something couldn't be repaired properly and wouldn't hold up, he would refuse to do the job, even when his customers insisted and even when he needed the money, and even when he knew they could go down the street and get it done by someone else.

I remember when I was first learning the trade. As an eleven-year-old my work was not always perfect. He would take one look at a job I had done and all he would say was "do it over" or "finish the job." I heard those words a hundred times. "Finish the job." He made sure that I learned, even if I was to be his savior. All humanity was depending on my completing a greater task. One day I had to be able to say to the whole world, "It is finished."

I learned from him to observe small things about people and about nature. He was always asking me questions such as, "Did you see how that man didn't answer my question? He didn't want me to know that he doesn't have enough money. It hurts when you are poor." Or, just before spring when the trees and plants were still barren and the land gray, he would say, "Did you ever notice how, just before the trees are at their brightest, they are at their darkest? That's the way God works."

My earthly father knew how to raise a child, how to give him room to grow. Even though I always knew he was the authority in the home, I was comfortable with him. I enjoyed him. He was particularly good for a teenager because of his sense of humor. Another thing I enjoyed about him were his stories. He was a master storyteller. I can still hear my brothers and sisters after supper saying, "Father, tell us another story, tell us another story." Later on they were to call me a good teacher.

I learned how from both my fathers. That's where I learned to teach in parables.

I saw Joseph's faults, too, but no son was ever closer to his father. I think because he knew who I was, he was more open with me. For over seven years we worked side by side every day, and then suddenly he became ill. I was frightened, concerned. I prayed and fasted for three days, asking God to heal him. Joseph died early one morning after I had stayed up all night praying.

I felt defeated. I was God's only son and he didn't hear me. Why would my father do this to me? He knew I was to suffer enough and probably in the near future. Why did he add this to me? He knew how much I loved Joseph. My mother was left with a house full of children and now no husband. My little brothers and sisters lost their father, Joseph, who had so much to give to them. It was almost more than I could bear.

At that moment I had a choice. I could have become angry with God and called him a liar. "You are not my father in heaven. You don't have any power; you don't care." However, in my pain I was able to cling to his words, "Many are the afflictions of the righteous: but the Lord delivereth him out of them all."[63] And "when you pass through the waters, I will be with you."[64]

He was there. I was finally able to say to him, "I do not understand this. I hate it. I do not know why you allowed this to happen but you are still God Almighty with all your mercy and kindness, and you are still my father."

I could not see into the future, but he could. He wanted me to be the most compassionate man who ever lived. The price for compassion is pain. God was asking me to look at death and say to him, "You are still good." When it came time for my own death, he would ask me to say the same thing to the whole world.

My father was preparing me for the awesome test ahead when the temptation to renounce him would be so much greater, when he would again have to say, "No," to my prayer on another night of, "Please let this cup pass from me." He was developing me into his son, a man of character, who in the face of adversity did not desert his friends or his father. He wanted a son about whom he could say that he was well pleased.

At the moment Joseph died, it was the furthest thing from my mind that my father was shaping me into the savior of the world. The loss was so great that all I had was his word that he would work it out. You have to be in a situation like that to understand the incredible comfort of my father's words. They have always ultimately overcome pain of whatever type—fear, grief, poverty, and oppression. His words will always overcome the world.

In the middle of all my grief, I developed such a hatred for death that I thought I would be willing to go through death itself to destroy it. A tremendous hope began to grow. "So this—death—is what I am taking away. This is what I am going to do for the world." Now I desperately wanted to be the savior of the world. When I looked at my brothers and sisters and my mother, I was more determined than ever to do what God was asking. That helped to ease the pain. Satan had really made an enemy.

What other events made your life hard?

It was all hard. As I told you, the older I got, the more I wanted to be a teacher—to show others who my father really was. When my father Joseph died, suddenly I had to put aside my plans to be a teacher. My father worked it out and taught me the high cost of being a teacher—experiencing the pain of life that teaches you. Although I was only seventeen, I was the oldest son, and the responsibilities for our large family fell on my shoulders. I became the father. I took Joseph's place. I became the teacher for our family.

Nevertheless, raising my brothers and sisters was difficult. That was one reason I had to wait so long to be the Messiah. But, of course, my father wanted me to experience the pressures of being a father myself.

It wasn't the most pleasant household in the world. My brothers didn't respect me. Have you tried to raise an adolescent who doesn't respect you? I was also under the same curse every other person had been under since the fall. As the third chapter of Genesis states, "From this day on, you shall earn your living by the sweat of your brow."[65]

More than once as I was carrying the responsibility for my family, I remember thinking, "Doesn't it ever get any easier?" Even after Joseph died, the rumors continued about my birth. Some neighbors spoke of Joseph's death as being "God's judgment on Mary." That hurt.

Money had never been plentiful, but after my father died, making a living became such a struggle that I had to sell my gifts from the Magi.

What good came from all this for you?

It helped me understand my mission. I remember gradually selling what was left of my frankincense and myrrh to make ends meet. Finally, they were gone, and the day came when I had to sell my box of gold so I could put food on the table.

At first I was very sad. It was the only tangible gift I had left from my own father. How many times I had sat there and looked at it, but then I realized how fortunate I was to have a heavenly father who had given us savings to fall back on. I was able to give my best for the people I loved. One day I would say to the world, "That bread that you must eat in order to live is better than gold, because that bread is the body of a king." My gold was sacrificed for my family, just as my life was sacrificed for everyone.

Notes

1. Luke 1:42–45 TLB
2. Psalm 69:7b–8, 10–12 NIV
3. Luke 2:34–35a TLB
4. Luke 1:32–33 TLB
5. Psalm 89:35b–36a
6. Psalm 72:10 (implied)
7. Isaiah 11:2 NASB
8. Psalm 132:11–12 NIV
9. Psalm 121:1–2

10. Psalm 122:1
11. Psalm 122:7–8 TLB
12. Isaiah 11:2a NIV
13. See Daniel 11:3–4
14. Psalm 89:4 (implied)
15. Galatians 4:4 (implied)
16. Luke 2:48b TLB
17. Luke 2:49 (implied)
18. Luke 1:38b
19. Luke 1:47–48 TLB
20. Luke 2:10–12
21. Luke 2:14
22. Luke 2:29–31 TLB
23. Isaiah 7:14b NASB
24. Isaiah 53:5, 12a, c
25. Psalm 121:1
26. Psalm 121:2
27. Psalm 16:10 TLB
28. Luke 2:52 NASB
29. Hebrews 2:14b TLB
30. Matthew 4:4 NASB
31. Psalm 40:6–8
32. John 8:12
33. Psalm 22:1, 6–8, 12–18 TLB
34. Psalm 23:1–4b
35. Psalm 24:7–9
36. Psalm 25:2c
37. Psalm 27:1
38. Psalm 27:14
39. Psalm 27:1
40. Psalm 34:4 NIV
41. Isaiah 53:7b–c NIV
42. Psalm 118:6a
43. Jeremiah 1:8b
44. 2 Peter 1:4b NIV

45. Matthew 7:23a
46. Psalm 139:23–24
47. Romans 1:18–19 NIV
48. 1 Corinthians 13:4–8a NIV
49. Matthew 24:35
50. Psalm 45:7
51. Psalm 16:5c TLB
52. Psalm 56:8b TLB
53. Job 22:21
54. Psalm 30:5c
55. Zechariah 4:6b
56. Psalm 91:15
57. Psalm 55:22a NASB
58. John 10:10 (implied)
59. Matthew 7:3 (implied)
60. Jeremiah 17:9
61. Psalm 49:14 TLB
62. Colossians 2:2d–3 NIV
63. Psalm 34:19
64. Isaiah 43:2a NASB
65. Genesis 3:19 (implied)

CHAPTER TWO

BAPTISM, TEMPTATION, SELECTION

The Announcement

Between the time when you were twelve and found out you were the Messiah, and when you were thirty, when you "went public," you had to wait for eighteen long years. Did you know exactly when you would begin your ministry or did you have to wait with some uncertainty?

I knew I had to wait for my "announcer." The "voice in the wilderness" about whom Isaiah spoke. While I waited, I asked myself numerous questions. When would I start? What if the prophet showed up now? How would I begin? With my new sense of responsibility from being head of the household, I began to get a sense of the process in which I was involved. I saw how my father was preparing me.

It was always very clear to me that I had a lot left to learn about my father. His personality was so varied that I could take one verse of Scripture and meditate on it for a month. God gave me the brightest mind in history and it still took me many years to know him. I learned something new about him every day until the day I died.

The Scriptures implied that the Messiah would come in the fullness of time. I felt that meant two things. The stage would not only be set historically but the Messiah himself would also go forward when he was ready. It was a historical and a personal "fullness of time." When I began to understand that my becoming the Messiah was a developmental process, I was led to a deeper awareness of my father as someone who was in no hurry.

As time went on, David's life had new meaning for me. How long he had waited to be Israel's king! God promised him the throne when he was around twelve, but he was thirty years old before he got even a part of his kingdom. He was thirty-seven before he got the largest part, including the great city Jerusalem. David was special to me. His words had comforted me many times, and my father had used his writings to tell me so much about myself that I began to wonder whether David's own life had even more parallels to mine. Both of us had found out about our royalty around the age of twelve. Was my father now telling me that I would be thirty when I got part of my kingdom and that I would become the Messiah publicly at that time? Clearly I could see that the biography of David's life could be telling me, "When you do get your kingdom, you won't get it all at once. You will get most of your power later." I began to understand that when I returned the second time, I would completely rule and have much greater power. That part of David's life also matched perfectly with mine. Jerusalem and his greatest kingdom came in the second part of his reign.

The awareness that David had been thirty years old before he had become king occurred soon after my father Joseph died. I remember thinking that when I became thirty, my youngest sister—the youngest child in our family—would be fifteen and more than old enough to care for herself. As it turned out, that was exactly what the Scriptures were telling me. I was to be thirty years old when I announced to the world that I was the Messiah. My father taught us all to wait, and I was no different. Abraham waited one hundred years to have his first legitimate child, including twenty-five years after God promised that he would have a son. Joseph waited as a prisoner and a servant for about eighteen years before he became prime minister of Egypt. Moses waited forty years as a farmer and eighty years altogether before he became the leader of Israel.

The people of Israel had waited four hundred years since the last writer in the Old Testament, Malachi, had "signed off." Malachi had promised that "the next voice you hear—the next prophet—will be 'the man from the desert,' the 'voice crying in the wilderness.' The one following on the heels of the 'desert man' will be 'the voice.'"

When John finally came, the plan was being carried out at last, just as my father had said. It was a very secure feeling. I was nearly twenty-nine when John the Baptist first came on the scene and began to attract attention, and I just chuckled to myself. I now felt very certain that my father was telling me, "You're right. When you're thirty—that's the time."

Before you began your public life, you must have been thinking about what you were going to do as the Messiah and what you were going to say.

I wondered many times where I was to go. Would I be like John and stay mostly in one place, letting people come to me? Would I keep my job as a carpenter and teach, or would I go out and travel from city to city? Once again, the Scriptures were my guide. All of God's men had to go into the unknown, trusting him alone. Abraham left his home. Moses went to a foreign land. Joseph had to live in another land. David spent years in the wilderness. Would I have any less adventure than they?

The nation of Israel had trusted God for over forty years every day to lead them by a pillar of fire. There was something challenging about letting God lead me daily, about not planning, but letting him plan. I was determined to present myself to the world as the Messiah in the Spirit of "Give, don't take. Trust, don't fear." Those words were at the heart of what I wanted to teach. I was privileged to live those words as well as teach them. Although I didn't know exactly what I would say or do, I had confidence in the leadership of my Father.

You waited over a year after John the Baptist first appeared before you presented yourself. What made you finally decide to go forward? Were there any special signs directing you exactly when to declare whom you were?

I had also wondered where I would start my career. Everything pointed toward Jerusalem. I had been born near there. I was circumcised there at eight days of age. That's where I discovered that I was the Messiah. David had reigned there. The Passover was held there—a time when everyone thought and talked about the Messiah. When John the Baptist began his ministry baptizing people in the Jordan River, not far from Jerusalem, I felt that I had been given further confirmation. I wanted to do it around the time of Passover, for I was the Passover lamb.

My identity led me to think about Jerusalem as the place and Passover as the time. After John came, I realized even more how much authority my father had given me. I was to pick the moment that I gave myself to the world just as later I was to select the moment I was to die.

As you said later, "No one takes my life from me, I give it."

That's right. For a few years, I'd waited as the Baptist prepared the way, bringing about a radical change in many people's minds. His message was simple: everyone was a sinner who needed cleansing, and the lamb of God, the Messiah who would do it, was on the way.

One day about three months before Passover, after I'd finished all the work I'd promised my customers, I closed my part of the carpentry shop. I had turned all of my new business over to my brother. The last night at home, the night before I went out to be baptized by John, I remember praying, "Father, I know your ways, I believe you are asking me to step out and trust that you have called me this far and that you will lead me on. Tomorrow, as the sign of my willingness to do what you have asked, I will go to the Jordan River to be baptized by John. Please confirm to me that now is the time for me to publicly declare I am the Messiah. So many times before, you have answered me; I know you will again."

Why did you get baptized? You didn't need to repent of any sins.

Besides being a symbol of forgiveness, baptism is a picture of death and of resurrection. The body first goes under the water—"into the grave." I was saying to my father and to the world that I accepted my death.

Your cousin, John, was a sight to behold, wasn't he?

At first glance he was frightening. He had a beard down to his waist and long, wild-looking hair. As a child he had taken the Nazarene oath and had not cut his hair or his beard. He dressed in camel skins and lived in the wilderness eating wild honey and locusts. He had an incredible booming voice that sounded like thunder! He was a picture of God—awesome, bold. He looked like someone from another world—and yet, at the same time, he was very comforting.

Imagine God's turning someone like this loose on the world and saying to him, "Get them ready." Do you think my father doesn't have a sense of humor? When he does something of this nature, he does it better than anyone! Think about having a "public relations" man like John.

John was unlike any other preacher the people had ever seen or heard before. It was as if Ezekiel had just stepped out of the pages of the Old Testament. When John finally got a chance to use his voice, he wasn't shy about it. "You followers of the one true God of Israel, you chosen people, you're fat and lazy. You're not ready for the Messiah who is almost in your midst. You think you can rest on your heritage: Forget it! God can raise up followers out of these stones. I am the one Malachi talked about, the man from the wilderness, and I tell you, repent. Turn away from your sins, all of you. Come be baptized to show you mean it. Say it: 'I'm sorry. I'm sorry.'"

Far from being antagonized, the people were drawn to John like a magnet. They all wondered if he was not the prophet they had been waiting for. He told them he was not worthy to be the slave of the one who was coming soon. Repeatedly he warned them that the Messiah was coming with a big stick, with a life or death matter; with an ultimate choice. "Take me seriously," John said. "He, the holy one will separate wheat from chaff, and burn up the chaff with an eternal fire. Eternal. Eternal fire."

John was given such a strong message to deliver. He didn't understand I was going to show more mercy than he ever thought about. Even though he knew I was going to die, he thought I was going to come in as he had and take the world by claiming that the world was mine and denouncing sinners immediately with judgment. Even though he didn't completely understand my role, he never backed off from his truth.

Since he was a teenager, he had spent his time almost exclusively in the wilderness alone with God. Imagine a man with that kind of fire and energy having to channel it all into one relationship—and, at that, with someone whom he couldn't see. I had tremendous admiration for what John had done. I also had some idea of what it was like to wait before the father when everything inside me was bursting with excitement to share, with conviction to teach the truth yet having to contain it all.

Truth can be a terrible burden. John lived with that burden for about the same length of time as did I. He went to the wilderness just after his bar mitzvah at thirteen and spent seventeen years alone with God, preparing to become my prophet. My father wanted someone to take the message to the people whose heart burned for him. It takes years to get a heart warm and longer to get one burning hot.

Jesus once said that there was never one greater among all the men who had ever lived than John the Baptist. Now I understood why he felt so strongly about John. John had walked where Jesus had walked, had traveled the same road of alienation, unbelievable self-denial, and waiting— waiting—waiting, all for the father. In the midst of his pain, John had nowhere else to turn but to God for the comfort a human being so desperately needs. There John drank deeply from the living waters of Scripture, of prayer, of meditation, like no one else had ever done except one. Jesus and John had had the same father, and both knew him better than anyone else ever had.

Day after day, John railed against the authorities of the time, screaming at the hypocrisies. The bigger they were, the harder he came down on them. Jew or Gentile—it didn't make any difference. That's what finally got him killed. He condemned Herod, the ruler appointed by Rome, the enemy who occupied Israel, for stealing his brother's wife. Yet John came down hardest on the Pharisees for teaching the people false religion. He was so genuine. He deeply loved God and was totally devoted to saying what God wanted him to say. He didn't care what others thought. That was one reason he had such strong personal appeal. John was a free man. He assured the people of the enormous blessings waiting for them if they turned from their sins. People came from miles around to hear John preach—common people, teenagers, Roman soldiers, even Pharisees. His fame spread beyond Israel, and you've never seen anyone who could reach a crowd the way he could. After he preached, hundreds of people would line up to be baptized by John.

Most of all, the Baptist talked about me, telling them that a light had come into their midst. The Messiah was here! John really did his job. He prepared the crowds for me.

According to the gospel accounts, when you were standing in line to be baptized, it seemed that John didn't recognize you. That suggests that you had not seen your cousin in years. Did you think about telling him who you were?

John hadn't seen me in years. I thought about telling him, but my father had been able to tell me who I was. I figured that he was just as capable of telling John.

It seems that your father did a good job of informing John. The Scriptures record a very dramatic scene when John did recognize you.

Just before it was my turn to step into the water, a little dove landed on my shoulder and John startled me as he shouted to the crowd, "Look, the Lamb of God, who takes away the sin of the world!"[1]

I can still hear his voice echoing across the water. After he said it, silence fell over the crowd. Later John told me that a voice from God had told him that the man upon whom the dove had just landed was the Messiah.

I recall thinking, "What a great appreciation for history my father has. How well he knows how to communicate and how much trouble he goes to in order to do so. The dove was the symbol of hope, of new discovery, and most importantly, of peace. He showed me that he understood down to the last detail. As Isaiah had promised, I was to be the prince of peace. My father's preparation was making sure that it would come true. That was enormously comforting.

What happened next?

What happened next was just as surprising as the dove. John didn't want to baptize me. He wanted *me* to baptize *him*, but I insisted that I be baptized. He paused for a moment, looked at me, and then finally baptized me in a way to let me know that he understood. He told me to take a deep breath, and then he held me under a very long time, much longer than anyone else who was baptized. It was so long that I started to get short of breath. I felt the panic that happens when you can't get enough air. I almost lost control until I realized what he was doing.

He wanted me to feel that pain so much like death to let me know that he understood what this was costing me. He knew that one day I would lie in a grave. Finally, he brought me up out of the water. I was gasping for air as he stood there with his hand on my shoulder. It was a strong hand. After several seconds, I finally caught my breath, and then it happened: I heard my father's voice for the first time, saying, "This is my beloved Son, in whom I am well pleased."[2]

God could have said anything, but listen to what He said to me, "This is my beloved son in whom I am well pleased." I can still hear that rich, majestic voice. Heaven had opened! I had heard my own father's voice at last!

After thirty years of waiting!

Many times I had wanted to hear his voice just as Moses and the other prophets. Often I wondered why he hadn't spoken to me directly, especially if I were as important as the Scriptures and the world around me was telling me. When I needed it most, he spoke. During the years I waited, I wondered what his first words to me might be. Would they be direct encouragement such as, "Keep fighting the battle," or "Never give up"? Would they be just a command as with Abraham: "Go to Jerusalem"? Would they be just a greeting of some sort: "This is your father in heaven"? I had always had a feeling that they would be very kind and special, because his written words were like that. The impact on me was startling. All those years of preparation, of making sure, of waiting, of living on his written words, of keeping the faith, had been validated firsthand.

Another thought that had occurred to me after I had heard my father's voice was that I should have expected it. When the prophet Ezekiel was thirty, as the first verse in his book records, the "heavens opened" and God spoke to him for the first time. This happened just before God had asked Ezekiel to go publicly before Israel as a prophet and deliver his message to the people. Like me, Ezekiel was from the tribe of Judah. As I had waited all those years to hear my father's voice I had always wondered if he were telling me that I would be thirty years old when it would happen. Just before my baptism my mind was on other things and I had forgotten that message. I'm glad I did, because it was such a nice surprise.

For days afterward, his voice kept coming back to me: "This is my beloved son." It was all I could think about. It was such an overpowering experience that I wanted to be alone to savor it. I almost had to be alone to contain it. Before I went out into the world, I also wanted as intense an awareness of him as possible. I knew from experience that the way to heighten my sense of him was to be totally alone with him and to fast. I had to go over with him what I was to do and what I was to say. That knowledge could come only by waiting before him.

That was when you went into the wilderness and fasted for forty days?

The time had come for me to go out into the world and I was faced with two extremely difficult tasks. I had to tell everyone, including strangers, "I am the most important person in your life. Your ultimate destination of heaven or hell, rides on my shoulders." That wasn't easy. It was one thing for me to know that I was the Messiah. It was another to tell the world, "I've got a surprise for you. All those years you thought I was just a carpenter with some of you even questioning my heritage, I have been growing up among you as your Messiah, and my hour has now come." If my father could communicate to me that I was the Messiah, I could say it to the world.

I was also going out into the world to die and I had total freedom to choose not to go. But he had said to me, "This is my beloved son." I would do anything for him, even give up my life.

Did you plan to fast for as long as forty days when you went into the wilderness?

As I said, my experience at my baptism was so intense, I had to get away. My desire to respond to my father was so strong, I wanted to tell him, "You are my beloved father." I thought of Moses and Elijah both of whom had been so consumed by the Lord that they fasted for forty days and nights before him. Someone was driving me to do that too; so I started toward the wilderness to be alone with God.

I also knew the rest of the script. Before a new beginning in Scripture, there were always waiting periods of "forty." To create a new world, it rained for forty days and nights. After the great flood, Noah's ark came to rest on the mountain and Noah waited forty days "in the mountains" after his great discovery before he opened the windows of the ark and sent out a raven to explore the land. Moses waited forty years in the wilderness before he led the nation of Israel out of captivity in Egypt. The Israelites wandered for forty years in the wilderness before they went into the promised land.

The Scriptures led me even further. On one occasion, soon after Moses heard God's voice, he fasted for forty days and nights on Mount Sinai, where God had called to him from the clouds. Years later, Elijah had fasted in the same place in the wilderness for an identical forty-day period. I wouldn't have tempted my father and fasted without water, too, unless I had thought the Scriptures were clearly leading me. I felt that I needed a testing, something to prepare me for the big battle to come. I had to have a major battle with my flesh and defeat it if I were going to win the "big fight" at the end of my life when I had to overcome all of my physical senses, when everything in me would call out to give up. As it turned out, he had a bigger test planned for me than I knew.

Once again, the Scriptures guided me clearly as I remembered what Moses said to the Israelites toward the end of their forty years in the wilderness,

> Remember how the Lord your God led you all the way in the desert these forty years, to humble you and to test you in order to know what was in your heart, whether or not you would keep his commands. He humbled you, causing you to hunger and then feeding you with manna, which neither you nor your fathers had known, to teach you that man does not live on bread alone but on every word that comes from the mouth of the Lord."[3]

I felt that my father was saying, "Before you go out into the world, go over my words one more time. Live on them. Fast for forty days to test yourself." I obeyed my father. He led me every step of the way. For forty days I wanted to eat almost continually, but I didn't. I was practicing.

Was this fast an encouraging time for you?

Fasting is rather like seeing in the dark. At first, everything is black and all you can think about is pain and food. After a while, you begin to "see things," to perceive things that you couldn't at first. When you don't eat, you quickly recognize how vulnerable you are, and I wanted to know that. Without leaning heavily on him, I could never go through with it. Once again I went over my role, and my mission became more focused than ever—even after I had already thought that it was clear.

My father had indeed filled me in a new way with his spirit and I understood more in depth what I was about. It was just as the eleventh chapter of Isaiah had promised the Messiah:

> And there shall come forth a rod out of the stem of Jesse, and a Branch shall grow out of his roots: and the spirit of the Lord shall rest upon him, the spirit of wisdom and understanding, the spirit of counsel and might, the spirit of knowledge and of the fear of the Lord.[4]

You mentioned you became more focused. What became clearer for you?

Everything depended on me. Salvation would be by me and me alone. No one else could please God ultimately. No matter how hard they had tried, they had all failed and always would. I would please him, though. He had promised. I was his son. For those forty days, I went over and over his words spoken to me. When I wasn't thinking about food, I thought only of my father and my role, and that experience took me to a new depth.

It became more and more clear that when I carried out this mission I would be changing the face of an entire religion, affecting ceremonies that were embedded in a way of life. Soon there would be no need for animal sacrifices, altars, or ceremonial washing. Yom Kippur would not be celebrated in the same way. If I understood all that I thought I did, the social implications themselves were enormous. Never again would people have to bring animals to sacrifice so that God would continue to bless them, because by then the sacrifice would have been made once and for all. The whole worship service would have to change its emphasis and everyone who was "sprinkled with my blood" would now be able to enter the Holy of Holies.* The Phari-

---

* Only one man in all of Israel, the High Priest, could enter the sacred room in the temple called the Holy of Holies. Then he could enter on only one day of the year— Yom Kippur—the Day of Atonement. At that time, the High Priest would take the blood of a goat and sprinkle it on the mercy seat that was atop the ark in the Holy of Holies. The blood represented a symbolic atonement for the sins of all the people of

sees would have a hard time with that one. No one likes to share power. My father was making me into a "radical," even if I didn't want to be. Truth is a sword that cuts wide paths wherever it goes.

As all of this went through my mind, I realized how much my father was asking of me. As is so characteristic of him, whenever he asks much, he gives much in return. His Spirit was there in a new way, even more alive. You know how someone's personality can affect you when they are there beside you. You can feel their spirit, their energy. I couldn't see him, but I could feel him. His words had never been more alive. I was completely one with him, and now I knew that my words would be his words. Everything I would say would have just as much authority as if he said it. Even better yet, he would be saying it through me when I spoke. As great as it was to hear my father's voice, the experience in the wilderness and the oneness I shared with him there was the greatest moment of my life. It was to be the central focus of my teachings. I never felt stronger than I did at that moment on the fortieth day of my fast. That's when "he" appeared.

He? You mean Satan? Did you know beforehand you were going to be tempted?

Not consciously. Unconsciously I knew everything. Consciously I knew that I could expect the enemy at some point.

But later on you were recorded as saying before you could take an enemy's house you had to defeat him. You clearly saw the world as Satan's house, didn't you?

That's what I learned when he tempted me. I didn't know exactly what Satan was going to do. I knew he would try to turn the people against me and that death was waiting for me eventually. I also knew

---

Israel. If God accepted the sacrifice that year, the Priest was allowed to live. It was a very solemn time, and the people waited outside while their High Priest went into that sacred room to meet with God. Every year there was a rope tied to the High Priest's leg so that if he offended God and the sacrifice was not accepted, then the people could pull him out if he were struck dead.

that he had tried to kill me as a baby and had tried to discourage me many times. In the back of my mind, I knew he would try to deceive me and, like a good soldier, I had trained my mind to be prepared for an unexpected attack.

Like the time your own disciple Peter tried to discourage you from going to the cross and you snapped at him, "Get behind me, Satan."[5]

At this particular time in the wilderness I was elated. I had just heard my father's voice. He was never closer. He was there beside me. I had just finished the forty-day fast when Satan surprised me.

You said he just appeared.

It had been forty days. I was thinking I would finally be able to eat something. As I was starting back to town I came around a boulder and suddenly a man appeared. He was a little on the short side, had a winsome smile and seemed to be exceptionally gentle and kind. After a few minutes with him, I decided that he was perhaps the most striking person I had ever met. He radiated warmth. We began talking and it was obvious that he knew what I had been doing. As time went on, I began to think that was perhaps one of my father's ways of revealing himself to me. After all, God had just spoken to me for the first time, and in the Old Testament angels had often appeared to various men.

I halfheartedly wondered if this were a trick but he was the kind of person who dispelled doubt and put you at ease. Besides, I hadn't talked to another human being for forty days. He seemed to take delight in me and to revere me. I told him about my joy and he seemed to understand. He even brought up the fact that I would overcome the evil in the world. It crossed my mind that he might be the enemy, but he was so convincing. We talked some more about fasting and what a great experience it had been. We both laughed when he said, "I don't suppose you are hungry." I had not asked him who he was, but ever so gently he volunteered, "I have been in the heavens with your father and I have come to talk to you."

That part was true about having been with God.

He said, "We both know your uniqueness, your special role, and how your father wants to give you everything he has including his power." He said, "Read the Old Testament. The Messiah will make the blind see and the lame walk. He means that literally, he is going to give you that power by faith. All you have to do is believe him." He continued, "God wants you to use your power. He doesn't want you to suffer any longer. He knows how hungry you are. Go ahead. Use the power he's given you. You are hungry." In an encouraging manner, he said, "If you are the son of God, turn these stones into bread."

Things were really moving fast for me. Was God, my father, pushing me to trust him more? This man was so encouraging! It seemed exactly the right thing to do. I was starving. Two things made me wait. One, I didn't really know this man, and there was just the slightest hint of urgency in his suggestion—of impulsiveness—of acting without thinking. And there was that one little word thrown in almost offhandedly—"if"—"*if* you are the son of God." More importantly, I knew the code—and the code was "wait." Abraham, Joseph, Moses, David—all the prophets had waited for God to put them in a place of power. Just as the Scriptures that had led me to fast for forty days said, "He humbled you, . . . to teach you that man does not live on bread alone."[6]

The Scriptures seemed to be saying to me that he would feed me; when he was ready he would send the manna. I had never done anything ahead of my father's command. If I were to do something more, this man-angel, if that's what he was, would have to show me out of God's word something that I didn't know was there. Or I would have to hear it straight from God.

That's what the whole test for forty days had been about, to learn to put his words ahead of everything, my instincts included, just as the Scriptures had led me to do in the first place when I began to fast. Besides, I was here to use my father's power for humanity's benefit, not mine; so I told Satan the same thing that Moses had just told me: "Man shall not live by bread alone, but by every word that proceedeth out of the mouth of God."[7]

I really wanted to turn those stones into bread. I thought I had that kind of faith and that kind of deity.

How did Satan react?

He was cunning. He dropped the subject immediately and acted as if it didn't bother him one bit. That relaxed me. I recall thinking that perhaps I wasn't trusting God—maybe this was his way of communicating with me and I was not pleasing to him.

The little man said, "Come with me." He whisked me to the top of the temple, miles away, and that power frightened me. We were sitting on top of the magnificent temple on the southeast corner, with the Kidron Valley four hundred and fifty feet below. He began talking about the power that God had given to me and how it was God's will that I use it. He could understand my reluctance, he said, but he told me that God had sent him to teach me and that now was the time for me to live out my faith in God just as my mother had. Then he looked down at the ground and said that there was a message for me hidden in the Scriptures just as all the other secrets were. He said it was the same kind of message that had led me to fast for forty days without food and water like Elijah did. Then he quoted part of Psalm 91: "For he will command his angels concerning you to guard you in all your ways; they will lift you up in their hands, so that you will not strike your foot against a stone."[8]

Satan said, "You can see that the Scriptures have prophesied this moment and are telling you to jump to the ground from here. The angels surrounding us will catch you. Listen to what your great, almighty father says to you. He will guard you in all your ways. He really means your ways, whatever you want to do." Quietly, almost in a whisper, but firmly, he said, "Use your power! Use it. Don't lack faith, believe! If you are the son of God, cast yourself down."

It was difficult for me to think. There was something daring in what he was saying. I loved the challenge. This man-angel had taken me right to the word of God. Was God reading my mind? Was my father again going before me as the Scriptures had said he always would? On top of that, it seemed as if my every thought had been anticipated and the Scriptures seemed so specific for this moment. I had always wondered what that verse meant. There was a godlike power in faith, and nothing pleased my father like our having faith in him. It was a totally new world that was being opened to me and I wanted to experience his power in a new way. I wanted to jump! Could I fall from this building and be caught by angels? Is God that real? To be caught by God six inches before I was to be bashed to death. What a challenge! I needed that much confidence in him to go out into the world to do what I had to do. After all, to be the Messiah was a supreme challenge of faith. Shouldn't I go ahead and use my power if I were really the Messiah?

I already knew that I would perform miracles to get the people's attention at some time in the near future. Prophecy told me that. Why not start now? I had always planned on making as bold an entrance as possible. After all, my father was bold. He had sent my cousin, John the Baptist. He had chosen Solomon at one time to make a bold statement. David charged boldly down the hill to meet Goliath. Maybe that was a picture of me jumping down from this building. I wanted to jump. That challenge was within my power. My father was greater than material power, greater than those rocks below.

My thoughts also went back to Moses' sermon to the Israelites just before they entered the promised land after wandering for forty years on a journey that should have taken them only about eleven days. It had been prolonged because the people didn't trust God. That part of Scripture was so fresh in my mind because it was about how the Jews were to handle their new blessing, their new land, after such a long wait. This was precisely what I had been thinking about. I needed to know how to handle my new role, my new power.

One of the things Moses told them was not to push God, not to demand or complain, but to accept what he had given to them. Here was Israel's great leader at the end of his life leaving them his final words, even though he couldn't go with them because of his own disobedience. He had pushed God and demanded more than God had wanted to give. So Moses told his people, "Ye shall not tempt the Lord your God."[9]

Moses had learned the hard way and, through Moses' example, I thought I had my answer to this man-angel's urgings. Moses' disobedience had come when he smashed a rock that he wasn't supposed to strike. It occurred to me that perhaps I wasn't to smash the rocks either.

This particular place on the temple was also known as "blasphemer's corner" where the authorities on occasion pushed blasphemers to their death. Was this location a message from my father saying, "Don't blaspheme me?" Quickly my mind flashed through the remainder of Scripture and immediately I thought of David, my character. God had told him when he was twelve that he would be Israel's next king. This had come about because God was extremely displeased with the man who was then king, Saul. After David's anointing by the prophet Samuel, Saul made several attempts to kill David and David spent twelve years living in caves, hiding from Saul.

David had two specific opportunities to kill Saul, and he would have been justified in doing so. After all, Saul was attempting to kill him unjustly. But David decided if he were to be king, he would wait for God to make him king. Again the message was, "Wait." Even more specific was the message, "Wait for the power."

As I looked at this man-angel who was urging me to act, the same doubts flashed through my mind. The subtle word, "if," was a problem. What did it remind me of? What was it? Then I remembered! There was the same doubt in the first book in the Bible when Satan used doubt to deceive Eve as to what God had said. Satan had asked Eve, "Did God really say, 'Don't eat the fruit of that tree?'" when he knew very well that God had. Satan had urged Eve to eat something, too, like this man-angel had just urged me to eat minutes before.

Something else reminded me of that garden. The garden was a deserted place. Satan suddenly appeared out of nowhere and started talking. He had obviously been very charming. The confusion started to clear for me. Was this man really trying to push me just for my own good? This was the second time he had wanted me to act quickly. The first time he had wanted me to use my power. Now he wanted me to force my father to use his power. There was just a hint of urgency, of manipulation. That had been Eve and Adam's mistake. They had been manipulated into action. "Watch out, think, don't act. Wait on the Lord," the Scriptures seemed to be screaming at me. David's answer to uncertainty had been wait on the Lord. I thought I had my answer, too.

It occurred to me that if I jumped, popularity would be mine. Then again, I knew I had not come to win a popularity contest. I knew I would do miracles, but somehow the idea of "jumping off a building" onto some rocks below seemed to draw more attention to me without having much value to others. The rocks themselves seemed to be images of deadness as I looked at them. Right then I also had the thought that surely God wouldn't believe that I would do anything without him. "Surely this isn't that kind of test," I thought. "I haven't eaten in a long time. Maybe I'm not thinking clearly." I thought of Job and David and others. God did allow tests, but God wasn't the tempter himself.

I still wasn't absolutely sure what it was intended to test—my faith or my pride. My father knew I had faith. I definitely had my answer. God did not tempt me and I would not tempt him. There was no manipulation, no coercion in our relationship. He was God Almighty and I was his beloved son. I could still hear those words. Whatever he gave me, *he* gave me. I didn't take it. I waited on his gifts. I answered the man-angel, "Thou shall not tempt the Lord thy God."[10]

What happened then?

After I had refused him a second time, he acted again as if nothing bothered him. I sensed something unusual about him then, because if he had really been an angel of God, I don't think he would have been able to be so indifferent if it were a true test of faith.

His third temptation came quickly and was exceptionally blatant. In the blink of an eye, he once again transported me to a distant place. This time it was to a tremendously high mountain, actually to several high mountains, over a short period of time. There were all the kingdoms of the world below us. What a magnificent sight it was! That kind of power display could take your breath away. The little man was god-like. Then he showed me his kingdom—all the kingdoms of the world below us. As he saw me looking around almost in a state of shock at what I was seeing, he said to me, with all his cleverness, "I know you won't do this," and he paused ever so slightly, "but if you will bow down to me, all of these are yours." For a brief moment it was so appealing. All that power offered with no pain, and I was meant to rule. As always, if you wait, evil becomes obvious. It was clear that this one last effort was utterly evil.

Just a good old bribe?

When all else had failed, his true colors showed. He used the oldest trick in the book: offering riches, power, and fame for my soul. Now I knew who this angel was. I had an eerie feeling. I was indeed in the presence of Satan himself. For a minute, I saw how great he could have been. He was powerful, persuasive, charming, but so unlike my father. My father doesn't offer riches. He offers himself. I detested Satan. He wants to take my father's place. I shouted at him, "Away from me, Satan! For it is written: 'Worship the Lord your God, and serve him only.'"[11]

It was really my father's world, not Satan's. A mean and most hateful look came over Satan's face. I had never seen anyone's face change so drastically. He was gone in a flash! Suddenly I found myself back at the boulder in the wilderness. Immediately, the loyal angels came and brought me food, and we talked about why my father had let me go through these temptations. This, too, was similar to what had happened to Elijah. An angel had brought him food and water in the middle of a wilderness after his great spiritual battle. Manna.

All three of your answers to Satan came from Moses' sermon at the end of his life, recorded in Deuteronomy.

It wasn't a coincidence that I had just been dwelling on Moses' words for forty days. The Scriptures were telling me that this was what I should think about before I went into public ministry. Those were the same words that my teacher, the spirit, used to lead me into the wilderness.

Moments After

How did you feel after the temptation?

I had vindicated my father's methods. He had taught me to know him through Scripture. And when the test came, I showed that I understood him very well. I thought of all those times I had questioned him. "Was he going to lead me to be the Messiah of the world without ever directly communicating with me?" I had wondered.

He had taught me to put his words above everything. If he said an event was going to occur, no matter what the odds seemed against it happening, it would happen exactly as he said it would. If he said I could do something, no matter how strong my feelings to the contrary, I could do it. If he said I was the savior of the world, I was the savior of the world. If he told me he was guiding me, he was guiding me even when I didn't know it. Many times I could see his guidance only "after the fact," just as he had guided me into exactly how to answer Satan. When I read back over the Scriptures I could see that he had even told me ahead of time what I was to say. I had learned that reality was what he said it was, not what I or anyone else thought. Reality was his word. I learned to live on those words and I never forgot how.

Suppose you had gone ahead and performed either of those two miracles. If it were an honest mistake, what would have been wrong with that?

The thought that "It doesn't matter" is the most subtle of Satan's voices. It would still have been a sin, no matter how small. You can see how deceitful his appeal is. Leprosy starts from the smallest sore. All Satan wanted me to do was to sin once. Then I would have the disease, too. Another reason I waited was that, as much as I wanted to see God work with my own eyes, I knew it was this same idea that led to idol worship. The people couldn't wait for God. They had to see him with their eyes and not with their faith. They got so tired of waiting that they made their own gods out of wood and stone and gold. I would see God when he wanted me to, not when I wanted.

Satan was particularly clever in the second temptation when he tried to make
you think that you had already tested God by fasting for forty days without
food and water. What was the difference between the fast and the temptation?

The difference was that God led me to fast. He didn't lead me to jump off a building. When I went into the wilderness to fast I had never felt more led to do something in my life. The writers of the New Testament report that I was driven into the wilderness by the Holy Spirit and that's exactly what happened. I had just been baptized and filled with the Holy Spirit in a special and new way.

Certainly a man has to be careful when he says God leads him to do something because his feelings can mislead him. There was also an impulsive quality to Satan's urgings. He gave me no time to think it over, and that's usually not God's way. When I was led to fast in the wilderness, I had the whole way out there to think it over.

Some people still have difficulty with the idea that you did not use your
omniscience at all times. They would see that as denying your deity.

If you understand the incarnation and that I constantly possessed my omniscience but chose not to access it, you can see how I was fully human but never lost an ounce of my deity. In fact it was crucial that I didn't use it to remain fully human. Those people who fear me losing my deity should be equally afraid of me losing my humanity.

The second I used my omniscience I would no longer be fully human and I would be unable to atone. My atonement only counted if I was fully human and could pass the test of all the human temptations. Like I told Peter when they came to take me prisoner I could have used all my power and stopped them. On the cross I could have come down, but I chose not to. Long before I came to Earth, I obviously had had a plan, and was determined to carry it out. In a real way I submitted to myself as well as my father, just as all believers must do.

Once I knew I was God, I realized everything was mine. At the same moment, though, I came into an awareness of my self-denial, of how much I had laid aside to come to earth. I chose to continue with what my father and I had started. People who focus excessively on my deity to the exclusion of my full humanity are in denial about the extent of their sin and fail to see how badly they need me to be fully human.

Coming back to the temptation, Satan must have made a strong impression on you.

I knew then firsthand why he was called the "angel of light." How subtly deceitful he was, and how appealing and harmless he made evil seem. The only way to counteract him was to know God's mind and to wait for God. I had waited all those years, and even after I had heard my father's voice, I still had to wait.

The more I thought about Christ's three temptations, the more human and divine he became at the same time. His first two temptations touched on probably our two most basic fears. The first temptation had to do with sustenance, "Will we have enough—enough food, enough love?" The second temptation had to do with our ever-present fears of annihilation.

The third temptation is also ours, but not exactly his. Forever do we, in secret or not so secret ways, crave fame. Ironically, the most famous man in the history of the world couldn't have cared less about fame in the sense that we think about it. He cared only about loving just as his father who gives us the freedom to choose him. Who waits patiently on millions of his people for thousands of years. I wondered if we were God, how long we would wait for "our human beings." Three weeks, maybe?

I was comforted by the thought that while Christ didn't crave fame, he did want recognition. As the New Testament says, "Who for the joy that was set before him endured the cross, despising the shame."[12]

The third temptation revealed even further how unlike us he was. We would have been tempted just to bow down to Satan and "not mean it." We would have missed the fact that at the exact moment we deceived anyone to the slightest degree, we would have become deceitful ourselves. Jesus was so pure that the thought of a tacit bow never occurred to him, as evidenced by his vehement response. There was only one person to bow before—the Lord God Almighty.

I reflected, too, on Jesus' comments about his self-imposed veiling of his omniscience. He was right. He depended on the Scriptures as we do. At the same time he revealed his innate difference from us, he was also one with us. There in the second temptation, Satan had tried to tempt Jesus with the Scriptures. If Jesus had immediately used his omniscience, it could not possibly have been a temptation. The verse in Hebrews again came to mind, "For in that he [Jesus] himself hath suffered being tempted, he is able to succor [aid] them that are tempted."[13]

With overwhelming clarity, the Scriptures were revealing how much like us he became. Once again, I saw how much restraint was to characterize his life. By not acting as Adam and Eve did, but rather by controlling himself, first at his temptation and later at his crucifixion, it was as if he were putting back in their place all those terrible forces which had been unleashed at the fall.

The Rewards of Waiting

All through this interview you have mentioned waiting a lot. Waiting seems to have been a constant theme that permeated all your teaching. For example, you said, "Blessed are you when people insult you, persecute you and falsely say all kinds of evil against you because of me. Rejoice and be glad, because great is your reward in heaven."[14] The so-called beatitudes in the sermon on the mount all had to do with waiting: "Blessed are the meek, for they will inherit the earth."[15]

One of the great tests of faith comes as we wait. That's why I emphasized it so. We all have to wait. The question is how to wait. Should we be complaining or waiting in expectation? Freud's thinking is not far removed from mine when he talks about delayed gratification as a sign of maturity. There are rich rewards for waiting. Some of those rewards we even get here on earth just when we need them.

After the temptation, I remembered distinctly my prayer before I journeyed into the wilderness on my forty-day fast. As I meditated on my mission, I said, "Father, show me the way. Help me to make sure of my way. This has to be for you, father, for your glory." Look what he had done! It was so like him to work all things out for good. He had used the devil himself to show me how important my life was. I was worth all the kings and kingdoms of the world. I could do miracles now if I wished. Finally, through Satan my father showed me the tremendous protection that surrounded me because I knew I could have jumped from the temple at that moment if God had said so. My father had trained me and I had won the first battle. It encouraged me and prepared me for the next battle I knew was to come eventually. Then, as is so characteristic of him, he gave me rewards beyond anything I had imagined for winning my battle with Satan. He sent a group of angels to minister to me.

What did you and the angels talk about? I'm assuming you had a conversation.

There was immediate intimacy. The first thing we discussed was my victory over Satan. We talked about how clever he was up to a point. I was awed by how impressed the angels were with him. They spoke of how great he had been in heaven before he fell. At one point, I remarked, "If he was so great, how could he have done what he did?" One of the angels answered, "I suppose it had to happen. He had so much intimacy with all of you, and that freedom made him think he was as great as God himself. It was much the same with Adam."

I had many questions for those angels about my role, about heaven, and about my previous life. First I asked them if they had permission to answer my questions. "Your father said you could ask anything," they said. "All that he has is yours."

So I inquired about my father and his glory and what I'd been like before. They answered me, "You were just like your father, and that words can't describe. You were both awesome and comforting—all at the same time. You've never seen anything like it. Words don't even come close to describing your father or you. Heaven is the same way.

You can't imagine the joy or the freedom there. All you're working for is worth it. You will bring happiness beyond belief to your followers—to those you and your father have chosen. There's so much love there, and absolutely no fear." Another angel spoke up, "We constantly see your place at your father's right hand. It's waiting for you to return. The reception that is planned for you will surpass the party we gave you when your father sent you to the earth."

I wanted to know if my understanding of the Scriptures was correct. They had already alluded to the trinity, and I went over my understanding of it with them. I began in the first chapter of Genesis, "Let us make man in our image."[16] Then, in the psalms, David had prayed to his Lord the Messiah who was already at God's right hand. In Isaiah, God the father, himself, called his only begotten son not only "Wonderful, Counselor, . . . The Prince of Peace," but also, "The mighty God, The everlasting Father."[17]

The father and the son were so close that the son was to be called father also. We are distinct identities and yet have such an incomprehensible oneness that we both have the same name. I didn't understand all of that then, but I went on. Throughout the Scriptures there were continual references to God pouring out his spirit upon certain people, and promises to do so even more in the future for all believers. The spirit of the Lord was often referred to in such a way that he began to take an identity of his own.

Then it occurred to me that perhaps the godhead had another partner—a "silent partner." How like God that would be—to be as great as God the father and yet so humble that you would never draw attention to yourself even to the point of keeping your identity almost secret. That meant my teacher had been not only my father but also his Holy Spirit, another member of the godhead, which now one could call the trinity.

The more I looked at the Scriptures, the more signs there were pointing toward a triune headship. God was the God of "Abraham, Isaac and Jacob." Joseph, Moses, and David all had three distinct periods in their lives. Joseph was the favored one, the prisoner/slave and finally the prime minister. Moses was the favored one, the rejected farmer and then the elder statesman. David was the anointed one, the hunted criminal, the great king.

The Scriptures also proclaim, "the heavens declare his handiwork," and when I looked at nature there were "threes" all around. There are three obvious parts of the environment—the earth, the sky, and the sun, and on the earth we notice land, sea, and sky. There are three kinds of objects in the heavens—the sun, moon, and stars. Water itself can take three forms. There are three primary colors—yellow for my father as king, red for me and my sacrifice, and blue for the Holy Spirit. Today you know that there are three parts to an atom (proton, neutron, and electron), the basic building block of the universe.

So the son of God had to wait to see all his glory?

Just like you.

The angels gave me a foretaste of my glory when they repeated exactly the proclamation that the angel of the Lord delivered to the shepherds the night I was born: "Behold I bring you good tidings of great joy, which shall be to all people. For unto you is born this day in the city of David, a savior, which is Christ the Lord. . . ." Then all the angels spontaneously sang the chorus that followed knowing I had never heard it either, "Glory to God in the highest, and on earth peace, good will toward men."[18]

It was the best music I'd ever heard on earth. I knew again that heaven was going to be beyond our wildest dreams.

After the Angels

After that talk with the angels, I was a different man. Before, I was in the passive role—being baptized, waiting in the wilderness, being challenged and tested by Satan, being fed and ministered to by the angels. Now I was taking over. I was going to let my light shine. Until I assumed the passive role for one last time at the end of my life, I would be the active one.

After listening to his interpretation of the Scriptures, it occurred to me that as human beings our present knowledge of God is limited by the boundary of Scripture. Having voluntarily become a man, Jesus limited himself, with a few exceptions, by that same boundary—and yet look how much more he discovered within the same boundaries. Among his many accomplishments, he was also the most brilliant student who ever lived. I wonder if one day "after it's all over" if he won't pick up these Scriptures just as he did with his disciples after his resurrection, and say to us, "Let's go through them again; I want to show you some things that you didn't see the first time."

When did you begin to use this power you were now aware you had?

Not right away. I knew he would show me when.

How did he show you?

Of all places, I was at a wedding party where they had run out of wine and my mother asked me to use my power to provide more.

I remember that story of your changing water into wine. Did you believe your mother's encouragement was a message from God? Or did you feel that perhaps your mother was asking you to use your power apart from God as Satan had?

This wasn't the first time God had used my mother to get a message to me. Mother knew about the recent events, such as my baptism and the temptation. She was well aware that the Scriptures had promised me power, and she knew I was waiting to use it. God encouraged her to give me a "motherly" push. When they ran out of wine at the party, the hostess was understandably upset. My mother was sympathetic with her friend's embarrassment. Because of the anxiety associated with her own wedding, mother always had a particular fondness for and sensitivity to weddings. She especially wished for them to go well. It was almost as though she was making up for what she had missed. When she saw her friend's distress, she said, "I might be able to help you."

She immediately came to me with the story and with some servants. Incredulously, I looked at her and said, "My time has not yet come."[19] She didn't reply to me, but simply spoke to the servants: "Do whatever he tells you."[20]

At first, I was caught completely off guard. It was so out of character for my mother, but then I wondered. "Is my father trying to tell me something?" Immediately, I recalled Moses' first miracle. He had turned the water in the Nile River blood red in order to get Pharaoh to set the Jewish people free. My first miracle would be to turn water into red wine as proof that I came to set all people free.

I also saw the beauty in what God was doing. Here was the woman who had given me life, who had sacrificed her life and her reputation for me. This beautiful lady had taught me all my life about God. She had confirmed who I was and encouraged me along the way, accepting my role. Now she was given the honor of launching me into the world as the Messiah. Her request was quite different from Satan's. She left it entirely up to me. "Do as he says." Satan had wanted to tell me what to do. He had wanted to control me.

Water into wine is an amazing miracle, but it seems insignificant in comparison to healing the sick and raising the dead to life. What significance did you see in this first miracle?

My father had set the scene. His message confirmed my mother's. The symbols around me were from Scripture. Water was the element used in Moses' miracle and John's baptism. When my mother asked me to produce wine, it was just as though my father said, "I know what I am asking you to do. The river of living water is a river of blood. Look at Moses. The deliverer has to lead his people across the Red Sea.

I even had them name that sea for you, for your blood. I've had it waiting for you all these years. Also, hear what your cousin John is saying. He told them that his baptism with water was not enough. It had to be your baptism with blood. I want the world to know the cost of the baptism, the cost of the new covenant you are negotiating on their behalf.* Go ahead, turn the water into wine. 'The seers' need to see it."

It was both a sermon and a picture of the great party to come. This impression of God's disliking pleasure is far from the truth. C. S. Lewis talked about my father at heart being almost a hedonist. The writers of the *Westminster Catechism* understood that fact well when they wrote, "What is the chief end of man? To glorify God and to enjoy him forever." Enjoy him! Pleasure will permeate all of heaven. Heaven will be so continually full of surprises, it will be beyond belief.

By that miracle, my father also was saying that I would make a drastic change in every believer's life. No longer were people to be burdened by the cumbersome ceremonies of the Law. After my death and resurrection, those who believed in me would be instantly changed—as quickly as the water was changed to wine—into righteous priests before the Lord. He would indwell them, and they would be his people.

The first miracle must have had quite an effect on you. Now you knew and had experienced that power.

It made me feel as though I were God. Before I told them to fill the containers with water, I remember asking myself again, "All I'm going to do is speak and the water will change to wine?" Then it went through my mind, "That's the way the Scriptures tell me we created the world.

---

* Through the sacrifice of his own life, Jesus negotiated a new covenant with God for man. Prior to this, the old covenant between God and man, which the Jews lived under for twelve hundred years, was basically a contract in which God had said to man, "If you are good and keep my commands, I will bless you." The new covenant takes into account man's basic nature as a rebel and says, "If you will repent and accept Christ's punishment as your own, I will forgive you and then, furthermore, I will give you the ability to walk in my way."

God spoke, and out of nothing the world came into existence." If I had done it before, I could do it again. I had known all along that one day I would perform miracles. When you do something for the first time, it feels strange, unfamiliar. My father had prepared me by letting me know in advance what I would do.

I told the servants, "Fill those containers with water and bring them to me." While they were gone, I thought about the temptation and my encounter with Satan. I thought of all the power Satan had. If the "rebellious one" had that much power, then the true son would have more. When the servants returned with six huge vats, I looked at all that water and thought to myself, "It's never going to be the same after this. Crowds will come. And, in the end, my blood will be spilled, enough to wash away the sins of the world." I looked at that water again and prayed, "It's my blood to do with what I want, but father, I give it to you. Accept it as my sacrifice for them. May many come and drink of it. World, I give unto you my blood. Here it is. Now."

Immediately, the water turned to the bright red wine. The partygoers said it was the best wine they had ever had. This kind of dramatic change was what our whole plan was about. The most bitter persecution and oppression the world had ever known would also be the sweetest event in history. Death would bring life. It seems paradoxical to say it, but that miracle increased my faith in what I was doing. It also humbled me.

Miracles

You are aware that some theologians say that your miracles didn't actually happen. They say that people in your day were so primitive that they explained things in magical ways that really weren't accurate.

You must realize that the writers of two thousand years ago were educated men who could read and write and who worked for a living. They also had difficulty believing in miracles. Could these men have consistently misinterpreted these events?

Another matter to consider is that God in his sovereignty has arranged trust at the heart of the universe. Can you take the word of these writers, which is really his word, or is his word no good? If you can't begin to try to trust an essentially honest person, then you can't begin to trust God. If that is the case, then you wouldn't be very comfortable in heaven, for heaven will be filled with people trusting one another.

What many modern professors are really saying is that they are better observers than people of biblical times. They mistake so-called knowledge for wisdom. They don't want to trust because they want to exalt themselves over their neighbors as well as over Moses, David, Paul, and me. It always comes back to pride, doesn't it?

My miracles were my calling cards, my personal trademark. That was the way I backed up my words. I was God before I came. I was God when I came here. I will be God for all the tomorrows.

My father worked in the same way. Almost every major character in the Old Testament is associated with a miracle: Adam and Eve's creation; Isaac's supernatural birth; Joseph and Daniel becoming national heroes in a foreign country after a supernatural interpretation of a king's dream; Moses parting the Red Sea; Elijah overwhelming the false prophets of Baal by setting water-soaked wood on fire.

One wonders how such brilliant people who deny your miracles can be so mistaken.

Look at Lucifer. He was more brilliant than any of the angels. Brilliance doesn't rule our pride. Usually the two go hand in hand. Many modern day teachers don't want me to have power they don't have. They don't want me to be God because they're not.

There have been scattered miracles performed in recent years and Christians continue to report unbelievable answers to prayer; but why don't you do these spectacular miracles anymore?

The greatest miracle of all is the fact that you have been blessed with God himself in you and that you have his very words to you anytime you want them. That's far more than most people in history have had. The Bible is a true miracle—words even angels longed to see for centuries.

Cleaning Out the Temple

Shortly after that miracle at the wedding in Cana, you went to Jerusalem for Passover. You began to testify to your messianic identity not only with your miracles, but also with other actions. You surprised everyone with your grand entrance at the temple when you introduced yourself to the moneychangers, the first of two such introductions you made to them.

For eighteen years I had gone to Jerusalem for Passover and I had watched the corruption in the temple get progressively worse, particularly as the moneychangers became more prominent. Jews came from all over the known world to celebrate Passover. Among the Jews were Gentile proselytes—converts to Judaism as a result of the dispersion of the Jews to many nations. They came from their pagan lands and were joined by their fellow Jews from all over Israel to meet their holy God in Jerusalem in his house as he had commanded.

What did they find in the temple? Moneychangers and merchants allegedly there to serve the people, but in reality, they were in business to sell animals, which the pilgrims couldn't bring long distances for sacrifice, and to exchange foreign money for Jewish coins that alone could be used to pay temple dues. They were victimizing the travelers. Here in my father's holy temple, people who had come hundreds of miles to worship were being forced to haggle over goods and were being cheated. These merchants and moneychangers, who paid well for the right to set up in the Court of the Gentiles, derived a goodly portion of their income from cheating in God's name. They disturbed the only worship place available to the Gentile converts. The moneychangers, with the help of the Pharisees, had desecrated my father's own house.

Each time I visited the temple prior to my public announcement, my anger at the moneychangers and merchants grew. "Somebody ought to throw them out, animals and all," I thought.

The year before my baptism the moneychangers had been particularly corrupt and repulsed me even more than usual. For weeks afterward, I kept having the recurring fantasy of walking in and cleaning out the temple. Then, one day as I was reading the Scriptures, I saw something else from that familiar messianic Psalm 69, which had often comforted me as a young boy facing ridicule, "Zeal for Your house has consumed me."[21]

Was my father telling me that one day I would be the one to clean out the temple? How like him to confirm my intuition and put my "instructions" in that particular psalm—the one that described the degradation of my mother and earthly father by some people I had wanted to throw out of town when I was ten years old. Then I could only take the abuse. Now, as I watched my heavenly father being degraded, I wondered if he were telling me I could defend his honor just as I had wanted to defend that of my parents before.

I knew that if I took action against the moneychangers, many people, particularly the Pharisees, would not like it. I was coming to understand why the Scriptures said what they did about my death—why the authorities were going to be the ones who ultimately would kill me. They were not doing their jobs; I would do it for them, and they would hate me for it.

I had also often wondered how I would make my announcement to the world as to exactly who I was. I searched the Scriptures for clues. Psalm 24 said that Jerusalem was to open her gates for the King. That was where my father's house was, and where the Messiah's throne was. I had already made two journeys there from Nazareth with great revelations occurring each time. The first was when, at eight days of age, I was circumcised in the temple at Jerusalem and proclaimed to be the Messiah by the two prophets, Anna and Simeon. The second was at age twelve when I discovered who I was at Jerusalem during Passover. I was the Passover lamb. Would it be proper for Israel's long-awaited Messiah to make his announcement at any place other than Jerusalem or at any time other than Passover?

Finally, I saw the plan. I was coming in my father's name to his house in judgment. That was how I was going to make my announcement.

Just as Samson had cleared out a temple of pagans, I, too, would do so. After all, I was paying the same price that Samson had paid to do it.*

When I came to my first Passover after publicly being declared the Messiah by John, I once again saw this beautiful majestic temple built for the glory of my father being turned into a marketplace. I could not go into the temple without being furious, and now I knew what my father was saying to me: "Your feelings are my feelings. It is my house. Go, throw them out—in my name." So I did.

When I got to the temple I saw the same corruption. I saw merchants selling cattle, sheep, and doves for sacrifices. I saw the moneychangers, and I went to work. First, I made a whip out of rope and then I struck quickly. I lashed at the moneychanger to drive him from behind his table, scattering his precious money across the court-yard. I had no favorites. One by one I went to every table as rapidly as I could. A few of the men, whose initial impression was that a mad man was loose in the temple courtyard, thought they could stop me. When they saw me using a whip with one hand and turning over an eighteen-foot-long, three-hundred-pound table with another, they suddenly realized they couldn't. Samson was loose in the temple!

Next the merchants selling animals for sacrifices felt the sting of my whip as I overturned their benches and began cutting loose their sheep and oxen, separating the merchants as I drove them out, "Get these things out of here. Don't turn my father's house into a market." The sheep and oxen I had freed noisily made their escape as the doves madly flapped their wings amidst the chaos. Now all of these animals were loose in the great courtyard of the temple. Some moneychangers scurried out. Others wanted to stay and protect their property. Some merchants who were trying to get out, bumping and pushing, with their cages of doves, converged and caused a chaotic roadblock. There I was, coming down the great Court of the Gentiles from one table to another right behind them, lashing away. Fear was in their eyes. This was judgment day!

---

* To rid a pagan temple of the enemies of God, Samson gave his life and pulled down the pillars of the temple, destroying himself and all within the crowded temple.

All was confusion when I had finished. I was so angry! I had run five hundred or more moneychangers and merchants along with all the animals out of the temple.

Gentle Jesus, meek and mild. That's not all there is to you.

Then the Pharisees arrived. Some of them had been inside the temple. Most had been in the hallways of the porches just outside the courtyard when they heard the commotion and looked around to see people and animals flying out of the courtyard. The Pharisees came running to me, demanding to know on whose authority I had just done this, and demanding that I show them a miracle at that moment to back up my deed. I told them, "All right, I will perform a miracle for you. Destroy this temple and in three days I will raise it up."

You confused them intentionally, it seems.

Those who wanted could hear what I was saying. I was telling them, "Stay around, for you will see a great miracle—the greatest—which gives me this authority. When you kill me, I will come back to life after I'm in the grave three days." The Pharisees missed the announcement I made to them. I had walked in the temple, changed things around, told them it was my father's house, and they, as T. S. Eliot once said, "had the experience and missed the meaning."

All they could do was to demand a miracle immediately. If they had just given me a chance, they would have seen miracles. I understood that a man who claimed to be the Messiah had better be able to back it up. Already I had given them a hint as to who I was when I performed my first miracle at the wedding in Cana. News spread quickly in the small country, particularly around Passover, but these Pharisees were not going to hear of it.

During that time in Jerusalem, I performed several miracles, but I saw that the Pharisees were not going to respond. I also understood that people needed much more preparation if any of them were going to hear me; so I picked up the message of John the Baptist, and, with several disciples, began baptizing people in the Jordan River. For almost the entire first year after my announcement, all I did was baptize people. As I had told my mother, the fullness of time for my ministry had not yet come. I had to do all I could to prepare the people's hearts to hear my real message. The work of repentance, of humility, still had to be done to open their minds.

Crowds came, bigger than those that gathered around John. The Pharisees became agitated to the point that they tried to incite envy in John. Unflinchingly, John told them that he must decrease and I must increase. The viciousness of the Pharisees was more apparent. I had done my work in Jerusalem, and now I had to take my announcement to the rest of the people.

I would return to Jerusalem on my last tour and make one final major offer on Palm Sunday. Before I did that, however, I would spend the next year and a half in northern Israel, in Galilee, with only a few brief trips to Jerusalem for religious holidays. I went to Galilee to gather a following who would stand by me.

On the Road Again

You had an interesting encounter on your trip back to Galilee from Jerusalem.

About midway on my journey I became fatigued and stopped at Jacob's well that was near the land Jacob had given to his son, Joseph. In my day the area was part of Samaria. Samaritans and Jews were enemies. Jews would have nothing to do with their "unclean" neighbors. The well was famous for its great depth, which brought forth wonderfully cool water. As I sat there resting, a Samaritan woman came to draw water. She had come alone in the hot part of the day— obviously at a different time from the other women who came in the morning or evening when it was cooler. She was an outcast.

I asked her for a drink. Indignantly, she informed me that I was a Jew and she wanted to know how I could dare ask her for water. When she made that comment, I was sure she was an outcast because she had tried to make me feel like one. I told her, "If you knew the gift of

God and who it is that asks you for a drink, you would have asked him and he would have given you living water."[22]

My father led me to this metaphor, I was thirsty, at Jacob's great well, and water had been at the center of my life for the last eight months, as daily I had watched hundreds be baptized.

The woman then asked me where she could get this living water and, in the same breath, asked me if I thought I was greater than their father, Jacob, who gave them this very well and drank out of it himself.

I told her, "Everyone who drinks this water will be thirsty again, but whoever drinks the water I give him will never thirst."[23]

I even added that a person who drinks this water would live forever. Very sarcastically, this feisty woman retorted once again, "Sir, give me this water so that I won't get thirsty and have to keep coming here to draw water."[24]

I told her that if she really wanted this water, to go get her husband and come back. Abruptly, she told me she had no husband. I told her I knew that was true. My father had given me the information I needed. I knew that she had had five husbands and that she was not married to the man with whom she lived.

With that, she realized there was something different about me, and the expression on her face changed dramatically. This revelation didn't slow her down entirely. She said, "I can see that you are a prophet. Our fathers worshiped on this mountain, but you Jews claim that the place where we must worship is in Jerusalem."[25]

She felt discriminated against. I told her the Jews had understood things correctly in the past, but a time was coming and indeed was here, when the true believers would worship God wherever they wanted. Only they would worship him in spirit and in truth, for God was a spirit.

At this point, she looked completely puzzled, but fell back on the comfort of her limited knowledge and informed me that one day the Messiah was coming and he would explain everything. I looked straight into her eyes, and slowly said to her, "I who speak to you am he."[26] For once, she had absolutely nothing to say.

My disciples arrived at just that moment. They all had that "What's he up to now?" look on their faces. During our years together that became a look I saw many times. Once again, my disciples were puzzled by my behavior. All wanted to rebuke me or at least to ask why I was talking to this outcast, but they didn't dare. By now they were beginning to learn not always to trust their natural responses, which pleased me.

The Samaritan woman, leaving behind her water jar, immediately hurried to tell her friends who I was, and very soon there was a crowd of people from the nearby town approaching us. My disciples urged me to eat something since they knew it had been a while since my last meal. I told them I had food to eat that they knew nothing about. My food was to do the will of him who sent me to finish his work. By now I wasn't hungry, because I was so thrilled at this lost woman's response and the response of her friends.

Whenever someone made a heartfelt commitment, I could see into the future and know better than anyone else what it would mean to him, and I know the pain and suffering from which he had just been delivered. At that moment, another person had been freed to one day be the most glorious creature imaginable. She became a person who would experience eternally a love, my father's love, and the depth of which she had no conception. She had been in a life or death struggle and I—life—had won another soul. Death—Satan—had lost another battle. Those moments of victory we will talk about forever.

Isn't that when you made the great statement about evangelizing: "Open your eyes and look at the fields! They are ripe for harvest"?[27]

I harvested that day and the next, too. That determined woman brought everyone she knew, and many of them became my followers. The Samaritans were starved for the truth. Their response came on the heels of a planned attack by the Pharisees—the people above all who should have received me. Yet here were these people whom the Pharisees would have considered "spiritually ignorant," pleading with me to stay longer. They proclaimed for all their neighbors to hear that I was the savior of the world. I was so moved by their warmth that one day when the opportunity arose, I made them the central characters in a parable and honored them forever. My disciples and I learned an important lesson during that unexpected two-day stop: because of me, many who are apparent enemies will become friends.

What happened next on your journey?

After I left Samaria, one of the first towns I visited in Galilee was the town where I'd performed my first miracle, Cana. A Roman government official from the nearby town of Capernaum heard I was there, sought me out, and pleaded with me to come to his home immediately to heal his dying son. This man was so desperate he didn't even acknowledge me. He just begged me to come home with him. I looked at this desperate Roman and, although my heart went out to him, I wanted to teach him that there was more to my father and myself than just our power. So I asked him, "Won't any of you believe in me unless I do more and more miracles?"[28]

He was so distraught that he could hardly comprehend what I was saying. He pleaded with me again, "Sir, please come home with me before my child dies."

I told him, "Go back home. Your son is healed!"[29] Suddenly, the man had a startled look on his face. He started to ask me to come home with him again, but thought better of that and eventually said only to me, "Thank you, sir." He walked off believing me. One thing the Romans had learned was to respect authority.

When he was about halfway home, his servants met him and said that his son was healed. The official asked them what time the boy had begun to improve and they told him at one o'clock the afternoon before—the exact moment I had commanded the healing. The Roman official had received the message, and he and his entire household came to understand that I was the Messiah. Then they gave me the acknowledgement I had wanted: they trusted me.

The heart of salvation is saying to you, "I trust you."

Trust is the ultimate compliment. Everyone who has ever lived, or will ever live, must say to me and my father one way or another, "I trust you" or, "I don't trust you." There's no room in our family for distrust. That's why heaven is going to be so unbelievable. Just as every moment of life on this earth is filled with anxiety or potential anxiety—death is only a heartbeat away—every moment in heaven will be one of absolute, unwavering trust. Trust will replace all fear. Trust is the one attribute you must have to get into heaven. It's a particular kind of trust; a test. One must say to God either, "I trust you, God," or "I trust myself, my own character, my own judgment." There's not room ultimately for completely trusting both.

All of life is designed to show us our need to trust. Trust or faith is woven into every moment of our beings. We are surrounded by organizations, businesses, governments, and leaders who constantly ask us to trust them. Every map you ever read asks for trust. Every time you go to bed, you trust the sun will be there in the morning. The very nature of history demands trust. You can't see a hundred years back or even back to your own birth. You have to depend upon someone else or someone else's book to tell you. God put history at the heart of the universe to testify to his book. The intellectual who is always saying, "None of this faith business for me, I only believe what I can see," doesn't live in the real world. He or she is just like the Pharisees who didn't trust me and didn't live in reality either. How hard it is for one to give up the old faith in self. How hard it is to trust that someone else's mind is better than yours. That's the danger of power; it freezes your mind. Be careful about mindsets.

Another one of your bold moves shortly after you began your public ministry in Galilee was to go to your hometown on a Sabbath and proclaim the fulfillment of the messianic prophecy recorded in Isaiah.

On the Sabbath, someone in the synagogue was to read from the Scriptures. As I was visiting my old synagogue on this particular day, they passed to me the scrolls to read, which "coincidentally" happened to be the book of Isaiah where more is written about the Messiah than in any other Old Testament book. I marveled at the way my father would lay these things in my lap.

Before I read the Scriptures, the rabbi introduced me and the people spontaneously applauded—something they were allowed to do in the synagogue in my day. They had heard of me—my preaching and some of my miracles. Although many were skeptical because they had known my family and me all my life, and I had been "just a carpenter," still I was one of theirs and a celebrity. After the applause died down, I read the messianic prophecy in Isaiah:

> The Spirit of the Lord is on me, because he has anointed me to preach good news to the poor. He has sent me to proclaim freedom for the prisoners and recovery of sight for the blind, to release the oppressed, to proclaim the year of the Lord's favor.[30]

When I finished, I rolled up the scroll, paused for a minute as I looked at everyone in the room, and then said, "Today this scripture is fulfilled in your hearing."[31]

The people were stunned. Their silence was broken as they reacted violently. "But we know you—you are just a carpenter—you are Joseph's son. You're a heretic!" I informed them that I knew they would react that way. Both Elijah and Elisha had been rejected by their own people but believed in by foreigners. This only made the congregation angrier.

Suddenly they shoved me out of the synagogue, and immediately a mob formed. They began to push me down the road leading out of town, shouting at me, until we came to the cliff outside the city. They intended to cast me to my death. I was just a few steps away from the edge, but up to this point, I had not resisted. For a moment, I wondered if this would be where I would jump and the angels would protect me. When I got one step away from disaster, I simply walked right through them as though they were not there. Their strength was nothing compared to mine. When I got to the other side of the crowd, I walked away from them.

It was at that moment I realized what I had done. God had rescued me again in a surprising way. He had not planned a rescue for me after I would have been pushed over the cliff. That would have put me in a completely passive role. Instead he had done something so typical of my father. He had let me—forced me—to use his power again, which was now my power. He wanted me to know that I had power over everyone on this earth, including an unruly mob, so that when that mob came for me at the end of my earthly life, it would be apparent to everyone that I was giving my life away. Nobody would take it from me.

I thought about Jesus' entrance into the world as its Messiah. He had done it in such a subtle way that at first glance one could miss the boldness that surrounded his claim. Even the Scriptures told the story in parts. One has to read all four gospels to get the whole story, as if God were trying to say, "If you want to get the full impact my son made, you're going to have to work."

Here is how Jesus made his entry. First, he came on the wings of an introduction by a dynamic, frightening prophet, to this point the greatest and most awaited prophet in Israel's history. Then he began performing extraordinary miracles in Jerusalem at Passover. This was only after, however, he had had his "coming-out party" at a most fitting location—a wedding where he performed the first of thousands of miracles. It was as if Jesus were saying to his people, "I am wed to my followers for life." Then, like a ruler taking charge, he immediately cleansed his father's temple— the only territory, the only thing close to a material possession he ever identified himself with, and even then it was his father's house, not his.

A short time later, Jesus fearlessly made his startling proclamation in his hometown of Nazareth. He was saying to the people he grew up with, "Whether you love me or not, I am a loyal son, and you who knew me first will have one of the first chances to see who I really am." Surely Jesus came in like a king, but it was as his kind of king and not the world's kind. He remained humble, full of grace and truth.

A New Base and a New Team

After that experience in Nazareth, it's obvious you wouldn't spend much time there.

I had to find another place to establish my base. I headed for Capernaum. It was not far away, a beautiful town on the edge of the Sea of Galilee. It was an ideal location for travel to other towns either by land or by water, and I planned to travel. Besides, a certain Roman official in Capernaum had a boat, and I felt sure it would be at my disposal any time I wanted it.

The more logical reason for choosing Capernaum was that Isaiah had prophesied that I would live in that area. I had my instructions even as to where my base was to be.* After making that decision, I began to determine who would be charged with carrying on the message after I left.

I'm glad you mentioned your disciples. I was interested in the way you selected them.

Andrew and John had been disciples of John the Baptist. They had heard John proclaim one day as I walked by, "There is the Lamb of God." Immediately, these two future disciples followed me to the place where I was staying. Later that day, Andrew introduced me to his brother Peter, and told him that I was the Messiah. We talked late into the night. Some time later when I was in Galilee, I was walking by the seashore early one morning. I saw Peter and Andrew out on a boat not far from the shore where they had been fishing all night. Until that time, Peter's catch had been very poor; so I shouted at him to cast his

---

* "In the past he humbled the land of Zebulun and the land of Naphtali [on either side of Capernaum], but in the future he will honor Galilee of the Gentiles, by the way of the sea, along the Jordan—The people walking in darkness have seen a great light; on those living in the land of the shadow of death a light has dawned" (Isa. 9:1–2 NIV).

nets on the other side of the boat. He did so, and immediately his nets nearly broke from the huge catch he made. He was overwhelmed. There in the boat, he fell to his knees and loudly proclaimed to everyone around that I was the Messiah. Then I told Peter and Andrew to come with me and I would make them fishers of men. They did so.

And you did!

Peter was a leader. He responded quickly and wholeheartedly. He was a large redheaded fisherman who was afraid of nothing. Fear only overtook him on that day when he denied knowing me. Even then, when I was taken prisoner, he followed me all the way to the Roman headquarters.

Two of my other disciples, James and John, were very responsive, also. These two brothers, like Andrew and Peter, were fishermen. They were also my first cousins, sons of my mother's sister Salome. I had known them for a number of years, as we would see each other on holidays or on an occasional visit. The same grandparents had reared our mothers, and I knew what kinds of hearts they had.

Shortly after Peter's big catch he came to shore and told James and John what had happened. That's when I walked up to them and said, "Come, follow me," and they did. These three—Peter, James, and John—were natural leaders of the group. They were very aggressive. Because they were such effective leaders, I spent more time with them than with the others.*

I nicknamed James and John the "sons of thunder" because of their temperaments. One day John "caught" a man casting out demons in my name and rebuked him because the man wasn't a part of our group. I had to tell John that "he who is not against you is for you."[32]

Later toward the end of my public ministry when I was making my final trip to Jerusalem, we needed a place to stay in a nearby Samaritan

---

* Often Jesus took just these three disciples with him at special times. They went with him to observe his Transfiguration. On the night before his death, these were the three he asked to stay with him and comfort him while he prayed in the Garden of Gethsemane.

village. I sent several disciples ahead to make arrangements. Before we got to the village, the disciples came back and told us that the Samaritans refused to give us accommodations because we were from Judea. Immediately James and John asked me to call down fire on that village. I had to rebuke them.

Another time, the mother of these two, my Aunt Salome, asked me if her two sons could sit on my right and left when I attained my kingdom. James and John were nearby, with the other disciples not very far away, and their eyes indicated that they, too, would like those seating arrangements. I told them that they didn't know what they were asking, that the honor was up to my father. I also asked them if they thought that they could drink from the same bitter cup as I. Did they want the same type of baptism that I was going to have?

You were implying suffering and death.

That's the cost of being close to me. They said they did indeed want the same baptism I would have. They still didn't know what they were asking, but I gave them what they wanted. As it turned out, they both suffered tremendous persecution. James was beheaded for being a follower of mine. John was persecuted throughout his life and eventually exiled to the Isle of Patmos where he wrote the book of Revelation. How John learned to channel all his assertiveness into an aggressive love! He was the one leaning on my shoulder at the last supper. He was the disciple who comforted my mother at my crucifixion. He stood by her side throughout the entire ordeal. He and Peter arose early in the morning to be the first disciples to visit my grave.

Later John wrote four great books on love included in the New Testament. For sixty-five years after my death, he was known to the early church as the "apostle of love." The story has been told often that even at age ninety he was a revered old saint. When asked to speak, John would still be telling the people to put their differences aside and would say, "Little children, love one another." He never quit talking about love.

After John came Nathaniel and Philip. Actually, they were chosen before James. They were from the same town as the two pairs of brothers—Peter and Andrew, James and John—and Nathaniel was a lot like Peter. He had been standing beneath a fig tree when Philip, who had just found out about me, came up to him and said excitedly, "We have found the Messiah!—the very person Moses and the prophets told about! His name is Jesus, the son of Joseph from Nazareth."

Nathaniel's immediate response was, "Nazareth! Can anything good come from there?"* [33]

Philip finally talked Nathaniel into meeting me, and they walked several miles to find me. As they approached, I said to Nathaniel, "Here comes an honest man, a true son of Israel." [34] Nathaniel had been direct about what he really thought about people from Nazareth. Immediately he asked me how I knew what he was like. I told him I even knew where he had been standing two hours ago—by a fig tree—when Philip had found him. Nathaniel blurted out, "You are the Son of God," [35] just as quickly as he had doubted me initially.

Then you told him that he would see greater things—that he would see angels visiting you back and forth from heaven. How did you know all these things? You've told me you didn't constantly use supernatural vision.

Usually when these incidents occurred, one of two things happened. Sometimes it just came to my mind the way most of our thoughts come to us. That's what happened with Nathaniel. Read the Old Testament and you'll see that's not so strange. Many times a prophet just "knew" something. God uses dreams, angels, and thoughts. They're all outside our control to some degree.

Other times, as when Peter was fishing, I would privately ask God to do something for me, such as put fish in that particular place. Then I would just tell others it had been done. "There are fish over there."

---

* Jesus' hometown was considered to be both rural and pagan, as it was just off the great caravan route to the East.

Another disciple that comes to mind is "doubting Thomas." Was he as much of an "unbeliever" as tradition has it?

Every group needs a man like Thomas who, in many ways, was the opposite of Peter. Thomas was a thinker who usually asked questions before he acted. He had to know why he was doing something. However, when enough of his questions were answered, he was a man of incredible devotion and courage. On one occasion toward the end of our three and a half years together, I had received a message that our friend, Lazarus, was very ill. He was the brother of two of our other good friends, Mary and Martha, at whose house we had stayed several times. When I received the news I said that we would go to see Lazarus. Lazarus and his sisters lived near Jerusalem, but the last time we had been in Jerusalem the Pharisees had threatened to kill me. All the disciples except Thomas warned me about that and didn't want us to go. I had constantly tried to tell my men I was put here to die, but they couldn't hear me. Thomas had heard my talking about my death and all he said, when I wanted to visit Lazarus, was "let's go too [to Jerusalem]—and die with him."[36]

Of all my disciples, Thomas came the closest to understanding my mission. His mind just wasn't comprehensive enough to conceive of the resurrection. If he didn't understand something, he would speak up. At the last supper it was he who questioned my statement that I would go to prepare places for my people. Thomas was confused, so he asked how they could know the way when they had no idea where I was going.

That's when you made the great statement, "I am the way, the truth, and the life: no man cometh unto the Father, but by me."[37]

Yes. After my death, Thomas was crushed and simply withdrew from everyone. He was unlike Peter, who had to be around others. After my death, I appeared to a few of my disciples individually. The first time I appeared to them as a group, Thomas was off by himself grieving. Later the other disciples told him what had happened, but Thomas said that unless he saw the wounds on my hands and touched them, he wouldn't believe it.

Eight days later, Thomas was with them in another locked room. They were still afraid of the Jews. I had seen all the others previously, so the first thing I did was look at Thomas and hold out my hands to him, "Put your fingers on my hands, and touch my side; now believe."

Thomas fell to his knees and in utter amazement cried out, "My Lord and my God!"[38] That's as great a confession of faith as you'll find in all the New Testament.

Thomas wasn't one to give his loyalty cheaply. That was one of the reasons I chose him. For years to come I wanted the world to look at my disciples and realize that these men were not blind followers. They were rugged men, who had difficulty bowing to any man or to God. They asked piercing questions. My claim to messiahship was strong enough to withstand the scrutiny of a "doubting Thomas."

Another one of your men, Matthew, responded to your simple, bold offer, "Come with me." That was a very daring invitation, "Drop what you are doing. Risk everything. Follow me."

Matthew was a tax collector. He was a sneak and a thief, a part of the most hated group of the Jewish society that I grew up in. A tax collector bought his office, and since Judea was a Roman province, he was responsible to Rome for a certain amount of money each year. Anything over that amount was his. You can imagine how corrupt and manipulative the tax collectors were. Every one of them was wealthy. They were hated even more as Jews working for Rome. They were traitors.

One day I was walking by the booth of a tax collector named Levi. He was sitting in his booth with his fancy robes and all his rings, looking smug and in control. I knew he was miserable—he had to be. He was created to give and receive love and respect from others and himself, and he had neither. I wanted as one of my disciples somebody who would qualify as "the last person you would expect" so that he would give everyone else hope. No one is ever so far from me that he can't reach my hand. I was looking for a man like this, and as I passed by Matthew with the usual crowd of people following me, I suddenly turned and walked toward him. I stopped directly in front of him and with the crowd behind me, I said, "Levi, follow me."

"Risk it all."

Initially, to show me he was not intimidated, Matthew had remained seated. After my offer, his smugness evaporated. He couldn't believe that I would even talk to him, much less know his name and offer a personal invitation. There was a look of shock on his face but it was a shock of hope, and I saw him weighing the offer. He was getting one chance at a new life. He had to give up so much; at first, far more than any of the other disciples.

For Matthew, to come with me meant no turning back. Peter, Andrew, James, John, and most of the others had a trade to go back to. They could always return to fishing. Once Matthew gave up his office, that was it. He would have no career, no security. If he were mistaken about me, he would be unable to return to his friends. He would no longer be able to keep up with them socially, and they would all think that he was crazy. To find a place in society when you were a former tax collector was extremely difficult. The decision that I was asking him to make quickly meant giving up everything, all his wealth, all his comforts. I was asking him to turn his back on a glamorous lifestyle to follow "a religious fanatic," who roamed the countryside. These were "unattractive" people who had no gold rings, no fine robes, and no beautiful homes.

Was Matthew going to risk all of this because of me—an unknown man, physically rather plain, and yet who knew him and who asked him personally to be his follower? Should he give up everything because of this man? He had heard this was the Messiah and did the things a Messiah would do. That man now appealed to him boldly. This Matthew admired. He himself often shocked people to get what he wanted. Frequently, Matthew would quote an astronomical figure as a shock tactic to a person who owed taxes. Then when he lowered the amount to a price he knew that person could pay, the person in a way would be relieved and almost glad to pay.

As I looked in Matthew's eyes, I could see that he wanted to go but couldn't quite make the move. I began to walk away. After I'd gone perhaps twenty feet, I heard the sound of feet running after me. He had done it! Matthew became a beautiful man—a choice disciple. He was a man who once would have cheated a widow out of her last coin. Now, he repaid twice over all the people he had wronged. Over time, he became a generous, loving man. That's what conversion is all about. Every time I looked at him, he was grateful. He never got over the fact that I had chosen him. I didn't want him to. He was a constant reminder to me of why I was dying.

Matthew obviously was very special to you. Would that be any reason his book is the first book in the New Testament? Would you and your father honor someone in that way?

My father never forgot what Matthew gave up for me. He looks for ways to honor his people. You cannot imagine all the honors he has in store for his people.

Why did you change Matthew's name?

Levi was a despicable name to everyone who knew him. I changed his name to Matthew, which means "the gift of God." And, believe me, Matthew became a gift to the whole world. What esteem Matthew has been held in for centuries. His name has been repeated billions of times. Thousands of people have been named for him and he has been quoted by millions of people for years. Whenever the gospel writers are referred to, it's always Matthew first. "Matthew, Mark, Luke, and John." He's a perfect picture of "the last shall be first." He's the first picture in the New Testament of me. The hated man who was nothing is now "everything." Of the four gospels, Matthew emphasizes most my royalty, my claim to the throne of Israel, and my claim to being the Messiah.*

---

* The gospel of Matthew primarily emphasizes Christ the king. In it, his genealogy is traced from David. Originally this gospel was written primarily to the Jews. Mark

There's another message in why Matthew's book is first. He's the kind of person I'm after and the only kind, really. He was so far away from me, yet he ended up so close. The whole world is full of Levis. If one Levi can be saved, so can many more. Matthew never forgot where he came from. In the tenth chapter of Matthew when he lists all my disciples, he refers to himself as Matthew, the tax collector or publican. Like all my followers, the more Matthew realized what my father and I did for him, the more humble he became.

Matthew was an example to the rest of my disciples of the radical change that could take place in a man—a change I wanted to make in every one of them. I picked men who would dare. Sometimes faith is a better word than daring. I wanted to create enough faith and daring within them to make them the kind of men I needed. They were going to need that faith when I wasn't around.

Finally, Matthew exposed them to an entirely different segment of society, one I wanted them to see. If they were going to take my message to the whole world, they had to get their feet dirty.

Matthew hadn't arrived at his station in life without being aggressive. He turned his ambition to my use. He gave a party for all of his fellow tax collectors. You should have been there. There were well-dressed, cultured, but corrupt people, who crowded in with a group of mostly blue-collar fishermen, along with some radicals like Judas and Simon, who were advocating the overthrow of Rome's occupation. I was invited. The tax collectors had heard about me, and were skeptical, to say the least! You should have heard some of the conversations at the party. Of course, the Pharisees couldn't believe that I would go into such homes, even taking my disciples with me. Those religious leaders were quite vocal in their disapproval.

That's when you told them, "It's the sick who need a doctor."

As I looked around the room that night and talked with the people there, I saw on the faces of several of them the same look that I had

---

emphasizes Christ the servant; it is a very straightforward book written primarily to the Roman world. Luke emphasizes Christ the man, and John emphasizes the deity of Christ.

seen on Matthew's face when I first spoke to him. There was gratitude, humility, and a hidden desperation crying out silently for love. Matthew was our first great evangelist. Several of his friends became my followers.

Heaven is going to be very interesting. You won't believe the circumstances a lot of people will have come from. We'll probably spend the first million years just listening to their stories.

I made sure my disciples experienced the challenge of faith just as Matthew had. When we began traveling as a group in my second public year of ministry I wanted to teach them to trust God for everything. We set out with no money, no food, no water, no roof over our heads—and, of course, in the beginning, with very little faith on the part of the disciples. They had the desire to trust, but not the ability. That's why I spent all the night before I chose the final twelve disciples praying that God would give me the right men and that he would supply the courage they lacked so that they could truly follow me. He did, but it took time.

The Final Twelve

You picked twelve men to be your disciples. By the world's standards they were just average folk, mostly blue-collar types; not particularly intellectual, and seemingly not overly religious.

That is with the exception of Judas Iscariot, who was a "religious" zealot.

Why did you pick that type of man?

They are the best ones—the humble. They were the same kind of men my father always picked, the same kind of man he picked to be the Messiah. As I told you, Abraham, Moses, and David were just ordinary people. Don't confuse humility with lack of wealth and intelligence. Remember, the man who after my death became my leading apostle was Paul, who was both wealthy and brilliant. Once I broke through to him, what a heart he had!

For my disciples, I wanted men who were basically humble and who, despite their faults, would be teachable men, or at least want to be. Instead of religious professionals who would be so competitive with me that they couldn't learn, I wanted teachable men. Judas's problem was that he was unteachable. I also wanted followers who could understand what normal people have to go through such as worrying about money and struggling for self-esteem. I wanted men with no particular prestigious position. Most of them were laborers, like me. I wanted men around me who would respond, who would be grateful.

Another reason I picked these twelve was that they were real. Most of them were fishermen. They were rugged men who worked with their hands as I did. Before I learned that I was God, I appreciated plain people; false, overly pious folk never appealed to me. Such falsely pious people give God a bad name because they hide so much of the rest of themselves. They misuse God's name often.

One thing that I didn't like at first about Judas was that he was a little too pious. That's why I picked the unpretentious men I did. They were the best examples around of who my father was and eventually of the way he wanted people to be.

You picked two pairs of brothers—Simon and Andrew, James and John—and two other men, Philip and Nathaniel, from the same town as the four brothers.

I wanted the group to learn loyalty. Loyalty is at the heart of my teaching, and there's no better example than to see two brothers stick together. Brothers fight also, but remember that I was looking for a model, and there were no perfect models. I used the best available picture of unity and loyalty.

After picking twelve men from apparently a large number to be your primary disciples, you selected three of those to train even more intensely. Did the other disciples envy them?

You mean how much did they envy them? I was close to all of them but closer to some. That created envy, unfortunately, but Matthew was so grateful that he helped hold down the envy. Judas, by the way, hid his envy best of all. It showed up only in little ways. In his super righteousness, for example.

Tell me more about Judas.

His ideas were always slightly better than those of the others. His problem was that often his ideas were better and it went to his head. He was also very responsible; that's why he was our treasurer. When he had money, he always wanted to be the one to decide what to do with it. Of course, he rationalized his actions by appearing to be responsible, pointing out that we didn't have much money and we had to be good stewards.

Judas was the only disciple from Judea; the rest were from Galilee. The zealots were the radicals of my day who believed God had given Israel to the Jews and not to Rome or to anyone else. They were committed to bringing about the return of Israel to the Jews. Secretly, they wanted to overthrow the Roman government in Jerusalem and were prepared to make any sacrifice, even that of their own lives. There was something noble and bold, and seemingly righteous about them. Judas was a very appealing man—intelligent, articulate, unafraid. The other disciples were so impressed they made him treasurer.

I recall that Judas didn't like it when Mary, sister of Martha and Lazarus whom you raised from the dead, poured a bottle of expensive perfume over you. Judas said that the perfume could have been sold for a year's wages and given to the poor.

You see, Judas was so smart that he thought he knew everything. He believed he was righteous and became overly impressed with himself, just as Satan. His greatest strength, his brilliance and righteous determination, became his greatest weakness. He reached the point where he thought he knew more than I did. When I didn't do things as he wanted me to, he took things into his own hands. Judas wanted to be God, just as Satan had.

Neither Judas nor Satan was satisfied with the gifts of God. They both became just as Psalm 109 describes them—wicked. Dissatisfaction is at the heart of sin, just as learning to be satisfied is at the heart of faith. Two men named Judas might represent all people. Judas Iscariot called himself my follower but grew more and more dissatisfied, and eventually became my betrayer. Judas, my half-brother, started out disliking me and being dissatisfied with my reputation. He disliked me because I wasn't as good a father to him as Joseph, whose place I had taken. Later, my brother learned I was not only his loving big brother, but also his savior. Eventually my brother Jude came to terms with who I was. Learning who I am is the essence of life, but it takes time to see who I am.

Before you chose your disciples, you knew from the Old Testament prophecies that one of them would betray you, but you didn't know who it would be.[39] *You must have done a great deal of wondering about each one.*

I wondered about every one of them. I began to look at all their strengths and weaknesses. Nathaniel was critical; Thomas tended to have doubts. Matthew had been corrupt all his life, and he continued to fight being a manipulator. All of them had major flaws. Remember the time I had just finished teaching them that I would sacrifice my life for them? The next minute James and John were talking about which of them would be the greatest in heaven. They all wanted power, and any one of them could have betrayed me.

In the New Testament in John's gospel, it says you knew who would betray you from the beginning, implying you knew before you selected him who the traitor was.

It wasn't that pain-free. My friend couldn't betray me until he was my friend. I had to invest in twelve men, and find out which one I would feel a particular kinship with because of his brilliance. Then I would know. In essence, I had to find out which disciple I enjoyed the most. When a man is betrayed, it means he first trusted someone a great deal. The greater your trust, the greater your pain. I was a man, and I know how it feels to be betrayed even if I did know eventually before the actual event who the betrayer was. That's what the Scriptures are trying to say.

The Scriptures record that you were betrayed by an "old, familiar friend."

Judas had a heart for what I was doing. He was a man of extreme devotion to what he believed in—strong-willed like myself. In many ways, he was the brightest of the lot. We had long, enjoyable theological discussions that the others sometimes couldn't understand. I was aware that I would be betrayed by a close friend. The prophecies in the psalms and Isaiah had made that abundantly clear, but Judas was the last one I suspected initially. I remember thinking when we would have our talks and I felt so close to him, "I know it will be a friend; surely this is not the one." The same thing had happened to my father. His best and brightest angel, Lucifer, was the betrayer.

The Old Testament had all these coded messages for me. There were *direct* messages: one of my disciples would betray me, the one with whom I loved to have discussions—in conjunction with the *indirect* messages: the leader would be betrayed by his most gifted follower (Satan betraying God). All of these communications pointed toward only one man, Judas. This is exactly what the angels I talked with had hinted at, after my temptation, when they told me the clues as to who would betray me were in the Scriptures. At first I could see Peter, because he was so impulsive, betraying me more quickly than Judas. It took some time for the depth of Judas's flaws to surface—the extreme piousness which eventually caused him to see himself as above the Law, to steal from the treasury, and ultimately to betray me. Three years later, even after I had watched Judas subtly slip away, it was still hard to believe.

Times Alone . . . Times Away

What were the times like when you were alone with your disciples?

Most of the time we were surrounded by tremendous crowds. The demands on us were so great that when we did have time alone, all of us were ready for intimate discussions as well as merriment. They would ask me what I meant by a certain parable. Sometimes they would just ask me to repeat a parable they had particularly liked. Many times they would ask me the same questions that you have. How does it feel to have all that power? When did you know you were the Messiah? How did you feel when you found out? What was the temptation like? Did you really see Satan face to face? How did you decide to tell the world? Why did God place you in a poor family?

What else did you talk about?

With six fishermen in the group, we shared a lot of "fish stories." Peter would argue with James and John over who had made the biggest catch. He didn't count the time I had helped him. Or they'd argue over who had been in the roughest storm. None of these three strong-willed men would give an inch, and the rest of the group took great delight in their ongoing battle.

Then I'd tell them about another fisherman, a man by the name of Jonah, who hooked the biggest fish in the world. For three days he battled the fish to a standstill, all without using a pole. Who else had battled a fish a hundredth that size for anywhere near three days? And this was Jonah's first experience with fishing. I told them, "Imagine what he would have done if he had stayed at it." We had a laugh. We would often just sit around and enjoy each other.

A frequent topic of conversation was my power. The aftermath of a miracle was one of their favorite topics, and mine too. No one could believe it at first, and that is exactly what I wanted them to experience—especially the intellectual types.

The Pharisees provided us with many laughs. I don't know how many times we sat around the fire talking at night and someone, often Peter, would provide the evening's entertainment by mimicking a Pharisee. In a deep "religious" voice Peter, mocking one of these men, would say, "'Jesus, is it really lawful to heal on the Sabbath?' and the Lord said, turning to the man with the withered hand, 'Let me answer that brilliant, penetrating question in this way—you're healed.'" Then Peter would say, "Did you see the look on the Pharisee's face?" He would open his eyes mockingly very wide, and everybody would begin rolling with laughter.

At other times I told them what my power had done for my faith. I constantly had to make sure they didn't see my power as a self-centered thing. The power was for teaching and for staking a claim. I never used it for selfish gain. I wanted them to be able to handle power, because after I was gone they would have the same power.

We were quite a group. There was a lot of action in three and a half years. We experienced big crowds, tremendous excitement, and great controversy. We were frequently on the road, and slept outside many nights. Those were some of the best memories, just sitting around the fire at night under an open sky, talking. There wasn't much we didn't talk about, and there weren't many experiences we didn't share—loneliness, uncertainty, tension between each other, and moral dilemmas.

Did you ever talk about sex?

Of course. What do you expect a group of young men alone at night to talk about? Several of them were away from their wives for weeks at a time, so the subject did come up.

In the New Testament, it says you were tempted in all ways as we are. It makes me want to ask you something but I'm hesitant to do so.

I'll tell you if I don't like the question.

Were you ever tempted sexually?

The Scriptures say, "tempted in all ways." Do you think that wouldn't include one of the greatest temptations? As a man, have you ever seen anything more striking in all of creation than a beautiful woman? Do you think I wasn't attracted to women, particularly knowing my father had invented the whole idea of sex? I was a normal man with normal human instincts, but, while I was close to many women, I abstained from impurity.

The sexual relationship was created for the most permanent, deep relationship—marriage. That's the mystery about sex. Sexual fulfillment and commitment are inseparably linked in ways beyond comprehension. Sexual fulfillment without commitment is an illusion. Even more, a sexual relationship outside of marriage is an abuse of oneself and of one's partner. At the moment one participates in such a relationship one repeatedly says, "I don't love you enough to form an unbreakable bond."

That's not a very popular opinion in today's world.

I'm not talking about an opinion. I'm talking about truth. That's a word that modern man has forgotten.

Did you ever think about marriage?

I was in love once. Unfortunately, I had to give her up, and I was a man of passion. She eventually married someone else. It would sadden me at times to see her with him, having his children when she could have been having mine. I loved children, and I had to deny myself that privilege, too. I loved her and the children I would have had enough not to leave them widowed and fatherless. I knew what that felt like firsthand, and I wouldn't inflict that on anyone if I could prevent it. Not marrying was another one of the sacrifices that I made—willingly, but I felt it. Losing her was nearly as painful as losing my father Joseph. To add to the pain, the second loss brought back all the grief of my father's death. I really learned the meaning of the word, "No." She was the most beautiful woman I ever saw. My life was incredibly fulfilled, however, as I went about my father's business.

A few moments ago, we talked about miracles. Was there one miracle that seemed to stand out more than others to your disciples?

The one they talked about the most was "the storm." We were out in a boat on the Sea of Galilee. I was exhausted and had gone to sleep in the tent-like cabin toward the back of the boat. A short time later a huge storm hit us, and the winds brought waves higher than the boat. The waves were unrelenting and powerful. Even the experienced fishermen on the boat who had grown up on the water were afraid. My disciples kept thinking I would wake up, but I didn't.

They waited and waited and waited until finally their panic became so great that they awakened me. I was in that half-dazed state when you're first awakened and being screamed at: "Don't you care about us?" Then I felt myself being slung roughly back and forth by the momentum of the waves. For some time I had been teaching them not to get anxious in difficult situations. I wanted them to understand that God would take care of them. When I stood up and got my balance, I looked at the raging storm and thought of Psalm 89, which unquestionably referred to the Messiah who will sit on David's throne: "You rule the oceans when their waves arise in fearful storms; you speak, and they lie still."[40]

Images of Elijah stopping the rain and of Jonah stopping a storm at sea with the sacrifice of his life also flashed through my mind. I knew what to do. My father was showing me. I walked to the side of the boat, looked at the storm and then commanded at the top of my lungs, "Peace, be still."[41]

The storm was over instantaneously. The disciples would always talk about the strange sensation of the abrupt end to the storm and of the boat rocking to a halt on a perfectly calm sea.

How uncomfortable did these displays of power make your disciples feel?

I made them uneasy. One other time when they were out on the Sea of Galilee, in the middle of the night, I walked out to their boat and got in it. That shook them up a bit. When I had first come near the boat and before they could recognize me, they thought I was a ghost. Then when I raised Lazarus from the dead after he had been in the grave for three days, he came out of his tomb with his head and body wrapped in white funeral clothes. That got their attention.

Often after a miracle they were a little frightened of me. Most of the time they were comfortable enough with me to tell me what to do. They told me when to get rid of the crowds. The people were hungry, they said, as if I didn't know it. They told me with their eyes that I shouldn't be talking to the Samaritan woman at the well. Peter assured me that I didn't have to die after I told him I did. I had to rebuke him for that.

My disciples were secure enough with me to ask me to call down fire on some people who didn't believe. I had to teach them again what I was about and why I couldn't do what they wanted with that fire.

Did you and your men laugh much on these journeys?

One of the great things about our group, about any good group, was the camaraderie. We'd be in the middle of a serious conversation about power and how to use it, and Thomas, or somebody else, would jokingly say, "If I had all that power I would make myself a big farm with a lot of cattle and a big house on it and retire." Frequently they joked about my power. One of them would say, "Lord, it is so late and I have to cook breakfast in the morning and all I have are some old beans. Could you muster up some fresh, broiled fish and wheat cakes?" I remember comments at night, before going to sleep, such as Philip's saying, "Lord, when your father made this earth, he missed this spot of ground I'm sleeping on; it's a little hard. It's probably his only other mistake besides Peter." Those were the times I'll always treasure.

You loved your men.

I would look at my disciples and think, "This is who I'm dying for. Is it worth it?" The answer would always be, "Yes." There was the indescribable feeling I had about each one of them. Real brotherhood would probably be the best way to define it. With all their faults, I loved them. I could see the worth in my men despite the stain of their sins. That's when I best understood how my father could look at a man like David—an adulterer and murderer—look past his sins and say, "There's a man after my own heart."

My disciples were one big reason I could go to the cross. Those men, whose fellowship I shared, were doomed to death. They were desperately trying to believe, but they didn't know how to trust. They wanted to be courageous, but they were cowards. They wanted to love, but they were filled with envy. They wanted to be honest, but they were all secret manipulators. All of them wanted to be devoted, but couldn't do it. Every one of them was terribly flawed, and I knew it. In short, they were sinful. Sin is not a popular word but that's what it was. Those self-destructive flaws were literally killing the disciples. I saw there was only one way to get rid of those flaws, and that was to judge them as they deserved and then get rid of them. I was to take the judgment my friends deserved. That's why I had to die. They could then be all they were capable of being.

Why death? It's so severe.

I must have asked myself that question a thousand times. The answer is both simple and tremendously complex. I was the only person who could satisfy God's conscience and everybody else's conscience too. Do you think people don't punish themselves terribly for their sins, even the nonbelievers—especially the nonbelievers? Everyone knows he or she is evil enough to deserve death. Think about that phrase, "I am so mad at what I did I could kill myself."

Are you saying that there is a universal death wish, a wish for punishment?

It is for justice. Deep down everybody knows they deserve death. I was the only man who ended up in a grave who had the right to come out. If I didn't overcome death, everybody was doomed.

Is this punishment wish a conscious or an unconscious thing?

Consciously, very few people think they deserve death because of their sins. Unconsciously, they know it.

With all they witnessed and with all you talked about, it seems your disciples never really understood what you were about and, in a way, lacked faith in you.

They never understood I had to die until after it was all over. Many people who attend Christian churches today don't understand what I was about either. One reason is that the price I paid is so high—death is so frightening.

In fact, I remember as I was coming to terms with my own death, it was constantly on my mind. I knew what was going to happen, and even though I dreaded it, I always tried to face it.

It was while my death still weighed heavily on my mind that the mother of James and John wanted to know if, when I reigned, I would let her boys sit on my right. How absurd it all was. I was thinking about sacrifice and obedience, surrounded by envious, selfish people—even my own men . . . particularly my own men. That was why I was dying. I can tell you they surely forced me to seek out my father. He was the only complete source of love.

The way you answered James and John's mother was interesting. You never put her or them down for wanting to be important.

They were created to be important. The whole question was how to do it. You should have heard the other disciples when they found out what James and John tried to do. The way the other disciples reacted revealed very quickly that secretly they all wanted those places. I told them that among the heathen, the leaders lord it over those beneath them. That's the world's greatness, I said. Among my followers, if you want to be a great leader, then be a great servant. If you want to be recognized, then sacrifice your own interests. That's what I was doing. As I told them, "I, the Messiah, did not come to be served, but to serve, and to give my life as a ransom for many."[42]

That was in truth living and why I always emphasized that if you want to find your life, lose it, for my sake and the gospel's.

Essentially you told them to give themselves up for the good of the team. I was interested that the Scriptures report that even you wanted recognition and that you sacrificed to get it. In the book of Hebrews, it says that for the joy awaiting you, you endured the shame of the cross.[43]

My father's the same way. He is pleased to be honored and he made his creatures like that, too. For anyone who will recognize his glory and appreciate him, he will pour out every blessing upon him. Heaven will be a place where everyone is recognizing his brothers' and sisters' glory. If you've ever been part of a crowd and cheered for somebody—for a team, a performance—you know what I mean.

Miracles Enjoyed

What were some other miracles you especially enjoyed?

One day I was walking down the road to Nain, a city in Galilee, with my disciples and hundreds of other people. Just as we got to the city gate, we had to stop and wait for a funeral procession. From the mourners, I learned that the only son of a widow had died. As I saw this procession and the mother who was overcome with grief, it moved me to tears.

I thought of my mother, a widow, who in just a short while would lose her oldest son. I went to the dead boy's mother and said, "Don't cry!"[44]

I walked over to the coffin and put my hand on it, looked up to my father and said, "Young man, I say to you, get up!"[45]

The boy sat up, looked around as if he had just awakened from a nap, and asked what was going on. First there was silence and then the crowd went wild. That miracle had great meaning for me, because one day I would be dead and my father would bring me back. The joy that I saw on that woman's face would be my mother's joy.

Another time, I was standing in the middle of a crowd and Jairus, a Jewish rabbi, came up to me, fell down at my feet, and begged me to come home with him. His only child, a twelve-year old daughter, was dying. Here was a proud rabbi with his heart breaking who was turning to me in utter desperation. He had put aside his pride, humbled himself, fallen on his knees, and pleaded for mercy. I couldn't refuse.

We fought the crowds, pushing them back, all the way to his house. About halfway there, I felt someone touch me, then felt the healing power go out of me for just a second. I stopped, turned around, and asked my disciples who had touched me. They looked at me as if I were crazy, "Lord, we're surrounded by crowds; everybody's touching you." Then suddenly the woman who had done it, fell to her knees in front of me, telling me she had touched me because she wanted to be healed and now she was. Then I said to her, "Your faith has healed you. Go in peace."[46] Jairus continued to stand beside me, watching all this.

Immediately after this incident, a messenger from his house arrived telling him there was no use to trouble "the teacher" any more because his little girl was dead. The effect on Jairus was devastating. The look on his face changed from great hope to total dejection. Before he could say anything, I told him to trust me, that everything would be all right. We walked the rest of the way and I could see it was almost too much for him. He wanted to believe, but he was fighting back the tears.

The house was packed with mourners. Remember, he was the preacher, the rabbi, with a large following. I told everyone in the room to "quit crying, the little girl isn't dead, she's only asleep." Some of the people became furious with me, and others began jeering. They tried to throw me out the door, but I took Peter, James, and John, along with Jairus and his wife, to the little girl's room.

There lay a pretty girl with long, beautiful curls and the sweetest look on her pale face. Her eyes were closed. She was not breathing. This helpless young person was dead. Then I took her cold, limp hand in mine, looked at her, and thought of the day when my hand would be cold. I said, "Get up, little girl." Suddenly, her hand was warm and alive. She sat up in the bed. I looked at her big brown eyes and said, "I'll bet you're thirsty. Get this wonderful little girl something to drink."

The people in the room heard Jairus's wife screaming ecstatically and watched her run to get the water, smiling and shouting: "She's alive! He's healed her!" When I walked out of the girl's room, I looked at the people who had been so angry and hateful just a few minutes before. They hated death as I did, but now they had the most incredible look of joy and gratitude on their faces. I thought, "This is the kind of change that I will bring about in people. Many who hate me will one day love me.

How did you feel after a miracle like this, after seeing you had a tremendous power that no one else had?

Both the moments before a miracle and those after a miracle, had an equally powerful effect on me. I would look out at those crowds coming to see me. No matter where I was, people came leading blind relatives by the hand. Others were carrying the paralyzed on stretchers. There were crippled of all types. Some were on makeshift crutches, some were deformed, and, of course, the lepers came if they could get anywhere near me. The sheer impact of those crowds was overwhelming. Never was I any happier as the Messiah, than to be the world's doctor.

I also took particular pleasure in being able to perform miracles, because it enabled me to defend my father's honor. There were people then, just as there are today, who said that God doesn't care about suffering. By so doing, they made him the author of evil and pain. Every miracle was a message from my father. It thrilled me to be able to say, and I always did: "Be healed in the name of God"; "God blesses you, be healed"; "Your father in heaven heals—you are well"; or, "You are healed in the name of the God of Abraham, Isaac, and Jacob."

Today, nearly two thousand years later, many theologians allegedly from your own church deny your miracles.

Why shouldn't I have done miracles? Creation is a miracle. Every single human being is a miracle. I am the greatest miracle the world has ever known. I am the prophet—both God and man. Moses, Joshua, Elijah, Elisha, and Daniel all had done miracles or participated in them. Can't those theologians see that I was bringing in a new day? I was a living testimony of what each person was meant to be. Those who disdain miracles should at least wish with all their hearts that they were true. It would make all of humankind so much greater.

Are these theologians afraid you'll lose your humanity if you performed miracles?

Maybe on the surface, but the real reason is that, just like the Pharisees, they don't want anyone to be greater than they are—so they change the words of God on their own. Secretly no one wants anyone else to be greater.

Tell me about the messages behind the miracles.

My miracles always had two messages. One was physical, and one was spiritual. It takes the spiritual side of a person to make him or her truly great. I came not only to heal the blind but also to give people the vision of faith. I healed "untouchable" leprosy and I was there to heal everyone's untouchable sins. I healed the deaf because I had come to help people who had been deaf to God's voice. Every miracle I did was a triumph over the misery of the world. All of my miracles mattered to me. It was an incredible experience to watch someone hear who never had heard before, or to watch a grown man walk or talk for the first time. It was particularly special to watch a blind man see.

The most powerful statement of grace, though, was the cleansing of lepers. After a miracle, I often was surrounded by people with expressions of overflowing gratitude. There were thankful relatives. There was a look I can hardly describe in a person's eyes when he or she was not only healed from disfiguring leprosy but also physically touched for the first time in years. Lepers were not only untouchables; they were unreachables. They couldn't even be touched emotionally. Because lepers were banned from the rest of the populace, they would see me after the crowds had gone late in the evening. Or they would catch me before I entered a town.

Once toward the end of my life, as I was heading toward Jerusalem, I came near the border of Galilee and Samaria. I was far outside any town, but ten lepers waited for me. I healed them instantly and told them to go to the Jewish priests and show them they were healed. All ran for town, except for one. He was the "foreigner" among them, a "despicable" Samaritan. This man shouted and fell face downward in the dust in true joy and humility. Finally I picked him up and told him, "Stand up," and he did. Now, with his face covered with dust that only accentuated his marvelous eyes filled with indescribable gratitude, he looked at me and I told him, "Go; your faith has made you well."[47]

I knew a day was coming when I would lie face down in the dust underneath the load of the cross and, at that moment, I would think about that leper and his eyes. During the crucifixion, I would think about the faces of all those I had healed and their relatives who had watched. They would be part of the crowd inside me, urging me on to climb that impossible mountain.

Your miracles are so different from those of fabled ancient wonder-workers in pagan literature. Your miracles were first and foremost for the purpose of helping your fellow humans. They were miracles steeped in love, gifts reserved for those who trusted you to the slightest degree. You did not do them just for popularity. Nowhere was this more obvious than at your temptation and also you refused to do miracles for a sign when the Pharisees or your hometown skeptics demanded one.

The miracles helped others and also demonstrated who I was. It may seem strange, but when I was on the cross and I'd given up the privilege of using my power, I didn't feel I was God. I had to look back on those miracles of faith to believe that I was God. It's strange—the thoughts and feelings that different circumstances produced. Even though I knew I could call on my power any moment I wanted to, as long as I didn't use it and as long as I was hanging there engulfed by pain, I didn't feel particularly like God.

Often before you performed a miracle, you told the people you were doing one "so that they might believe." Building faith seems to be the constant goal of your teaching.

My goal was my father's. The Jews, the "chosen ones," would forget about him; so he wouldn't do anything for them. He would let things get worse and worse—persecution, fear, famine. Midway through this process, God would bring in a prophet to warn his people. If they still wouldn't listen, he would finally tell them, "So that you will know that I am the Lord, your God, this is what is going to happen to you." The Israelites would then be told that they would be slaves of Babylon or that Jerusalem would be destroyed or some other prophecy would be given. The event would happen exactly as the Lord had said. Things would go from bad to worse until Israel was finally humbled. Then some of the people would return to God and there would be a great deliverance.

Take courage when you see things getting worse and worse in your world—pornography, murder, crime, infidelity, materialism. My father's deliverance always comes when things couldn't be any worse. When it comes, you will know who did it.

Many of your followers today feel as if they can't relate to miracles.

A follower of mine with the slightest spiritual awareness, who knows anything about prayer, has seen God work supernaturally in a situation. Always, after the brief period of ecstasy that accompanies a definite experience with my father, a person must return to the darkness of the everyday world. It is a world where, in their flesh, people can't see the other world, the real world. Only those with other-worldly vision see that real world very clearly.

Even at best, there are great challenges in the seen world to divert and to block our spiritual vision: glitter; glamour; and, most of all, clamor. There always comes a time after an experience with God when people find themselves beginning to doubt, to fear, and to live strictly in their humanity. An individual then has to start all over with the skills of faith.

In a way it was the same for me. Every time I performed a miracle, I always had to return to my humanity and, once again, overcome the limited vision of my retinue. Miracles didn't stop my need for faith, just as they don't stop yours. In a way, miracles increased my need for faith. It was the miracle of the Scriptures, the fact that there existed an absolutely accurate communication from my father about what was happening now, and what was going to happen to me in the future, which caused me to have a terrible burden. Because of my faith in my father's omniscience, I knew death was staring me in the face every day. Omniscience doesn't always remove pain. My father had known all along how things would work out and even he had to wait on it to happen.

You say you always had your humanity waiting for you after a miracle, but several times, particularly in John's gospel, you said you did only what you saw the father doing. That implies you saw things we couldn't. It hints that you used your omniscience.

I could have been talking about what I saw him doing in the Old Testament. I was completely human, but I could still see my father at work, and everything I saw him do, I was allowed to do. Every miracle I performed had been done in the Old Testament or was alluded to, except for casting out demons. That was my idea, but then my father had already led me to conquer Satan himself. Then I knew I had authority over all the evil one's followers.

The Pleasure of Faith

Anytime you saw faith, it pleased you tremendously. Why?

Because it shows so much respect for my father. My father's honor was at stake, and anybody who had faith took my father at his word. Anyone who lacks faith at that moment does not believe my father. It's a rare thing to find a person of faith. It's the most precious commodity in God's economy.

I remember the Roman officer whose faith was unshakable. His servant was ill; so he sent several Jewish elders to ask me to heal him. Even though he was a Roman, the Jews loved and admired him for his kindness to them. Because of this, these elders came to ask me a favor. As I went with them and approached the Roman centurion's house, he sent one of his servants to tell me not to come into his home. He said he knew he wasn't worthy of that, but if I would just say the word, he knew his servant would be healed. After all, he was a man who gave orders, who understood the chain of command, and he knew of my power.

An untaught Roman had more faith than a Jewish rabbi. He didn't have to see me. He didn't have to touch me or to have me touch the sick. He didn't even have to hear my voice. All he needed was to know that if I was willing to do something for him, it was as good as done.

As I recall, you healed that servant.

That Roman was like the millions of people I ask to believe in me who have never seen me or touched me or heard my voice. Another reason I love faith is that it is the vehicle through which people know God. You can't see God with your eyes or hear him with your ears. You have to look for signs that he's there, and that always involves faith. If you miss those signs, you miss his magnificence. If you don't believe he answers prayers, that he really affects circumstances, then you will miss him. If you don't believe he has written down his words to you, you won't hear him. You will miss all his guidance for you. You will miss his attempts to comfort you and love you through friends, his blessings, and his Scriptures. You won't see his work in the circumstances of your life. You have to have the eyes of faith.

As the apostle Paul told the believers later, "We are those who walk not by sight, but by faith."

There is nothing like the victories faith brings, the last-second relief when all seems lost. It is joy indescribable. Faith is the key to that joy.

My father is a master dramatist. Drama is tension, and he works in the resolution of that tension. Without conflict, you'll never see God. Next to healing lepers, I always got my greatest thrill out of watching blind people see for the first time. That was the essence of what I was doing—helping my followers to see.

The Roman soldier obviously inspired you with his faith. Who else did?

Many times someone would inspire me. Often the inspiration would come from the least-expected source. Once in Capernaum, I was staying at a friend's house, and news spread excitedly that I was in town. Before we knew it, the house was packed so tightly that there was not room for even one more person. Even outside, the crowd was so great that no one could get near the house.

As I began teaching the people, all of a sudden in the middle of my talk, clay started falling from the ceiling. I looked up to see what was going on, and I saw someone digging a hole in the roof from the outside. At first the hole was small, and I could barely make out a face peering down through it. Then I heard the man who was doing the digging yell, "We hit it. He's directly below us." He and his friends began digging some more, until there was a large hole with three faces looking down at me through the roof. The diggers paused for a moment, and, with smiles on their faces, began lowering a stretcher with ropes. On the stretcher was a paralyzed man. The ingenuity and determination of his friends moved me. They had incredible perseverance! You don't think I would disappoint them, do you?

There were scribes, "learned scholars," standing around, and it was obvious they disapproved of the sick man's friends. It's bad manners not to knock at the front door, and some of the clay had fallen on their precious robes. I was moved by the moment; the hunger of my father's people, my people. I looked around at the clay that was still in our hair and on our robes. Everyone around me was a little dusty, and I thought, "I want all of you to see that what I am doing is more than just healing someone so that he can live a few more years. It's a lot bigger than that. I'm here to remove your dirt—your sins—and I want you to know it." So I looked at this pale, thin man who had no strength even to hold up his head and who just lay there staring at me with those pleading eyes. I said, "Your sins are forgiven."[48]

That made the scribes furious. I could see it in their eyes, and I knew what they were thinking: "Only God can forgive sins." Several of these scribes had been in the synagogue and had tried to kill me the day I had made my announcement. I looked at them and told them, "Which is easier: to say, 'Your sins are forgiven,' or to say, 'Get up and walk'? But so that you may know that the Son of Man has authority on earth to forgive sins . . ." I turned to the paralyzed man and said, "Get up, take your mat and go home."[49]

Before you could blink an eye, this man jumped to his feet and was staring me in the face with a big grin. He was so excited that he picked up his bed and pushed his way through the crowd. He hadn't walked in years, and now he wanted to get outside and *run* as soon as he could.

As I watched him part that crowd, that man made me think of my father when he parted the Red Sea. The scene was that compelling!

As they witnessed this miracle, the shock that went through the crowd turned into the most joyous shouting and singing to my father you have ever heard. I was especially pleased that they were thanking my father, for they understood for the moment whose power it really was. The people kept saying, "We've never seen anything like it!" What a special time! We were so tightly packed together in that house that you could really feel the crowd in a unique way. We were one. I remember thinking, with that electricity flowing through the crowd, "Heaven is going to be like this."

Finally, I looked up at the ceiling and there were these same three faces, now with incredible smiles, and they were laughing and singing with me. Then before they left, they fixed the roof.

That particular miracle had a special impact on me. People were surrounding me in that tightly packed room, desperate for good news and new life. More and more, I began to see the hunger in every person. If I could just satisfy that deep spiritual need. My heart was moved for humankind. So many people wanted God so much, but many couldn't admit it.

All of this was going through my mind as I walked down the road after leaving that house with the crowd still following me. Suddenly, I felt the strongest urge to ask my father to lead me to the most despicable person around, who I knew deep inside was yearning to know God. My father answered that request and there I saw Levi, the tax collector, sitting smugly in his booth. He was about to have his life and his name changed.

You are unpredictable. You've done everything possible to urge the worst sinner into heaven, thereby bringing tremendous comfort to the people—"If Matthew can make it, I can, too." At other times, you often intentionally increased the people's tension, as you did with the scribes in the house with the hole in the roof. You warned them frequently that if they didn't listen you would disown them. You backed a wealthy potential follower into a corner when you told him to sell everything if he really wanted to follow you. You asked your disciples to do things they couldn't do. This seems largely to contradict the image the press and the media today have created for you.

As I made plain, I came to bring a sword. Truth is never comfortable in this world.

There was tension in my life, and I was the son of God. Do you think anyone will escape it? Pain made me cry out. It taught me to wait, to pray, to trust, to look for answers, to be humble, and eventually, best of all, to be rescued.

Your life was a drama. It has often been called "the greatest story ever told."
What do you think of those today who are creating drama, the entertainment
industry?

The great danger is that your talent can become your idol, and then
you become your own god, the same temptation Satan faced. Throughout history, people are so quick to forget where they got their talent. It
always comes back to pride. I would remind the people in the entertainment world never to forget what my father said to ministers, that
he holds teachers more accountable than others.

Those in media or entertainment should not forget for a moment
that they are the most influential teachers in society. Every movie, every television show, every performance is a sermon, whether they realize it or not. The gospel they preach will be judged by the gospel that
will prevail.

When the Statler Hotel opened in Los Angeles, a number of actors
and actresses were invited to write their deepest wishes on a "wishing
wall." Ginger Rogers wrote, "I wish that all men knew that God is impartial." That would be another thing that I would say to the entertainment industry.

Did it bother you that many people didn't believe in you?

My father had told me in the Scriptures to expect unbelief. I saw
everything coming true just as he said it would. The people really were
lost, and the Pharisees really hated the truth. Miracle after miracle
had no effect on them except to make them determined to destroy
me. That increased both my confidence and my dread.

At the same time, my followers were confused, the Pharisees were
planning to dispose of me, and all the time I was wondering, "What
do I have to do to convince them? I've healed the sick, raised the dead,
walked on water, turned water into wine and fed twelve thousand
people with five loaves of bread." I knew they were blind, but I couldn't
stop trying to convince them.

Still, it hurt when they didn't accept me; I was as sensitive as my father. He made himself vulnerable to you. Listen to him: "No, my people won't listen. Israel doesn't want me around. So I am letting them go their blind and stubborn way. . . . But oh, that my people would listen to me! . . . How quickly then I would subdue her enemies!"[50] His promises comforted me, I knew that one day truth would reign.

The response of many people was more than I had expected even with all the prophecies telling me that I would someday be famous. My popularity became so great that I couldn't enter a city without a tremendous crowd. That's why I spent so many nights in the wilderness with my men. My heart was moved, though, by the hunger of the people. They were crying out for a shepherd.

Everything was coming to pass just as it was supposed to happen. The Pharisees saw very clearly that they either had to kill me or make me their king.

Notes

1. John 1:29b NIV
2. Matthew 3:17b
3. Deuteronomy 8:2–3 NIV
4. Isaiah 11:1–2
5. Matthew 16:23 NASB
6. Deuteronomy 8:3 NIV
7. Matthew 4:4
8. Psalm 91:11–12 NIV
9. Deuteronomy 6:16a
10. Matthew 4:7b
11. Matthew 4:10 NIV
12. Hebrews 12:2b
13. Hebrews 2:18
14. Matthew 5:11–12 NIV
15. Matthew 5:5 NIV
16. Genesis 1:26a
17. Isaiah 9:6c

18. Luke 2:10b–14
19. John 2:4b NIV
20. John 2:5b NIV
21. Psalm 69:9a NASB
22. John 4:10 NIV
23. John 4:13–14a NIV
24. John 4:15 NIV
25. John 4:19–20 NIV
26. John 4:26 NIV
27. John 4:35b NIV
28. John 4:48 TLB
29. John 4:50 TLB
30. Luke 4:18–19 NIV
31. Luke 4:21b NIV
32. Luke 9:50b NASB
33. John 1:45b–46a TLB
34. John 1:47 TLB
35. John 1:49 TLB
36. John 11:16b TLB
37. John 14:6
38. John 20:28 NIV
39. Psalm 41:9 (implied)
40. Psalm 89:9 TLB
41. Mark 4:39a
42. Matthew 20:28b TLB
43. Hebrews 12:2
44. Luke 7:13b TLB
45. Luke 7:14b NIV
46. Luke 8:48 TLB
47. Luke 17:19b TLB
48. Matthew 9:2b NIV
49. Matthew 9:5–6 NIV
50. Psalm 81:11–14a TLB

CHAPTER THREE

OPPOSITION AND CONFIRMATION

The Pharisees

You didn't care for the Pharisees very much, did you?

All those years I visited the temple at Passover, I listened to their "wisdom." Their hypocrisy was ever before me. They had created a religion of externals and had forgotten about the soul. They ate the right food, they had the right hygiene, they washed before eating. They spoke the right language in the sense that they didn't swear, and they went to the right places—the temple or synagogue—on the right day— the Sabbath, but their hearts were all wrong.

The Pharisees had started out with a good idea—trying to separate themselves from evil and to follow the God of Israel. They confused their heritage with their own spirituality, though, and thought themselves automatically to be God's special people. They failed to learn the same lesson most of their ancestors had failed to learn—that they were proud and spiritually blind and that only those who recognize their blindness and cry out to God for help are special. The Pharisees forgot that they belonged more on their knees than on their feet. The externals in which the Pharisees put so much stock were only to be representative symbols of what was inside. Inside, the Pharisees were corrupt.

They didn't love God or their neighbors as much as they loved themselves. Their way of life, with all their rules, was for one basic purpose—to gain control and to glorify themselves.

Secretly the Pharisees loved material things more than they did God—their long robes, their rings, their gold. How they loved power, the place of honor, the public recognition, the catering of others to them. They were good at keeping minor rules like fasting and tithing by which they could measure their performances, but they had no heart for the people.

To the ten commandments they regularly added laws of their own that they considered, "divinely inspired" and which regulated every aspect of Jewish life. They wanted control. They wanted to be God.

In response to this legalism came a reactionary Jewish religious group, the Sadducees, who rebelled against all the imposed restrictions and called for a return to the Scriptures as the only standard for life. Theirs was not truly a scripture-based reformation. Instead, it was based on their secret liberalism and their own materialism. The Sadducees had carefully maneuvered their way into the upper echelon of Jewish-Roman life, with a lifestyle more Roman than Jewish. This they wished to preserve at all costs. As materialists, the Sadducees didn't believe in a life beyond earthly existence, so they tried to get all they could while they were on earth.

These were the two groups of leaders responsible for teaching God's people the truth. The Pharisees, the more powerful of the two, had a tremendous opportunity to teach the people the word of God, the truth. Instead, they devoted themselves to keeping their rules and reading their words instead of God's word. Written commentaries and religious treatises on the Law were the focus of their teaching, discussion, and authority. They became experts on the words of their fellow Pharisees until the words of God were pushed backstage. That same thing has happened with some religious leaders today.

The Pharisees were charged with the responsibility of teaching the people to repent. They should have taught that all people are naturally far from God, do not really love others, and are selfish and self-centered. They should have called the people to humble themselves before God, as the writer of Chronicles said:

If my people, which are called by my name, shall humble themselves, and pray, and seek my face, and turn from their wicked
ways; then will I hear from heaven, and will forgive their sin,
and will heal their land.[1]

If the Pharisees had done that, they would have given the people
victory over their biggest opponent—themselves—and would have
made everyone a true neighbor. Unfortunately, the Pharisees didn't
believe their own religion and weren't true to their own faith. Worse
than that, they exalted themselves and their performances at the expense of their neighbors—the students they were supposed to teach.
They made their neighbors constantly feel inferior and carry their guilt.
The Pharisees were charged with lightening the people's burdens and
presenting them a God who would lift their spirits as he lifted their
guilt. Instead of humility and freedom, however, they gave their charges
slavery and oppression. The greatest oppression in my country at that
time in history was not from the Romans, but from the Pharisees. The
more I saw it, the more I understood the truth of spiritual blindness.
At first I tried to reason with the Pharisees about what they didn't see.
They were not men of reason, despite their continued attempts to con-
vey their intellectual integrity. I was greatly annoyed by what they were
doing to people. They took God's name in vain in the worst possible
way.

The Pharisees frequently harassed you.

They complained because my disciples didn't fast. They called me a
"drunkard" because I drank wine, after they had accused John the
Baptist of being too ascetic for not drinking wine. When I allowed a
prostitute in my presence, or when I associated with a tax collector, I
offended their self-righteousness. You're right. They never stopped
harassing me.

The Pharisees devised traps to get you arrested, but you were always one step ahead of them.

I remember the day a Pharisee named Simon invited me to his home for dinner. During the meal, a prostitute brought me a gift, some perfume. This prostitute didn't interrupt the conversation. She just knelt before me and began to cry. She washed my feet with her tears and dried them with her hair. Then she anointed me with perfume and kissed my feet reverently. My host obviously didn't like what was happening. I knew he was thinking, how could I be a prophet if I would even speak to a prostitute, much less let her touch me.

This condescending man hadn't even offered me water to wash my own feet, as was the custom. He had not treated me as a respected guest. He felt little need for the forgiveness that I had the authority to give. At the same time, here was a woman who cleaned my dirty feet with her own hair, literally begging for forgiveness. So I told the Pharisee a story.

"Simon," I said, "A man loaned money to two men. One he loaned $5,000, the other $500, but neither could pay him back. Being a kind man, he forgave both debts. Which of these two men do you suppose loved him most?" Simon, not knowing I was talking about him, answered correctly, "The one who is forgiven the most must love the most."

Then I interpreted the parable for him. "You didn't even offer me water for my feet, but she washed them with her tears. You denied me the customary kiss of greeting, but she has not stopped kissing my feet. You neglected the usual courtesy of oil to anoint my head, but she has covered my feet with rare perfume. Therefore, her sins that are many are forgiven. The one who is forgiven little has little love."[2]

In moments like this, the spiritual world was manifested. It was clear whether the spirit of humility or the spirit of pride dominated a person.

When you forgave sins, you did that in a way on credit. You were banking on the fact that you would complete your task. With all your troubles, you were very confident.

I can never say it too much: "Man shall live on every word that proceeds out of the mouth of God." I had his word that I would complete my task and that I could forgive others. There's nothing that makes you more confident than that.

As he talked about his confidence, I realized how closely confidence and faith are related to each other. True confidence looks not only to the past, but largely to the future. Of all the men in history, Jesus was the most confident, the most certain that events would take place.

You were constantly outsmarting the Pharisees. You knew the Scriptures better than they did and turned the questions meant to trap you back on your accusers.

Once when I was teaching the people, a group of Pharisees and political leaders tried to trap me into an offense against Rome. They wanted the Romans to have a reason to arrest me. They asked a question they were sure would entrap me: "Sir, we know that you are very honest and teach the truth regardless of the consequences. . . . Now tell us, is it right to pay taxes to the Roman government or not?"[3]

I told them they were hypocrites. Then I asked one of my disciples to give me a coin and he borrowed a penny from someone in the crowd. I help up the coin and asked the Pharisees, "Whose picture and whose name is on it?"

They replied, "Caesar's."

So I said to them, "Well, then, give it to Caesar if it is his, and give God everything that belongs to God."[4]

Another time you adopted their tact of asking a question from Scripture, and the Pharisees couldn't answer it. The question had to do with your divinity.

They pounced on even a hint that I was calling myself the Messiah, so I continued to say it indirectly. If they didn't get the message when I raised somebody from the dead, telling them in words would have little effect.

One day after they'd been trying to trap me with one question after another, I turned to them and said, "You've asked me a lot of questions, now let me ask you one. If the Messiah is to be a descendant of David, how could David write in the book of Psalms, "God said to my Lord, the Messiah, 'Sit at my right hand until I place your enemies beneath your feet.'"[5] I was asking how the Messiah could be David's Lord, if the Messiah hadn't even been born. The Pharisees stared at each other with puzzled looks, each hoping their fellow scholars had the answer, and of course, they didn't. There were no more questions from that faction that day. The Pharisees walked away, muttering to themselves. Justice had been served.

More on the Pharisees

As I read the gospels, I never cease to be amazed at the number of times you provoked the Pharisees. You said or did things that to us seem unnecessarily provocative.

Remember, I was the truth. Several times I told them that purity was best demonstrated in generosity and that they were fools. They washed the outside, but inside they were full of greed and wickedness. They wouldn't accept the truth—they hid it from others and prevented them from having a chance to believe it.

Once, a Pharisee informed me, "Sir, you have insulted my profession." I replied, "Not only are you Pharisees hypocrites, you are murderers, too. You killed all the prophets."[6] Never forget, "preachers" killed me. I hope preachers today don't forget that.

John Calvin declared that those with the most power are always the most dangerous. They have the greatest temptations. There have been plenty of great preachers, and some terrible ones. People shouldn't be surprised that Satan always tries to infiltrate his enemies' quarters. That's the first place he attacks.

Be wary of those hypocrites, those ministers who change my words and my father's words and say, "God didn't really say that, this is what he said. . . ." That voice goes all the way back to the Garden of Eden. Many a famous man by the world's standards has made the same disastrous mistake. They have taken that fatal step from which there is no return and have changed the holy words of Scripture into "what they really mean." This is where more than one scholar has been converted into a fool by his pride. This is exactly the place where man wants to become God, speak for him, even correct him. It is here that C. S. Lewis reminds them—it is impossible for man to be right and God to be wrong. Frightening, isn't it, to be so certain, and yet so potentially deceived by one's own perception? Everyone likes to forget that Hitler was really a human being.

I remember another incident with the Pharisees when, on the Sabbath, you were in the home of a Pharisee. A number of them were watching you closely to see if you would heal a man who had suffered chronically from fainting spells. You asked them if it was lawful to heal on the Sabbath day or not.

I took the sick man by the hand and gave them my answer. I healed him. Then I turned to them and said, "Which of you doesn't work on the Sabbath? If your cow falls into a pit, don't you proceed at once to get it out?"[7] The Pharisees, as usual, became enraged.

They were such religious zealots. Another time on the Sabbath I was teaching in the synagogue and a handicapped woman who was bent over and unable to straighten herself was there. Later I learned that she had been this way for eighteen years. I called over to her, "Woman, you are healed of your sickness!"[8]

Then I went over and touched her, and she immediately stood up straight and began thanking me profusely. The local rabbi at that synagogue became very angry because I had healed her on the Sabbath. He shouted to the crowd, "There are six days of the week to work.... Those are the days to come for healing, not on the Sabbath!"⁹

The Scriptures say that you had a quick answer for him.

I told him just what he was—a hypocrite. Their hypocrisy was beyond belief. Imagine standing there with a woman who was dying and who now is tremendously excited to be free of the pain that has enslaved her for eighteen years. Imagine having the capacity to totally ignore that, and at the same time the audacity to tell the person who helped free her of her pain that you are better than he is.

The utter insensitivity of human beings at such moments amazed me, and I wasn't about to let any of the Pharisees continue teaching this false religion of "Look how good I am."

I wanted the people to know exactly where I stood and where the Pharisees stood. I was going to be murdered, and I wanted it well known who did it. I didn't want the Pharisees coming back and saying, "We were really on your side." Remember, I was a prophet, and it was my job to warn the people about the Pharisees and about the potential Pharisee inside each of them. I wanted to let the light shine on the real fruit of the Pharisees. If you wish, you can call that provoking.

You called the Pharisees on different occasions "egotistical," "corrupt," "fools," and "murderers." Somebody might get the idea you called them names.

Once I told a story about the typical Pharisee:

Two men went to the Temple to pray. One was a proud, self-righteous Pharisee, and the other a cheating tax collector. The proud Pharisee "prayed" this prayer: "Thank God, I am not a sinner like everyone else, especially like that tax collector over there! For I never cheat, I don't commit adultery, I go without food twice a week, and I give to God a tenth of everything I earn." But the corrupt tax collector stood at a distance and dared not even lift his eyes to heaven as he prayed, but beat upon his chest in sorrow, exclaiming, "God, be merciful to me, a sinner." I tell you, this sinner, not the Pharisee, returned home forgiven![10]

You never let up on the Pharisees.

The Pharisees were everything my father wasn't. I told my followers to watch out for the Pharisees. The men who claimed to be the best were the most evil. I thought the people ought to know.

I also tried to teach the people that life is not in what you have. It's not what you store up, as the Pharisees were teaching, but living is in spending—in giving. Big spenders are a lot closer in some ways to my father than people think they are. Spend your time, your money, your beliefs, your heart, your soul, your life. Spend it. Spend all you have on my father and me and on your neighbor. Then you will see the kingdom of God.

As I reflected on Jesus' persistent attitude toward the Pharisees, I became more aware of his extremely subtle but powerful intensity. Fire burned deep within him, and it became clear how much of a radical he really was in his day—ruthless in his confrontations with the authorities, the false shepherds. After all, they were in charge of guiding his flock. Indeed, he had come to bring a sword, too. Yet even when his sword was out of its sheath, his winsomeness must have shown through, for several Pharisees did invite him home for a meal, even after getting "an earful." Even at his most confrontational, Jesus was always open to reconciliation with whomever would accept the truth, just as his father was.

Some people think there are plenty of Pharisees still around in the churches today.

Every person who enters a church, whether he or she stays there fifty years or not, has a blacker heart than one can ever imagine. Many people in the church have admitted to that in part and have some understanding of why I went to the cross, but very few really see themselves as deserving of capital punishment. That was my message to every person from the cross. There's more envy, anger, slander, and materialism in any church than you can believe and plenty of lust—however mental. That's why I had to die.

Someone ought to stand outside the church door on Sunday morning greeting each worshiper kindly with, "Good morning, murderer. . . . Good morning, lustful one. . . . Good morning, envy. . . . Good morning, greed. . . . Good morning, evil one."[11] Then right inside the door should be another minister greeting them again, saying, "Welcome. Come and receive forgiveness. Come and receive Christ's gift. Welcome to the house of peace. Good morning, saint by his righteousness. Good morning; receive his righteousness."

There are many people sitting in church every week who deep down don't really feel like they need to be forgiven. I'll tell you what makes great Christians and a great church—humble hearts. Of course, the price for humility is the same as the price for compassion—pain. This means death to the myth of the good self, the good person, the "sweet lady," the "gentleman." Myths die hard.

Nicodemus

There were a few Pharisees who listened to you, weren't there?

There's always a remnant of truth-seekers, but even they didn't come out boldly and declare themselves at first. I remember one night a Pharisee named Nicodemus came to see me long after dark, dressed plainly and not in his bright, tailored robe. He didn't want to be recognized, but had the courage to be honest and consider new truth from outside himself. He came directly to the point. He told me that everyone could see by my miracles alone that God had sent me to teach. I didn't want Nicodemus to see me as just another great teacher or prophet. I wanted him to know I was *the teacher*. So just as forthrightly, I told him, "You must be born again."

"But how can an old man go back to his mother's womb?" he asked. I told him that he didn't understand that I was talking about a spiritual life. I was talking about "life from heaven," which could only be gotten from God, who gave the spirit of life when he wanted to do so. I explained that anyone who believed in me, in fact, had this spiritual life, which was also eternal life, now. I explained that one was born again, and had a new spirit when he linked himself to my spirit, and not until then.

Nicodemus looked at me incredulously. He had come for a discussion. He hadn't come to meet the only begotten son of God. He never expected me to tell him that he wasn't born again, nor did he expect me to make the claims that I did.

I told him that I would be lifted up on a pole just as Moses had lifted up a brass serpent on a pole, saving from death all the people of Israel who looked at the serpent.*[12] God had sent me, his only begotten son, into the world to save the world, and I implied how I would do it by my death. I told Nicodemus that I was God's only son, the light from heaven. I said that many people loved darkness more than my light, because they were evil and the light would expose them. I told him that some would come gladly to the light to see who I was and who they are. I was encouraging Nicodemus to continue to search for who I was.

---

* After the people of Israel had been delivered miraculously time after time from all kinds of enemies, they continued to complain because circumstances were not as they wanted them. God sent punishment on one occasion through numerous poisonous snakes. In a panic, the Israelites repented and cried out for the deliverance that Jesus refers to here.

During that talk you told Nicodemus that you were giving him special knowledge as to what was going on in heaven. You said you had seen things others hadn't. Were you manifesting your omniscience at that time?

I was talking about how the spirit moves and causes men and women to come alive in a new way. I was thinking of my own baptism when unexpectedly the spirit of the Lord came upon me in a new way, the time when "I saw the heavens open" and a dove come down and I heard my father's voice. Remember, too, I had talked with some angels shortly after my temptation and they had told me some of the events that were taking place in heaven. I was only telling Nicodemus about my experiences as a man.

Nicodemus left that night with much to think about. He was a remarkable man who had the humble strength to accept truth. So few people can do that. Many don't want to admit that someone else might know something more.

You were an enigma to the Pharisees. Every time they asked for a miracle, you wouldn't perform one. Yet you did miracles freely for others. The time immediately after you cleared the temple, throwing the moneychangers out for the first time, the Pharisees asked you to prove that you had authority to do it by performing a miracle and you gave them a seemingly bizarre answer: Here's your miracle. "Destroy this temple, and in three days I will raise it up."[13]

They just wanted to destroy me. I wasn't going to cast my pearls before swine. I was going to warn them. They were throwing down the challenge, "You're not God." I was answering, "Stay around, and you'll see."

You had them all figured out.

Jealousy is easy to spot.

Many times Jesus gave brief but to-the-point answers to my questions just
as he had done centuries ago, "He that is without sin among you, let him
first cast a stone at her."[14]
"Get thee behind me, Satan."[15] "Thou shalt love thy neighbor as thyself."[16]

That fact impressed upon me how perfectly his use of parables fits him.
The parables reveal everything or nothing in a brief moment. They were
never gushy, rarely overwhelming. They combined his desire to teach with
his need not to intrude. He was the same way with his miracles, often
letting them speak for themselves, and certainly never pushing them at
the people.

Restraint and brevity characterized his whole life, not just his words or
deeds. They pointed to a remarkable self-containment, particularly evi-
dent after a miracle. Jesus never flaunted his power, but used it to draw
attention to his role, "I am the bread of life."[17]

Jesus was like his father, who in the thousands of years of human his-
tory available to him, chose just three years to make a public statement
with his son. The father and the son both thought there was something
powerful about brevity. After all, they just spoke and the world came into
being, and they put all of themselves into the size of a man.

There were other times you responded to the Pharisees in surprising ways. On
one occasion, you refused to answer a Pharisee's question.

The closer I got to my destiny, the more aware I was of the tremendous price I was about to pay, and the more aware I was of the Pharisees' attitude toward me. They had no use for me or for what I was
doing.

They came up to me the day after I had cleaned out the temple and
said, "Tell us, by whose authority do you remove the merchants from
the temple?" They didn't care about the answer, so I judged them. I
told them I would answer them if they would answer me. "Was John

the Baptist a prophet sent from God, or was he deluded?" I asked. John was very popular with the people, and the Pharisees wouldn't answer me. So I refused to answer their question.

Your work finally became intolerable for them. They had to get rid of you.

From the beginning of my ministry, it was obvious that they couldn't live with the differences between them and myself. Finally, the Pharisees became terrified that the people were about to make me king.

Closed Minds, Closed Eyes

These men were ambitious, educated, intelligent. With their own eyes, they had watched you heal hundreds of people, turn five loaves of bread into fifteen thousand, raise the dead; still they didn't believe in you. You even fit many of the messianic prophecies that they understood from the Old Testament. How did they miss you?

Oh, they were intelligent, capable, determined, and they were from elite families. They were the chosen people of the chosen nation. They wanted a messiah, a deliverer, who would usurp the power of Rome— the kind of messiah they deserved.

Certainly they didn't like my origins in contemptible Galilee— Nazareth, of all places. It was on the road to the corrupt pagan world. They knew the Messiah had to come from Jerusalem. That was God's city. That's where he put his temple.

So they ignored the prophecies and invented their own messiah. Pride closed the Pharisees' minds, as it always does, even to the point that they couldn't see their own Scriptures. On top of it I wasn't trained in their schools. I was just a carpenter and a megalomaniac troublemaker.

They had to explain my miracles. They couldn't use the explanation that twentieth-century Pharisees use today, "The miracles never really happened." So they decided I was straight from Satan himself.

The Pharisees also had envy that obstructed their view. Not only could they not duplicate my miracles. Their characters were flawed and mine was not. They were jealous. I was God and they wanted to be.

So with envy in their hearts, they had to kill you on the pretext that you and Satan were in collusion.

They did, but, as Solomon said, "There's nothing new under the sun." Many of today's religious authorities are still "killing" me. Not only do they deny my miracles. Modern Pharisees water down my words. "I am the light of the world," becomes "I am a nice man and on occasion a nice symbol." "I am the way, the truth, and the life" becomes "I am only one among several important men in history."

Defenders and Deniers

You have indicated your strong feelings about those who water down your words. You must also have strong feelings about those who haven't toned down you or "the pure gospel."

They are the defenders of the faith: "Eye hath not seen, nor ear heard . . . the things which God hath prepared for them that love him."[18]

What about those who exalt humanity to the highest place and claim to have values such as compassion, sensitivity, and justice? They also deny a belief in God in practice if not in actuality. And, if they recognize you at all, it's only as a "good man" or "another prophet."

You're either going to say to my father, "Thy will be done," or "My will be done." The independent humanists, who deny any real significance to the spiritual world and feel that man is on his own, obviously think the latter. Secretly, they want to take God's place. It's an old story. Pantheism, which includes Hinduism and Buddhism, tries to take my father's place by claiming equality as the core of its teaching. It says we're all just drops in an ocean called God. Equal parts.

The western version of that is egalitarianism, one of the greatest counterfeits in history. In the name of justice, fairness, and equality, truth is forsaken. "All men are created equal," becomes, "All men's ideas are equal, all men's values are equal, all men's religions and religious leaders are equal." Finally, all ideas are equal with God's, and, thus, humanity has become God.

It's an uncomfortable thing to be just a creature when you can be God. That's primarily where the theory of evolution came from—secretly people were looking for a theory to get rid of God. Darwin and his followers should have been like the great, early modern scientists who happened to be Christians. Men who stood there with their hats in their hands in awe of the wonder of creation.

At this point, I couldn't help but think how differently Jesus did things, not by grasping for equality with his father, though it was his, but by humbling himself and becoming human. In so doing, he reversed all of human history, as do his true followers even to this day. Humility is the mark of the Christian.

How can you justify Christianity's claim to be the only way to God, a claim that offends many people?

Because it's the truth. I am the only God. In an egalitarian society, those are hard words, but egalitarianism is a Christian heresy. There's another side to life besides justice. It's called "truth."

I am God's only son. I am the only one who paid the price and could pay the price for the justification everyone so desperately seeks. No other important person in history has ever made the claims that I've made. I have been here once as the king in all of history and was refused. I'm the only one who came from heaven. That's either true or false.

The heart of the egalitarian gospel says, "there are absolutely no absolutes," thus revealing the intrinsic illogical nature of their faith. If you want pictures in nature of absolutes, they're all around you. You can begin with the law of gravity. The sun is absolutely the center of our solar system. You are either dead or alive.

Maybe in a dark and dead universe stretching billions of miles, God intended for there to be life on only one planet as a sign of an absolute—that there is only one way to life. Maybe the earth is a picture of me, a picture of the incarnation. One planet with human life. One man unique among billions—further confirmed by placing him on the third planet from the sun to signify that one of the members of the trinity lived here.

You see, independent humanists are self-destructive because they destroy the truth that a transcendent God exists. They try to give others purpose and meaning, while denying the importance of eternal matters. Lose eternity and you lose humanity, for nothing ultimately matters. Eventually that reaps a society that doesn't care, because there is nothing worth caring about.

The people of this world today are being fed one of the greatest propaganda lines in history, "You make up your own mind. Do your own thing; it doesn't matter." That's an age-old lie. "It doesn't matter, Satan. Overthrow the father." "It doesn't matter Eve. Eat that apple." "It doesn't matter, Judas. Betray Jesus; someone else can be a better leader."

It does matter. You matter. Your children matter. Your words matter. Your choices matter for all eternity. What a wonderful message I was privileged to bring to the world. Through my people and my word, I still speak every day to a world that's indifferent, and careless, and self-destructive, because nobody has given them a reason not to be.

To that world I get to say, "I am life. Come."

You were anything but dull and stupid, and yet there is a mentality that says that Christians are rather stupid, weak people. Many Christians themselves seem to have embraced such a self-concept, and quote verses like, "God hath chosen the foolish things of the world to confound the wise."[19]

Humility is the queen of the virtues, but my people forget about their heritage that was full of brilliant people whom my father used mightily. Moses was tremendously learned, educated in an Egyptian culture that was centuries ahead of its time. Daniel, as a foreigner like Moses, was a recognized genius in the powerful Babylonian empire. David was a brilliant poet and military leader. His son Solomon had wisdom far beyond anything this world has seen before or since with one exception. People came from all over the world to observe his wisdom.

Then, after my death came Paul, a brilliant Jewish lawyer and scholar who became the greatest missionary the world has ever seen. Few people know that Paul in his time was known as the genius of the Middle East. His teacher, Gamaliel, who is mentioned in the Scriptures, was the foremost teacher in the most respected school in the Middle East and Paul was his outstanding pupil.

I'll tell you how much my father loves wisdom and knowledge. He made his only son the most-quoted man in history just to show how much brilliance comes from walking in his light. Part of being almighty is being brilliant. I never felt handicapped intellectually. My father made sure of that.

Your teaching and your brilliance, just like your father's, penetrate all areas of life. You predated by about nineteen hundred years Freud's discovery of the unconscious and the particular unconscious mental mechanism or "trick" of projection, both cornerstones of modern psychiatry. Freud said that unconsciously people see in others what really is a part of themselves. You said it better so that everyone could understand it—the speck you see in your neighbor's eye is the log in your own eye. You weren't particularly bashful, either, about saying how gifted your father had made you. On one occasion when the Pharisees were ignoring you, you told them that "one greater than Solomon is here."[20]

One of the reasons my followers sometimes are more timid than they have to be is because they are correctly afraid of being like Satan. Satan had so much talent that he became proud and forgot that he wasn't

God. To protect themselves from their pride and their universal secret wish to be God, my people at times attack their own intellect.

Do you think that everybody secretly wants to be God, even the godly little old lady who bakes cookies for the church bake sale and raised two sons who became missionaries?

Within every sweet person lurks an Alexander the Great. It may take the form of just wanting your son to be "the great one" or making sure everybody knows your minister is the best in town. This desire to conquer the world, and the fear of expressing that wish and becoming like Satan, cause us to forget that we're like God. There is nothing stupid about God. People have stereotyped images of my father as being opposed to intelligence, but as I read the Scriptures I got a very different picture. I paid particular attention because this was my father talking. His character was stamped on every page. His personality exuded from this book.

Suppose I described my father as someone who loves beautiful things. He ought to like them. He made them. Read Ezekiel where my father talks about what he had given to his people, Israel:

> I gave you beautiful clothes of linens and silk. . . . I gave you lovely ornaments, bracelets and beautiful necklaces. . . . And so you were made beautiful with gold and silver, and your clothes were silk and linen and beautifully embroidered. You ate the finest foods and became more beautiful than ever. You looked like a queen and so you were! Your reputation was great among the nations for your beauty; it was perfect because of all the gifts I gave you, says the Lord God.[21]

Look how he dressed his priests and the splendor with which he surrounded his kings. People forget that the most splendid king in the history of the world was Solomon. As the Scriptures record, he was "richer and wiser than all the kings of the earth."[22]

The Queen of Sheba, who had heard of Solomon's fabled wealth and wisdom, made a six-month's journey of 1500 miles by caravan to see Solomon firsthand. She saw his great palace with the great room 150 feet long and forty-five feet high—with 500 huge solid gold shields on the walls. Then she saw his immense ivory throne, the most famous in the world, overlaid with gold and surrounded by six gold steps with two enormous gold lions on each step. On her visit the Queen of Sheba drank from nothing but solid gold cups at Solomon's immaculately set tables, surrounded by hundreds of beautifully dressed servants. She saw his stables and chariots and all the gold in his treasury.

All of this was as nothing compared to how Solomon impressed her with his wisdom. He was an architect, a musician, a composer, a poet, a philosopher, and a statesman, in addition to being a king. Before she left, the Queen of Sheba told him, "Everything I heard in my own country about your wisdom . . . is all true. . . . The half had not been told me! . . . How the Lord must love Israel—for he gave you to them as their king!"[23]

Everything Solomon has or had, my father gave to him. He was a picture of my father. Do you think of my father with that kind of passionate personality?

Piety

You never seemed very pious.

In many ways, I never wanted to be. That's why I did some of the things I did. I ate meals without the ceremony of washing. I allowed my disciples to gather grain on the Sabbath for a meal. I healed on the Sabbath and visited the homes of "pagans." I wanted to break through this phony pious image of what it meant to be spiritual. I wanted people to live out the exciting tasks of being believers, of having vital relationships with my father.

I hate hypocrisy and false piety. Religious hypocrisy is particularly offensive, because believers are supposed to represent the ultimate in authenticity. Remember, though, that there are hypocrites at the country club or at the "most honest business in town" or wherever people look in mirrors.

You don't expect your followers to be perfect?

How can you expect someone who has a heart so deceitfully wicked ever to be perfect? The flesh—that part of you that wants to sin—is always present. You may control it most of the time, but you can still feel its presence. It is the part of you that lusts after possessions, that secretly delights in gossip, that privately enjoys your neighbor's failures. It is the part of you that wants to look at a pornographic magazine or to watch an erotic movie. That's the curse, and one day it will be gone.

Many people think the church today is insignificant.

The church is not perfect and it won't be until my return, but it's not insignificant. In the first century, the church had its beginnings in a small, out of the way, "peculiar" country. To all outward appearances it was insignificant. Rome ruled the world.

Within three centuries, Rome was gone, and the church had a wide presence. Whatever you may think of the church, with all its factions and contradictions, it has remained on center stage all these years and will continue to do so until my return. I meant it when I said that the gates of hell will not prevail against my church.[24]

Preview of Pain

Luke quotes you as saying, "I have come to bring fire to the earth, and, oh, that my task were completed! There is a terrible baptism ahead of me, and how I am pent up until it is accomplished!"[25] Obviously you dreaded what was ahead. In your own parables and lessons, death and injury are recurring images. The good Samaritan was beaten. The crippled came to a banquet. A rich fool is going to store up his wealth and enjoy it, but he dies that night. On other occasions, you told your disciples not to be afraid of death. As you came into the city of Jerusalem, you proclaimed, "O Jerusalem, Jerusalem! The city that murders the prophets."[26] You called the Pharisees murderers. These images suggest that death was much on your mind.

The closer I got, the more sharply it came into focus. Every day it became more real. It was one of those things you know is going to happen, but you don't think it really will, and you half hope it won't. I felt the pressure. I thought about my crucifixion daily. I had waited for that day since before creation. One day of extreme suffering was all I had to take—one day out of eternity. At first I would tell myself, "Anybody can do that," but nobody ever had. No one had ever come close to what the Scriptures described.

The pain was horrible. Pain can break anybody. Dictators over the years have used pain to conquer. When all else failed to break a prisoner, they would send in the torturers. I was going to face the ultimate torture.

I was the world's prisoner. It may have been voluntary, but still I was their prisoner. They were going to try to break me. Their hope was that I would have so much pain I couldn't stand it and would give up. Or maybe I would lash out and become like them. Perhaps I would even lash out at my father as they did, blaming him.

I was determined to go through the crucifixion. My father had said I would make it, but how would I stand the pain? I had to wait until that day arrived to find out. I would have lost my mind had I thought about it all the time.

As you said, "Sufficient unto the day is the evil thereof."[27]

That's why I could teach the people, "Don't worry about tomorrow." I learned to go to my father and live in him, each day. I anticipated the pain of that short period of time, however, for most of my life. I fought to keep it from ruling my life. After that day was over, I would then ask everybody to make one decision upon which their whole life would hang. I, too, had to make such a decision, to choose my way or God's way.

The consistent theme in many of your parables is that the decision is now or never. One must choose God or the door is shut. When you think of "being saved" in those terms, salvation takes on a deeper meaning.

The spirit of this world has helped make *salvation* a trite word. The world has scoffed at the idea of being "saved." Many human beings fight that idea. However, you're in a terrific struggle for life and death, even if you don't know it.

When a doctor enters a patient's room and says, "You've got cancer," the normal reaction is denial: "Not me!" That's the psychological mindset of the world—denial. Everyone around you has a terminal disease, and so do you. The Scriptures tell you that you are utterly defeated, in turmoil, hopelessness, nothingness, and dust. Your deepest fear is realized—death. When the patient realizes he or she has the disease, cancer research takes on new meaning.

In the same way, when a person really gets to that same edge of reality in his or her life, *salvation* is no longer just a word. You can hear the "doctor's voice" in Scripture. That voice, for some, is hard to hear. Ask any doctor who has to bring painful messages. He or she is hard to hear. If you can hear those words, if you can hear how sick you are, how black with sin you are, then hope, cure, life itself is yours. Victory at the last minute is snatched from the jaws of defeat. One can look death in the face: "O death, where is thy sting? O grave, where is thy victory?"[28] You can say that with confidence, though, only if the word *salvation* is defined in your life by me.

You must have prepared yourself mentally for the crucifixion.

I can't tell you how many times my mind played out that scene, particularly the closer I got to it. I knew so well what was going to happen. I could see them beating my face, spitting on me, pulling my beard.

After my face, then came my back. Thirty-nine times they would lash my back, ripping it open. Perhaps I could meditate on the Scriptures as the punishment continued, particularly Isaiah, "He was wounded for our transgressions ... and with his stripes we are healed. ... He opened not his mouth."[29]

I also planned to think of people I loved, whose punishment I was taking, present followers and past as well as future believers. I was going to keep reminding myself I was their shepherd. Without me they were all lost. Moses would be lost. David, Elijah, and Daniel as well; I had to do it. I would remember that.

So from the start I understood that it would be a great battle. The question kept coming to me, "How am I going to do it and not say a word?" I knew that if my father filled me with enough love, I could do it. I knew he would help me.

By the time I was actually crucified, I knew what I was going to do. My father always prepares you. I didn't go into that battle untrained or undisciplined.

Signs of the End

Often persons dying of a terminal disease describe how the awareness of their death significantly affects how they look at the world. What effect did your being a "marked man," who was going to die, have on your perceptions of the world?

It caused me to see the world for the way it really is. It was obvious to me that nothing on this earth was going to last forever. The only eternal things besides the Scriptures surrounding me were my fellow humans, and even they wouldn't be in the same form or place forever.

The more I pored over the Scriptures, the more I understood my role and at the same time how transient everything is. That's why, when my disciples and I walked down the street, they could see a beautiful temple, but I saw its coming destruction.

You warned them that the whole temple would be leveled. As you said, "not one stone here will be left upon another, which will not be torn down."[30]

That same day we left Jerusalem and stopped on the Mount of Olives. At one point in the afternoon, I was sitting with four of my disciples. As we looked out across the Kidron Valley to Jerusalem on the opposite hill, we could still see the temple behind the walls. My disciples had been thinking about what I had said earlier and asked me when the destruction of the temple was coming to pass. They wondered if there would be a warning; so I told them the signs of the end time.

How did you know what the signs would be?

It was all there in the Old Testament, every sign. I told them that, just as in Jeremiah's day, it would be a time of false prophets and false messiahs. The prophets Daniel and Joel had prophesied that the end time would be a period of the worst and most horrible devastation in history, almost incomprehensible. It would be far beyond the suffering Hitler and Stalin brought about. The great tribulation would live up to its name. There would be wars everywhere, in nearly every nation.

Never before would my father have allowed humans on a worldwide basis such free reign of their basic instincts. This time they would be turned loose and would prove for all to see what humanity was really like. As if to match humankind's destructiveness, nature would have its own upheaval. There would be famines everywhere. Earthquakes would be commonplace. Untreatable diseases would abound. Even the oceans would be turbulent. Nature's chaos would also be an answer of judgment from my father on the destructiveness of humans.

Unless my father intervenes, the world will literally destroy itself. Humans will not wipe themselves off the earth with nuclear destruction, because my father controls even the buttons that set off the bombs. At precisely the preordained moment, I will return to take over the world.

You learned all of that from the Old Testament?

Remember, too, I was able to talk with angels. Of course, my father also arranged all of history so that I would understand what was going to happen. The prophet Daniel predicted that there would be four great world empires before the Messiah. These four had come— Babylon, Media-Persia, the Greeks, and finally the Romans, as I saw with my own eyes.

The Man and the Mission

Seemingly, you alone understood thoroughly your mission. The Pharisees weren't the only ones who misunderstood. The records indicate that even your own mother, who had participated in the miracle of your birth, didn't understand what you were doing. She once came with your half-brothers to ask you to restrain yourself.

Once I set out on my journey, my family quickly heard about my following and they heard the criticism, too, particularly that from the rabbis and scribes. Everyone in Nazareth was saying, "He is just a carpenter," and my family heard what a radical I had become. Not only was I talking to untouchables, such as the tax collectors, I was eating dinner in their homes and going to their parties. People said my followers were nothing but tax collectors, radicals, and fishermen. For the most part, they were right. My religious critics complained that those with me were not particularly learned, and certainly not men of God, true men of the Scriptures. That wasn't true. They knew the Scriptures.

My family also heard that I was deviating from the Law. I was not observing the Sabbath, not washing before meals. They were told I was making incredible claims: "I am the light of the world; I am the bread of life," and that I was, on my own authority, forgiving sins. People were saying then that I was insane just as some do today. Worst of all, my family heard that I was attracting my following by using demonic powers to heal, to drive out demons, and even to raise the dead.

The pressure on them became so great that they came to see what I was doing. My mother brought only my brothers. She thought they could best confront me without my sisters. They asked me not to stir up trouble, especially with the Pharisees. They felt so strongly that when they came to where I was one midday my brothers couldn't wait until I was through teaching to talk to me. They sent a message that they needed to speak to me immediately.

You sent them an interesting answer.

The messenger couldn't get to me because of the crowd. So he yelled loud enough for everyone to hear, "Your mother and brothers are outside and want to see you." Because they had to so obviously interrupt my teaching, I immediately surmised the reason. So I looked at the crowd and asked them, "Who is my mother? Who are my brothers?" Then I pointed to the people around me and said, "These are my mother and brothers! Anyone who does God's will is my brother, and my sister, and my mother."[31]

I am surprised that your mother reacted the way she did.

She was human. Just because she was the savior's mother, she wasn't perfect. If you were told by your rabbi and all the people you had respected all your life that your son had lost his mind and was attacking religion, you would go to see him. I was not around to defend myself, and my mother temporarily lost perspective. Like John the Baptist, she thought that maybe I didn't understand my role. She had been my advisor all my life. She wasn't prepared for all my teaching, either, and she didn't realize how evil the Pharisees were. She was my mother. She couldn't bear to see me die, and she knew that I wouldn't live long teaching what I did.

Your mother wasn't the only one who began to wonder about you. As you mentioned, even John the Baptist questioned whether you were really the Messiah.

John was making bold efforts to proclaim me the Messiah, and when he saw me "just walking around from town to town teaching," he began to wonder why I wasn't consistently denouncing the Pharisees publicly for their hypocrisy. Why wasn't I making bold efforts to become king? He himself would have done so had he been the Messiah.

John and I had very different personalities. That's why my father chose him to be my prophet. John got concerned, but true to himself, he handled things straightforwardly. He sent one of his disciples down to ask me if I really was the Messiah or if someone else were coming after me.

What did you tell him?

I reminded him of the fulfilled prophecies that the blind see, the lame walk, the lepers are healed, the deaf hear, the dead are raised, and the good news is preached to the poor. I reminded him: "Blessed is the man who doesn't lose faith in me."

John's death must have had an impact on you.

It shocked me. I wasn't prepared for it, though I should have been. Most prophets were killed by their own people. There's nothing like death to open the door to reality, and John's death brought home the reality that my own death was imminent. John was murdered for telling the truth, just as I would be. He had been a good man, and they took his life. I remember thinking, "It's all coming true, just as the prophets said."

In a strange but real way, John comforted me in his death as he had during his life, for I was not to be the only one who died for truth. My father had known that in coming to terms with my mission I needed confirmation that he was at work. As only he can work all things for good, he used John's death to encourage me. Just as John was similar to me in his birth, John was like me in his death. Later when I was being crucified, my tormentors tried to make me feel evil and dirty. Even then John helped me keep from being overwhelmed by shame, because I could recall that sometimes a good man is killed.

Nothing affects you like the death of someone you're close to. When

I heard about John's murder, I wanted to be alone and spend time with my father.

You left town for the country, but many people followed you. Why didn't you turn them away at a time like this?

I meant what I said: To live is to deny yourself for the sake of others. You don't simply deny yourself. That's the world's distortion of what I said. You deny yourself for others.

I saw people crying out for a reason to live, for a purpose, for real life. I began to teach them there in the wilderness. I stood in a little valley and looked around me at several thousand people scattered about on the sides of the hills, miles away from home, listening to every word I spoke.

That was one of the times when you fed a great crowd?

Yes. Late in the day, my disciples came to remind me that the people were hungry and that I should send them back to town to find food. Then I remembered the Scriptures. I told my disciples, "You feed them." They looked at me with one of those now familiar, "Are you crazy?" looks. They knew it would cost a fortune and there were no markets around anyway.

I asked how much food we had. Andrew was trying so hard to believe. He said meekly in a halfhearted way, "There's one little boy with five loaves of bread and two fish." I told them to bring that food to me. That was one of my favorite miracles.

I held the food up to my father and asked him to bless what I was about to do. I thought to myself: "You can kill John. You can kill me, but you can never stop me or my followers. My sheep know my voice, and I will feed them. I am the bread of life."

Then I took the five loaves and two fish and fed five thousand men and their families all they could eat. As I divided the food, I looked out at that crowd and kept thinking, "This is my body broken for you"— "The kingdom of God will multiply, just as this food is multiplied."

Was that when the people tried to make you king?

They had never seen power like that, and they were immediately ready to challenge Rome. If I could make food, I could do anything. I must be the Messiah, and in their minds that meant only one thing— power! A group of men tried to overtake me, throw me on their shoulders, and force me to be king. They were willing to participate in riots, rebellions, or whatever it took. Rome was coming down in their dreams.

These men had ignored my teaching:

> Blessed are the meek, for they will inherit the earth. . . .
> Blessed are the peacemakers, for they will be called sons of God. . . .
> Blessed are you when people insult you, persecute you and falsely say all kinds of evil against you, . . . because great is your reward in heaven.[32]

Blessed are those who mourn, not blessed are those who overcome others. They were going to do it the world's way—with muscle, with power, with rebellion. I came the first time to win men's hearts, not to overpower them. These men hadn't comprehended that.

I felt that my teaching had failed. These men coming to make me king didn't have the slightest idea about my thoughts or how heavy my heart was over John. There would be no reasoning with them. Before they got to me, I slipped away, high up the mountain.

I knew something had to change. Now I had the time with my father that I needed. I spent hours with him. It was one of those times when I needed him desperately—his confidence, his calmness, his vision. I couldn't get John's death off my mind. The shock. The grief now. The grief to come.

As usual, I had his peace. I was surrounded by people who didn't understand, who were trying to force my hand before I wanted it played. I needed to know where to go from there.

The Mountain and the Miracle

What did you and your father talk about on the mountain?

That night I asked the Lord: "Where now? What now?" Over the next hours it became clear to me. Many who followed me weren't my true followers. They were power-mongers. I could see the cost. Most would desert me, and I counted that cost.

Despite the tension that persisted, I had the most incredible peace from my father. For the next few hours before I left the mountain, I spent time thanking him, meditating on his words and singing songs of praise.

I remember how grateful I was that night that I had learned how to get that degree of oneness with him. How grateful I was that I had learned the skills of faith. I couldn't have been that comforted when I was fourteen, but now I knew how to abide, how to live in him.

What a thrill it is when you eventually come to know that your father in heaven is so omnipotent that he is your friend who constantly goes before you every, every step of the way. He looks for ways to reassure you and delights when you turn to him. He holds every situation in the palm of his hand. The verses "There is a friend who sticks closer than a brother"[33] and "Many, O Lord my God, are the wonders which You have done, And Your thoughts toward us"[34] kept coming back to me.

Before I left the mountains that night, I asked my father one last thing. I knew this was to be a major turning point in my ministry and I wanted to send the people, and particularly my disciples, one more important message about why I was here. My disciples could easily get caught up in this frenzy. They still didn't really understand who I was and what I was about. I was still grieving over John's death, and my own death was imminent, and I thought of the verse, "Cast thy bread upon the waters: for thou shalt find it after many days."[35] Suddenly, it occurred to me to ask my father for something special. "May I walk on my grave, on my death?"*

---

* The sea, the water, was the symbol of death and the grave. It's where baptism comes from, which also contains the picture of resurrection.

Just as I accepted my grave when I went to be baptized, might I now have the privilege of walking on top of it, a foretaste of the day that I would walk out of it? Immediately I knew I could—the Scriptures told me I would do awe-inspiring deeds for myself as well as for others. It was clear to me that all things that the father had were mine, and he held the oceans in the palm of his hand.

Moses had walked through the ocean, Noah had, in a sense, walked on "my grave," and Jonah had spent three days in it, and all three had come out alive. They were all pictures of my ruling the ocean, ruling nature as king, and ruling over death. Later I would further declare my lordship over nature by cursing a tree and causing it to wither. At this time I realize my father was guiding me to walk on water. It was another one of those moments when I bowed before the awesome Scriptures.

Where were your disciples all this time?

I had already sent my disciples across the Sea of Galilee in the only boat we had. Somehow, in the back of my mind I knew what I would ask my father, and I knew that he would grant it. I walked on the water to my disciples. I kept thinking of my father, how he never laid on us more than we could bear and how he often gave us a taste of our future glory to keep us going.

When I got to the boat, my disciples were, you might say, slightly alarmed. *(He laughed again loudly.)* They thought I was a ghost. They thought the crowd that wanted to make me king had somehow lost control, and I had been killed. Now here they were, huddled together on the far side of the boat afraid of a ghost. It was a very comical sight. Even after I told them who I was as I neared the boat, they were too frightened to do anything. That included, of course, everybody except guess-who?

Peter.

Peter was his usual self. He was leaning over the side of the boat toward me, looking at me, and saying, "Lord, let me do it, too." So I let him. He walked for a little way, but when he realized what he was actually doing he became frightened and sank. Peter's like a lot of folks. He lacked some of the faith he needed, but at that moment he didn't lack courage.

So if Peter had believed in you completely, he would have made it?

Absolutely.

Did you have some of the same feelings Peter did when you were out for your evening stroll on the water?

At first I almost always had the same sense others did that "This is strange." or "Is this a dream?" or "I'm a long way from the shore." I'd just come from six intense hours alone with my father, though, and I knew he could do anything. In the face of human doubt, I knew how to trust completely. Peter didn't. So I had to hold him by the arm as we walked back to the boat together. Peter was much more humble on the way back, but that wasn't too bad a lesson for him to learn. Without my father and me, neither he nor the rest of them could ever accomplish anything.

By the time you and Peter got to the boat, the New Testament indicates that the disciples had finally caught on or thought they had and said, "Now we know that you really are the Son of God." What brilliance! Whenever I read that, I always chuckle and think of the people who say that God has no sense of humor.

My father's sense of humor is seen all through the Scriptures and in nature. Remember the time God wanted to stop a prophet of sorts by the name of Balaam from taking a particular action? He had Balaam's donkey stop, turn around, and talk to Balaam. Changing an old man's name from Abram to Abraham which meant "the father of many nations" when the man at age seventy-five had no children and his wife, Sarah, was post-menopausal. She laughed herself until she was an expectant mother, eight months pregnant at age ninety-one, while Abraham, the proud father, was one hundred years old. Don't you think God had a good time dressing up my cousin, John the Baptist, "to begin his public ministry"? Anybody who created Peter had to have a sense of humor.

Surprised by the Spirit

How surprised were you with some of the things you did?

That was one of the surest signs to me that I was God, that my father lived through me. I would often ask myself after a miracle, "Where did that come from?" I would amaze myself because "I was not just I." At times I could actually feel his power in me.

That impressed you?

Many times I would sit and think, "So you're God." It was amazing to me. Psalm 45 described what I would do, and it was beyond my wildest imagination at first. The Scriptures even told me I would be impressed. Psalm 45 says, "Let Your right hand teach You awesome things."[36] In other words, my own deeds would teach me. Being one with the spirit was magnificent. The things he did through me inspired me. Isn't that the way he works with you, with all believers? Aren't you honored when he uses you to do good things?

Yes, of course I am.

It was the same for me. Frequently I felt like just another man, but the more closely I stuck to my father and his words to me, the more I realized that I was the Messiah and the more I thought like the Messiah. It's the same thing that happens to a man when he becomes a world leader. It's hard to believe at first, but one grows into the role.

The condition of the world helped to clarify my identity. One day before I went public with my announcement, I perceived that the world really had no leader. They were all sheep without a shepherd, and the more I saw that somebody needed to be the shepherd, the more I realized that I was the good shepherd.

My father also confirmed my identity by giving me miraculous powers. The Messiah's role itself demanded that he have some supernatural powers. He had to stand not only beside his fellow men and women but also above them, not just in character, but in power, too. My father obviously knew that in order for people to believe "a man was going to be God," that man must do some extraordinarily powerful things. That's why I appealed to my miracles when people doubted me.

To get back to my story, the next morning after their great push to make me king, all the crowds were down by the shore at the base of the hills waiting for me to come down. They knew I had already sent my disciples across the Sea of Galilee to Capernaum. After waiting some time, the people got into their boats and came on over to Capernaum where, much to their surprise, they found me already at the synagogue.

They asked me how I had gotten there, and I told them that they just wanted to be with me because I had fed them, not because they really believed in me. The people confirmed that impression, telling me if I wanted them to believe in me as the Messiah, I would give them free bread every day, just as their forefathers had been given nourishment in the wilderness. To add stature to their unrealistic desire, they manipulatively quoted the Scriptures, "Moses gave them bread from heaven."[37]

I hadn't come to remove the pressures of life from them, but to give them strength and character to face life's trials. My miracles were meant to testify to them that I was their Messiah. So I replied that Moses hadn't given them bread. God had. They should seek the true bread sent from heaven: "I am the Bread of Life. No one coming to me will ever be hungry again."[38]

The same day that I actually claimed to be the Messiah, many of the people were disturbed; particularly the ones who said they knew my parents. The crowd was confused. Some wanted to declare me as the

Messiah on their terms. Some didn't want to declare me the Messiah under any terms. I kept going. I told them that no one could believe in me unless the father drew him to me, and at the last day I would raise those believers from the dead. The look of unbelief continued to grow on all their faces, but I was not deterred.

> How earnestly I tell you this—anyone who believes in me already has eternal life! Yes, I am the Bread of Life! When your fathers in the wilderness ate bread from the skies, they all died. But the Bread from heaven gives eternal life to everyone who eats it. I am that Living Bread that came down out of heaven. . . . This Bread is my flesh given to redeem humanity.[39]

It was too much truth. They couldn't handle it, but I went even further:

> Unless you eat the flesh of the Messiah and drink his blood, you cannot have eternal life within you. But anyone who does eat my flesh and drink my blood has eternal life.[40]

That did it. They thought I was crazy. How could I say, "Eat my flesh; drink my blood"? It was too much. I could sense a large number of people pulling away from me, but it had to be. Many of those who wanted to believe I was the Messiah couldn't now. They didn't want a messiah who talked about his death, made his followers cannibals, and spoke of waiting for the last day and redemption. They wanted a messiah who talked about conquering Rome—now. They wanted a messiah who hated the Romans.

Other teachings confused your listeners. You said that no one could come to you unless the father attracted him to you. The debate in the church for years has been, "Can a person choose you, or does your father choose your followers?" It's the old free will versus predestination question. Your speech on that day seems to favor predestination.

Remember that in the same talk I urged people to eat my flesh and to drink my blood, to believe in me as though they had a choice. I also said at another time, "Whosoever will may come." You don't think you will understand everything about salvation, the incarnation, or my atonement, do you? That confusion is meant to lead to humility. It's a boundary between God's intelligence and yours, to highlight the difference in you. All of God's roads lead to humility.

Alone with the Father

During this time did you ever feel alone or abandoned?

Sin always extracts a high price. All of God's people have to spend time alone. I was like Job. None of Job's friends understood him, and the need to be understood is great. I was carrying a heavy burden every day. I wanted others, particularly my disciples, to see what I saw, to encourage me, and to share the battle with me. Instead, they could see only with their eyes. I knew great pain awaited us.

I kept thinking that they had to see what they were up against. After I was gone, they were going to have the challenge of taking my message—taking me—to the whole world. It was obvious that I was going to die soon. According to the Scriptures, I would come in my full glory and in judgment at my second coming. If the world was to be evangelized before that day—and my father had promised that it would be—I would have to do it through my disciples.

Because I had no one else to turn to, times alone with my father were especially rich. He kept me going. Again, through his word, he told me exactly what to expect, "Strike down the Shepherd and the sheep will scatter."[41]

My disciples would run from me. I knew that. I also knew that a good friend would lift up his hand against me. That was Judas. God left no illusions. He was saying to me, "Your disciples are blind right now, but take courage; I will establish them in time. I know one of them will betray you; be prepared. Only you can have faith and overcome the world's lack of faith in me. That's why I sent you."

You and your father repeatedly brought stress to your disciples to teach them. You constantly chided them about their lack of faith. They couldn't cast the demon out of the boy, and you easily did it. They had to go through the frightening storm at sea.

One of the best ways, and for many people the only way, to discover him is in the middle of impossible situations. My men had to learn to pray and to wait, particularly to wait. First would come my death and resurrection. Joy would come after the wait. To have joy, one must endure an element of the unexpected, the unknown. The greater the fear, the greater the uncertainty, the greater will be the joy. There's nothing more secure than when God rescues you.

Did anything else happen during those times when you went to be alone with your father early in the morning?

You feel the electricity when an "alive" person comes into a room? That's how you should come to feel about your devotional times—you are meeting with the most charismatic personality. My "sessions" with him taught me that.

How many people have seriously considered that God is the most exciting personality they've ever met? The central question of life is, "Can you really trust this personality?" You have to find that out. Quiet time alone with him is how to do it.

Teachings on Prayer

Tell me about prayer.

Prayer was a great experience for me. I went to my times alone with God to be treated as I would treat others. Daily it became an experience in which I would know by faith that I was in the presence of someone who personally cared about me beyond belief.

Because I constantly let God teach me through the Scriptures, I could respond to him in prayer. Often I would come to a point in my prayers where I knew I was surrounded by his great protective love. Faith eventually enables a sense of God's presence, that he's always there. Someone who feels that can go through anything.

He had a special love for me, so evident in those portions of Scripture that were meant just for me:

> I will appoint you . . . as a light to the nations.[42]
> Kings and queens shall serve you. . . . They shall bow to the earth before you, and lick the dust from off your feet.[43]
> I will fight those who fight you.[44]

It sounds like your prayer life was different from that of most people. They describe it more as a ritual and less as a passion.

That's why I often prayed for long periods. You have to work at prayer. You have to work to get the sense that he's there, that point of knowing. To do it takes time and often, initially, some rituals to help focus your mind. Some prayer times are better than others, just as some times with friends are better than others. I reached the point where all of the times with my father were good. Of course, when your needs are strong, your spiritual sense is acute.

Your disciples were impressed by the way you prayed and asked you to show them how. That was when you taught them what we call "The Lord's Prayer."

I tried to teach them to pray from the heart and to pray for what was most immediate, such as daily bread, daily failures, and daily temptations. I tried to teach them to pray wherever they were and at whatever they were occupied.

I wanted them to talk to God as they would talk to a friend who was really interested in them. Most of all, I tried to get them to accept who they were—human beings—and to let God be God.

So you opened "The Lord's Prayer" with "Our Father, who art in heaven. . . .
Thy will be done. . . ."

That is the heart of every prayer and the means to freedom. Once
you learn that you're not God but that he is, you're halfway there.

But you are God.

I was also a man.

You were so consistent in prayer, yet so many believers have trouble with their
prayer lives. As a friend of mine said, "We're all foxhole Christians." We're on
our knees in crises, but at other times we take prayer lightly.

There are different elements in prayer. One is asking someone to
do something for you. That's almost totally a passive role, and eventually there is tremendous relief to get to that point. Another element
involves work. It's asking frequently for what you want him to do along
with continually praising him for the power he has. To praise God is
to recognize his character and abilities, which helps you realize who
he is and who you are.

I also viewed prayer as joining a giant war between good and evil,
and continually praying for good to win out in the church. Prayer contains a built-in way of losing your life for God when you praise him—
offering the sacrifice of praying for others. That's one main reason why
people don't pray enough. They hold on too tightly to their time.

The opposite view of time can also present a problem. People think
that to really pray they have to be alone for long periods of time. They
don't realize that God is their friend, who is always with them, and he
is someone they can tell things to at any time, just as to a husband or
a wife or a dear friend.

Another major reason people don't pray enough is that they're afraid
of the power they've been given. Imagine this: you can move the hand
of God. Listen to what he says, "Call to me and I will answer you and
tell you great and unsearchable things you do not know."[45]

He's waiting to answer you. That's why I told my disciples so many times to ask. Six times in my last message to them before my crucifixion, I told them to ask. Power makes people uncomfortable. They back off from the influence they have, and then their God becomes too small. I hope my people never forget that they're made in the image of God.

Often people are unaware of how hard God is working to communicate with them daily. Remember, he is the one who said, "I will guide thee with mine eye"[46] and who said, "The Lord is my shepherd."[47]

Moses and Elijah

What were your difficult moments before your final Passover and crucifixion in Jerusalem?

I was so alone. I had been rejected in Judea and rejected in Galilee, when I wanted to be accepted. I was misunderstood by my mother and my family, by the people, by my own prophet, and continually by my disciples. It was as if my teachings were in vain, and the final Passover was staring me in the face.

I was now in the middle of the grief the Scriptures had told me I would feel, "a man of sorrows, and acquainted with grief,"[48] only I hadn't completely anticipated the grief of alienation. I had forgotten that I was to have Job's role as well as David's. How easy a role it was to forget.

It became harder to experience relief with my father and to focus on the future. One morning after this had endured for several days, I felt discouraged. Then I remembered something that Moses had done at a difficult moment all alone as Israel's leader. In his distress, Moses had reached the point at which he had to know for sure that God was still with him. Jehovah then personally guaranteed Israel's eventual greatness and, at the same time in a very intimate way, reassured Moses. As he said to Moses, "You are my friend."[49] Moses was so moved that he asked to see God's glory.

God's glory would be too intense for Moses to encounter, but God showed him part of it. On Mount Sinai, the Lord passed in front of him while covering Moses' eyes. God allowed Moses to see his back. I wondered if God wanted me to ask to see his glory, which was also my own. I was greater than Moses, and Moses was a picture of me.

I also thought of Elijah, when he was distraught to the point of wanting to die because of the constant persecution of Queen Jezebel, who wanted him dead. Elijah thought he alone still stood for God. God sent him to the same Mount Sinai on which Moses had stood. There God comforted Elijah.

Both Elijah and Moses had felt particularly alone, and God let them have a brief look at the unseen spiritual world. It seemed evident that I could ask him for the same privilege. Through all these circumstances in the Scriptures—always the Scriptures—I felt my father was leading me to ask him for the same privilege Moses and Elijah had received. So I did. I asked him to show me my glory on Mount Hermon, and let some of my disciples see it to build their faith.

You were so confident in your father's answer that you took three disciples—Peter, James, and John—with you to see God's answer.

I went in great expectation.

What happened?

We were on top of the mountain praying. Suddenly a bright light appeared. When I opened my eyes I saw that it was coming from me. My robe was the most brilliant white you could imagine, and my disciples said that my face shone like the sun. Then Moses and Elijah were standing there, and we began talking.

Why were these two men sent?

They represented the two pillars that always sustained Israel, the Law and the Prophets. I was the fulfillment of the Law. I was also the fulfillment of the Prophets. Now Elijah was saying to me, "You are the one we have been waiting for." I knew who I was, but I was a man and I needed to hear from my father again that I was *the* prophet, the last in the line.

Have there been none since?

None.

You obviously have a special attachment to Moses and Elijah. Why?

Both Moses and Elijah were surrounded by Jews who never quite understood them. Both were persecuted unfairly. With God's power, both eventually performed great miracles to deliver their people. Moses parted the Red Sea. Elijah performed some of the same miracles I had—raising the dead, supernaturally providing food, controlling the rain. Also the authorities of the day tried to kill him because of his loyalty to the true God. Also, Elijah never died. He was a picture of both my resurrection and of my ascension.

What did you talk about with Moses and Elijah?

Elijah said to me, "Lord, we all have waited for this for centuries." I told them, "I dread what is about to happen." Elijah said, "We know, Lord."

Very sensitively, Moses and Elijah began to talk about their hardships when they were here. Elijah described how he had battled almost a whole culture. His task had seemed impossible. As he said, "Israel had become so pagan, you can't believe how bad things had become. Temples to Baal, like the one standing over there," and he pointed to another peak of Mount Hermon, "were everywhere." Then he smiled and said, "You know how your father works—the God of impossible situations."

Elijah, who was as forthright as the Scriptures had described him, also told me, "Lord, just as Jonah rose from the deep after three days, you will rise from your grave. Then one day, Lord, you will do what no one has done—come back from the dead. You will honor us by giving your life for us."

"But it won't be easy, Lord. At the moment you are in the middle of your suffering, you will feel all alone and powerless. You will probably have thoughts that will surprise you—even after all God has shown you." Then he went on, "Moses and I talked to God directly, and still moments came when our faith wavered. It was as if we'd never heard God's voice."

Moses added, "Lord, I went into a rage over my people's disobedience and I exploded at them and dishonored God, I was never allowed to go into the promised land. In fact, this is the first time that I've ever set foot on it.* When you're on that cross, you won't lose your temper as I did. You won't retaliate. You're the lamb of God, chosen by your father before the foundation of the world. You have to do what none of us could do.

"This world thinks it is so mighty to retaliate, but one day the people will know the greatest deed, the greatest strength in history was shown not by retaliating but by an act of self-control beyond belief."

"It will be 'The great submission,'" Elijah said.

Moses said one more time, "Lord, look at your glory. You can do what we could not."

The last thing Moses said was, "Cherish those words." I thought about everything that had been said on that mountain all the way to the cross.

---

* Once when he was leading his rebellious followers, Moses had instructions to speak to a rock and water would come forth. That miracle was intended to help Moses quiet his people. Instead of just speaking, Moses was furious with his people and hit the rock twice with his staff as hard as he could. The rock was a symbol of Christ, the Immovable Savior, and was not meant for him to strike, but only for God to strike—and he would strike it only once. Because Moses had disobeyed God, he was never allowed to enter the Promised Land, although God permitted him to lead the Jews to the entrance.

What were your thoughts after the transfiguration?

As I told you before, when one of these things happened, it impressed me as much as it did anyone else.

When Moses and Elijah appear to you, tell you how important you are, call you Lord, and your garments and entire countenance turn a bright dazzling supernatural white, it's an experience you don't forget.

It was also clear that my suffering would soon be over, and then I would have my true glory back that I had now partially seen. I'd also heard my father's voice again telling my disciples to listen to me, emphasizing my authority and telling me how pleased he was with me. Telling me once more, "All that I have is yours."

I thought about this day over and over again, just as I had my baptism. I'd asked him to show me my glory and, as usual, he had done more than I expected. I had seen living proof of the resurrection—Moses and Elijah—just when I needed it most.

Before Bethlehem

Were there other moments when you wondered about what you were really like before you became a man; when you were God unveiled?

Constantly. I thought about what it would be like to know everything about the universe and every thought. To have all that power, to be able to create oceans and mountains. That seemed incredible. Yet I'd used just a fraction of that power when I healed the sick or turned water to wine. I had firsthand proof of the existence of that kind of power.

I thought about being omniscient, and yet having such a personal relationship with each individual. That for me was almost incomprehensible. Still, I had experienced his guidance and personal love. I knew how passionately I cared about every person I really knew, and it struck me that my father feels the same way. He knows *everybody.* I had this knowledge before—and I would again soon.

Some people will be puzzled as to how you could have been an all-powerful God and yet couldn't remember it.

My memory of eternity past with my father was one of those privileges I veiled. I'll show you a picture in nature of what I'm talking about. Can you remember the day you were born, or most of what happened to you at one or two years of age? In fact, God could have built in that memory gap as a picture of the incarnation.

I can think of two groups of people who won't like what you said about your omniscience. The nonbelievers will say you are just dreaming, and some believers will say you weren't that limited when you were on earth, that you always used your omniscience.

The unbeliever doesn't know how gifted he or she is, but my father communicates in nature, just as the book of Romans says. The average person knows about five percent of himself. By far the largest part of a person is buried in that vast reservoir called the unconscious, which shows you how deceptive feelings are, because we experience subjectively knowing all of ourselves. The unconscious mind is a picture of our greatness. One day every person will get his complete identity, and find out he was more deeply complex, much bigger than he imagined.

I understand humility is a virtue. Yet your father is generous beyond belief—he gave us his only son. If you were so loved, why did your father make you so poor financially?

He wanted me to have adventure. Usually, if you have this world's certainty, you will miss out on the other world's certainty. Then you really miss out on living. Above all he wanted to teach me how to get life.

Living is trusting?

That is what I said in chapter 12 of Luke. Living is not in the abundance of things you have, but is in giving and trusting that he will provide for you. Every day I went to the spiritual world to get what I couldn't get here. All this world offers is false certainty and fear. I needed peace and confidence and true certainty. The only place to get it was from him. I would go to my father to get his life, his certainty, so that I could give that to my people. I would give them God. We're always giving each other something good or bad in our interactions. We should be prepared every day to give someone the kingdom of God. To give others my life.

The God Who Is Love

You talk about how innately loving your father is, but some people criticize him for being self-centered. They say all he wants is to have others praise him all the time.

That sounds like projection. You can read the Scriptures that way if you ignore everything about God's giving, but that would mean ignoring a great deal of Scripture. In any case, when God says you were made to serve him, substitute the word *give* for *serve* and you will be all right. You're made to give to God just as he wants to give to you. C. S. Lewis called him "The Great Giver." As I said, all of heaven will be people giving to one another.

There are people who say you were a kind man, as the New Testament reveals, but that the God of the Old Testament is different. He is angry and cruel.

I was the Old Testament fulfilled. I came straight out of those pages. Everything he told me to do, I did. Whose idea was it not to retaliate on the cross? His. Read the Old Testament. He was the one who said for me to keep my tongue silent. He was the one who was giving up his only son. If you want to see what the God of the Old Testament was like, look at me. I'm no different in the New Testament, and neither is my father.

The people who say he is harsh have never read about his patience. Imagine someone who is the king, the Lord of the universe. He takes abuse and rebellion—not just for an hour or a day but for years, centuries; from people who do nothing but bring grief to him and to others, people to whom he gave everything, including the breath in their lungs. He watches them destroy themselves and others until they are a shell of who he made them to be.

People can worship pieces of metal called automobiles that race through space. They can worship one part of a person's life, such as sex, until it destroys the rest of their personality. God won't stand for it. After demonstrating incredible patience, he finally says, "Because you continually reject me year after year and spit in my face, I do the same to you. I will watch while your enemies kill your children, torture you and rape your wives, just as you have done to others, and I will do nothing."

Imagine someone that angry. At first I thought, "How could someone that angry be holy?" I didn't understand how great he was, how great his plans for his creatures were, how holy he intended them to be, how holy he was. That took me years. Once I did understand, I saw that only a God with that much feeling could send his only son to die. At the same time, it made me fear his wrath. I had to bear it, and that was incomprehensible.

On the other hand, this is how passionate he is when he is on your side.

> He brought you out of Egypt by his Presence and his great strength, to drive out before you nations greater and stronger than you.[50]
> Call to me and I will answer you, and I will tell you great and mighty things, which you do not know.[51]

Look how powerful he is!

> The earth trembles at his glance.[52]
> He counts the stars and calls them all by name.[53]
> Who else holds the wind in his fists, and wraps up the oceans in his cloak?[54]

Look how he makes you promises, how he guarantees them.

Never will I leave you; never will I forsake you.[55]
I will multiply your posterity as the stars of heaven.[56]

Isn't that the kind of God we want? Does that sound like someone who is weak or unconcerned? His anger was never wrong, and never will be. People just get what they deserve. Don't you see? God had to judge. His honor was at stake. Would he let injustice win out? Would he ultimately allow an unjust universe? Do you think he will not demand absolute fairness?

People are right when they see injustice. Do they think my father doesn't see it? Do they think they see more than God does? Or are they better than he is? Don't worry; God will take care of all of the injustice in the world. He's just trying to allow as much mercy as the world will permit.

When that great judgment day comes, people will truly understand how unjust everyone was, particularly themselves. Those who are Christians will then see the extent of God's great mercy. Those who are not will see how much they needed it and what they refused. There will be no complaints about injustice on that day.

Can you really love a spirit, "someone" you can't see, like God?

You can love him enough to die for him. We have all loved people we haven't seen through their books, and, in essence, we loved their spirits. Everything I did was because I loved him, and others have had similar experiences. That's why the psalmist could write, "As the deer pants for streams of water, so my soul pants for you, O God."[57]

For a long time, part of the Scriptures may seem just like words until repeatedly you experience that breakthrough phenomenon. One day you gradually come to see that you were made for these words, that they are you.

As Paul said, *"until Christ is formed in you."*[58]

God is good. That's why you can love him. If you're looking for him, he strengthens your faith at just the right time with tangible events and circumstances that carry the message, "See, I hear you."

I remember one particular time when I had been pressured by crowds for days. I had been healing late into the evening, usually sleeping on the road, and it was wearing on me. At the end of a long day John came and told me, "There's an old man who wants to tell you something that I think you'd like to hear." I nodded in consent and John brought him to me. This man, who looked twice my age, began to tell me about a night over thirty years ago when he and two other young shepherds had been tending their sheep outside of Bethlehem. All of a sudden an angel had appeared to them telling them that the Messiah had been born and was lying in Bethlehem in a manger. He remembered how odd that had seemed. The Messiah was in a manger, a feeding trough from which animals eat! Undoubtedly an angel was telling them that it was true.

Then the old man told me how hundreds of angels had appeared in the heavens and began to sing. After the angels had left, he recalled the three of them running into Bethlehem to find the Messiah, and how awestruck they were when they did.

Then he said, "I know you were that baby because I've seen your miracles, and I know where you're from—and your mother and father told me your name. They told me their names, too—Mary and Joseph from Nazareth. I've never forgotten your name, Jesus. I've never forgotten that night or your mother and father. It was such an incredibly beautiful and clear night. Your mother, who was such a pretty young woman, had the most radiant glow I'd ever seen. I didn't know the whole story, but the look on their faces was almost proof of who you were. They had a glow and also a look almost of shock, like they had just witnessed a miracle.

"Your mother and father were such gentle people, and they thanked us for coming. I'll never forget that night with you in that stable. The whole world seemed to be at peace."

Notes

1. 2 Chronicles 7:14
2. based on Luke 7:41–47
3. Matthew 22:16–17 TLB
4. Matthew 22:21 TLB
5. Luke 20:42–43 TLB
6. see Luke 11:45–51
7. Luke 14:5 TLB
8. Luke 13:12 TLB
9. Luke 13:14 TLB
10. Luke 18:10–14a TLB
11. see Mark 10:18
12. see John 3:14
13. John 2:19
14. John 8:7b
15. Luke 4:8a
16. Matthew 19:19b
17. John 6:35a
18. 1 Corinthians 2:9
19. 1 Corinthians 1:27a
20. Matthew 12:42c NIV
21. Ezekiel 16:9–14 TLB
22. 1 Kings 10:23 TLB
23. 1 Kings 10:6–9a TLB
24. see Matthew 16:18b
25. Luke 12:49–50 TLB
26. Luke 13:34a TLB
27. Matthew 6:34b
28. 1 Corinthians 15:55
29. Isaiah 53:5–7a
30. Matthew 24:2b NASB
31. Mark 3:32–35 TLB
32. Matthew 5:5, 9, 11–12a NIV
33. Proverbs 18:24b NASB

34. Psalm 40:5 NASB
35. Ecclesiastes 11:1
36. Psalm 45:4b NASB
37. John 6:31b TLB
38. John 6:35a TLB
39. John 6:47–51 TLB
40. John 6:53b–54 TLB
41. Zechariah 13:7b TLB
42. Isaiah 42:6 NASB
43. Isaiah 49:23 TLB
44. Isaiah 49:25 TLB
45. Jeremiah 33:3 NIV
46. Psalm 32:8b
47. Psalm 23:1a
48. Isaiah 53:3b
49. Exodus 33:17b TLB
50. Deuteronomy 4:37b–38a NIV
51. Jeremiah 33:3 NASB
52. Psalm 104:32b TLB
53. Psalm 147:4 TLB
54. Proverbs 30:4 TLB
55. Hebrews 13:5b NIV
56. Exodus 32:13a TLB
57. Psalm 42:1 NIV
58. Galatians 4:19b NASB

CHAPTER FOUR

Instruction and Celebration

The Teacher

Let's talk more about your teaching.

Everyone remembers my miracles, my birth, my death, and my resurrection. People often forget that my primary work during those last years was to teach. The people were getting such poor teaching.

How did you decide exactly what to teach the people about who you were?

I learned the Old Testament until I understood my father and myself and my mission. Then I knew what to teach. I did a great deal of thinking about how to describe myself. At first I wondered if he wanted me to use the names he did in Isaiah where he prophesied the Messiah's coming:

> For unto us a child is born, unto us a son is given: and the government shall be upon his shoulder: and his name shall be called Wonderful, Counselor, The mighty God, The everlasting Father, The Prince of Peace.[1]

I didn't have all my glory yet, and the government wasn't going to be on my shoulders on my first visit. I wasn't comfortable with all those names yet. I let him describe me in that way. I asked him to guide me as to what to teach in my own way. He did. For example, after I had fed the multitude, I told them I was the *bread of life*.

I always wanted people to get an idea of a relationship that was vital and alive. That's why I tried to use images that were essential to life, such as bread and water. That's why communion is so basic.

My father emphasized further the kind of relationship I would have with my people. I told them the same thing that he did: I was their shepherd.

You referred to yourself as "the good shepherd."

God used that image in Psalm 23 and elsewhere in the Old Testament. It was particularly in chapter 40 of Isaiah: "He shall feed his flock like a shepherd: he shall gather the lambs with his arm, and carry them in his bosom, and shall gently lead those that are with young."[2]

Remember, too, who David was before he became Israel's great warrior king. He was a shepherd who risked his life to protect his sheep. David, as I've said, was a picture of me. First, he was a protecting shepherd. Then, in the second part of his life, he was a king. The first time I came I was the shepherd. When I return I shall be the king.

Privately, before my death, the most common way I thought about myself was as the people's shepherd, who lays down his life for his sheep. Self-sacrifice was at the center of my teaching, and that was at the heart of the Scriptures about the suffering Messiah—especially Isaiah 53. It was that part of the Scriptures that Jewish scholars totally ignored. It couldn't have been more precise. It shows you, as T. S. Eliot said, how little truth human beings can tolerate. When I thought of my mission, the one verse that always stood out to me directly referred to my people as sheep: "All we like sheep have gone astray; we have turned every one to his own way; and the Lord hath laid on him the iniquity of us all."[3]

In one of your sermons, you forever stamped your identity as shepherd, "I am the good shepherd. The good shepherd lays down his life for the sheep. . . . I know my sheep, and my sheep know me."[4] *Then, with incredible authority you promised that there would be worldwide unity, one government with you at the head: "I have other sheep that are not of this sheep pen. I must bring them also. They too will listen to my voice, and there shall be one flock and one shepherd."*[5]

The idea of one world government with one ruler was distinctly there in Isaiah, "And the government shall be upon his shoulder."

I had two identities that I had to communicate to people. I commonly referred to myself as "the son of man." It was a name with two identities. In the book of Daniel, the title referred to the future divine Messiah. It was the way my father repeatedly addressed his very human prophet Ezekiel. Literally, son of man means "son of dust." He is vulnerable, perishable, finite—not eternal. The body that I had was going to die. I felt like a man; I thought like a man. I never wanted the people to forget that. At the same time, I was more than a man. I was God.

There were other titles the Scriptures led you to call yourself.

In Isaiah, my father talks about the farmer planting his vineyard. It is a beautiful parable and I often use his image of planting and growing in my parables, particularly at the last supper, "I am the vine, you are the branches."[6]

Another time, my father called me the light, "The people walking in darkness have seen a great light."[7] That's where I got the idea to tell them, "I am the light of the world."[8]

That is why I told my followers not to hide their light. That's the plan. Develop the lights and let the world see them. They point the way toward the light. Almost everybody has to overcome a reluctance to let his light shine.

Except Peter, you have noted.

Peter's personality sparkled from the first day he was born.

You understood so much. Did it take you a long time to comprehend just how fully you were the light of the world?

As I said, that's what I had to be about for thirty years, to work out my own understanding. When I finally understood I was the light—the pure light, the only light, then everything fell into place. I was the one who was to reveal the father. I was the one who would speak for him. I was to confront as he was to confront, as the prophets before me had, only—being *the light*—I had more light and power.

When I saw who my father was, felt his heartbeat in the pages of the Old Testament, it resonated deep within me with the passion I had for the oneness of humankind. I could see that I was pure, and I could see my brothers' blindness. I was prepared to put everything on the line for them when I came to see that my father had put out everything he had for them, too. He had sent his only son, and you don't think his only son was going to let him down. I wasn't going to ask anything less of my brothers.

For centuries, there's been a prevalent mentality among Christians that we're not to use our talents. Instead, we are to "lose our lives for Christ's sake," and deny ourselves completely. How does that fit with "letting your light shine"?

To give balance to the true meaning of "losing your life," I said, "Let your light so shine."[9] What kind of God would he be who gave us light and told us not to use it? Our light shines brightest when we use our talents to the fullest. When we do that, we're always serving, and we are also in the process of denying ourselves. When you serve, self-denial will take care of itself. Never forget that the second great commandment is, "Love thy neighbor as thyself."[10]

You're made in the image of God. To quit loving yourself would be in a way to quit loving God, but you've got to keep it in perspective.

As I told you, there is a feeling that comes with asserting ourselves that makes us cautious. I knew I was at the center of the human race and the central part of my message was at my atonement. "I have given myself up for you." Imagine having to say to every man alive, "You need me; without me you will perish. I am the light of the world." That was one of the most difficult parts initially. It took years before I could say that. Eventually, when I realized fully who I'd been chosen to be and particularly what it was costing me, I could state the facts. That's why I could say that I would make it through the cross. My father was sensitive. All the gifts he had given me were perfect. Through the Scriptures and through the events in my life, he revealed himself to me so clearly that my knowledge of him made me tremendously confident.

He gave me the ability to teach, to think, and to speak about what I had learned. From knowing him, there comes natural courage and peace at the same time. That's how he sent me into the world. That's why I love him so much.

Clarification

Let's talk specifically about some of the statements you made. In chapter 12 of Luke, you said not to worry about what we had no control over, such as tomorrow. That almost seems like hopeless counsel because it's so natural to worry.

Living in reality is difficult. What I was saying when I told people not to worry was that they should accept reality at every moment. If you're poor, you're poor. Don't fret about it. God knows it. If you have cancer, you have cancer. Accept it at first. You can fight whatever you don't like and try to change any situation, but not to the degree that it disrupts your entity as a creature, as a Christian.

All of life is to teach us to submit. As Thomas Merton said, "The will of God confronts us every minute."

Let's discuss swearing. Why is God so opposed to what seems at times to be such a natural expression of feeling?

Isaiah had the same problem controlling his tongue. The problem with swearing is that it's a lie. Think of every profane word you have used against a neighbor, who is made in the image of God. There's no person too far gone to become the most holy being you can imagine, and one must never curse holy beings. Every profane expression at a moment of frustration is a lie. No situation is too hopeless for my father, and there is no situation he doesn't permit. Every moment of life is holy if he is Lord over it.

How can you attempt to speak for God, trying to become the "word of God," if it's really just a lie? When you swear, you condemn, yet there is no person, nation, or situation that God condemns until he condemns it. He has patience and mercy and kindness.

You made statements like "I and the Father are one"[11] and "These words you hear are not my own; they belong to the Father who sent me."[12] Did you feel God inside you?

Can you feel your red blood cells or your liver inside you? Of course not! If they're missing, then you know it. I didn't usually feel God inside of me, although at times when I was healing, I literally felt a tingling throughout my whole body. It was my father's power and I could feel it going out of me to the other person. Most of the time I just felt like me.

For being a servant, you really said some very tough things to your followers. They were statements like, "If you don't stand up for me on earth, I won't stand up for you in heaven," or, "Unless you lose your life for my sake you won't find it."

I had to operate under the same demands from my father. What I did for them cost me everything. You must embrace my passion or reject it. Besides, I'm not only your servant, I'm also your sovereign.

Parables

Why did you teach in parables?

It's how my father told me to do it. It was prophesied in Psalm 78 that the Messiah would teach in parables. When God asks you to do something, he always prepares you. Both my fathers had taught me through parables.

As I told you, my earthly father Joseph was a master storyteller. Looking back after his death, I was amazed to learn how many of his parables had stuck with me. My heavenly father communicated with me through stories. He knew I had some powerful truths to communicate, and the only way I could do it without overwhelming the people was indirectly through parables.

If I had told them directly everything I knew, it would have caused so much chaos that my teaching would have been hindered. Think how many people would have reacted initially had I come right out and said, "I'm God." As Emily Dickinson was to say centuries later, "The truth must dazzle gradually, or every man be blind."

Is that why you said, a person could see a speck in his brother's eye and miss the log in his own?

Often the speck you see in your brother's eye *is* the log in your own. Another reason I taught in parables was to demand humility. The meaning of a parable is hidden and will forever be hidden to those who refuse to see. Parables are a test, and a prophetic one at that. It's how I was instructed to test the people.

You knew how you would teach. Did you practice making up parables?

I continued Joseph's tradition of telling stories, so that molded my thinking. My brothers and sisters were the first ones to hear certain parables. Also, for years I had thought about what stories I would use to tell people who I was and who my father was. Later in my public ministry, when I saw crowds gathering, I knew I would be speaking to thousands. I planned what I would say. I would often answer a question with a story, though. It was another personal confirmation of who I was.

Had you anticipated many of the questions?

Remember, I said to be as meek as doves and as streetwise as serpents.

He smiled slyly here, and it was obvious how much he enjoyed the give and take of human interaction, being the teacher who anticipated his students' questions and an adversary who outfoxed his opponents.

Not many questions came up that I hadn't thought about. And, because in my search for my identity I had asked myself most of the questions that came up.

Did you have a favorite parable?

The parable of the prodigal son was one I deeply felt. One of the reasons I appreciate that parable so much is that I'll never forget the experience in my early years when I felt as lowly as the prodigal son, and my father surprised me with greater blessings than I had ever dreamed of. To go from feeling that you are a stumbling block because people think you are "illegitimate," as I did in my childhood, to being the way to God and the redeemer does wonders for your self-esteem. It felt much better to be a stumbling stone than to be a stumbling block, although both roles hurt.

What other parables did you especially like?

I liked the growth parables. One such parable is about the seed planted in a garden. Soon it grows into a large tree and the birds live among its branches, but it all began from one seed.

I started out hardly believing that I was the Messiah, and I came to the point of knowing that I was God incarnate who could perform miracles. I started out trusting God to provide for my family when my father Joseph died, and I ended up trusting him to let me walk on water and to raise me from the dead. My life was like the single seed.

You told one of my favorite parables when an attorney tested you with the "great question," and you answered with the parable of the good Samaritan.

A scholar who had been listening to me teach for several hours approached me with a question. "How does a person inherit eternal life?" He had expected to find flaws with my answer, but instead I showed that I knew the Law and its summary in the two command-ments, "Love thy God with all thy heart, and soul, and mind. And love thy neighbor as thyself."

This attorney asked another penetrating question: "Who is my neighbor?" That's when I told him the parable of the injured man who was ignored by the people who should have helped, but was res-cued by his alleged enemy, the good Samaritan. I told him our neigh-bor is anyone who needs help, and I said, "Now you go and do likewise." Everyone should have the chance to be a good Samaritan. I did.

You seem to have a special heart for the downtrodden.

Life is so difficult. God made that plain from the first book in the Bible on. Since Adam fell, there has been a curse on man, but there is relief. I tried to get people to turn to God for everything, particularly when they were in trouble.

I tried to teach them, "When you're in trouble, and you don't feel you have faith even to go to God, go to him for the faith. Go to the

Scriptures." Our usual mentality is the opposite. We avoid God because we're embarrassed about our character flaws and our lack of
faith. If you need faith, read the Bible. It will provide the faith. It's the
most creative communication in the world.

Did you know that you would be written about later?

When he told me that I was to be the light of the world, those weren't
just nice, theological words. There were things I knew that no one else
knew, and the people had to learn them from me. I was the only person who ever really knew God. I was going to teach them how to love,
maybe for centuries.

The spirit had worked that way before. He was used to working
through one man at a time; taking the words of Moses or David, which
really were God's words, and giving them to generations beyond in
the written word. I knew the spirit was going to do it again. If my
coming was so important that it had been written about for centuries,
my deeds would be worth writing about, too.

The Scriptures said that one day the Messiah would come and teach
all. Since I knew there would be a significant period between my first
and second coming, just as the angel said and just as the Scriptures
confirmed, I knew that I would be written about. The words would be
the same and yet fresh, generation after generation. From then on,
every person who lived would have the same opportunity to hear me.

*It's interesting how your disciple John described you in his gospel after spending
three-and-one-half years with you: "In the beginning was the Word, and the
Word was with God, and the Word was God. . . . And the Word was made flesh
and dwelt among us."*[13]

That's why I could say, "Heaven and earth shall pass away, but my
words shall not pass away."[14] The Scriptures were explicit. My father's
words endured forever, the father and I are one, and all that he has is
mine. If that is true, why shouldn't my words endure like his? That's
why I could call myself "the truth."

If you knew words were that important, you must have felt a fair amount of responsibility for every word you said.

That's why I always studied the Scriptures. If you are going to teach people on earth for many centuries, and then in eternity, and if those words will be "the gospel" forever, you might think a few days or years about what you say. I was teaching people how to live before God, and that was important. Yes, I chose my words carefully.

Besides teaching, did you ever think about doing some writing yourself?

I didn't have enough time. I was a doctor, a teacher, and, besides that, a savior. That was one reason I could say to my disciples, "Greater things will you do than I have done." They would write the books.

Did you know in advance who would write the books?

I thought Peter, James, and John would write. Peter and John did, but James was killed before he had an opportunity. I thought that Thomas might, because he was a thinker, but he didn't. At first, Judas seemed the most capable. I knew there also would be surprises. Matthew and my half brothers James and Jude were surprises.

The Unexpected

You often did things that people didn't expect. Not only did you walk on water and frighten your disciples, you let one of them walk on water. You did other things unusual for a religion teacher: You had meals in the home of tax collectors, who were essentially criminals. You went to parties and changed water into the finest wine at one. You bodily threw people out of the temple. Why did you act this way?

Doing the unexpected brought people out of enslavement to their preconceptions. I learned that from my father, who planned to have me say to every human being who ever lived: "You think you are a bad person? You are. Even worse than you think!" Or to the good men, "You are nothing like you think you are; you are worse than evil." Or to both those who recognized their evil and those who thought themselves good, "You deserve death, and I so sentence you."

Can you imagine telling every person in all of history that he deserves capital punishment? Equally as shocking, he comes and says, "My only son is paying the price for you." Who is prepared for those kinds of messages? For that degree of truth? I had an important message to deliver to the world, and I tried to do it in as many creative ways as I could.

A characteristic of your teaching that stood out to people was the authority with which you taught.

It took me thirty years to understand my father completely. The price for true authority is always high.

You're saying that, even though the spirit of God indwells a believer, the believer still has to work to know the Holy Spirit?

You have to work on any relationship. Nowhere is that more true than with God. You always reap what you sow. That's why people need to pray and to read the Bible to get to know my father and me.

How would you define faith?

First of all, it's a belief, an awareness of your own limitations. Faith is also an awareness of what's really there. The book of Hebrews, where the most clear-cut discussion of faith is found in the Scriptures, defines faith as being "certain of what we do not see." Faith and truth are inseparable.

Faith brings patience and hope. It enables you to see beyond today or tomorrow, to get a glimpse of the day relief will be here, to see past the darkness of the moment. Faith is the only thing that sees that far, that can give you hope.

Faith really is a part of knowledge. It is knowledge of the unseen world. That knowledge perspective comes only from God. The awareness that faith brings is an antidote against the pain the world offers, but like an analgesic, it doesn't take away the pain. It helps you to live with it.

When you've lived with faith long enough to know how well it enables you to see, you have confidence about every moment you live. It makes you certain about things in the past "you didn't know."

A Word About the Teacher

I realized what a gift for word pictures, for images, Jesus had. Besides the good Samaritan, there is the prodigal son, the sower, the light of the world, the bread of life, and the good shepherd, as well as the vine and the branches. His ideas have penetrated our culture to the core. Besides being the savior of the world, Jesus was a remarkable teacher whose brilliance is sometimes taken for granted because his words are so familiar. Most famous people in history are remembered through one or two quotes, or maybe one speech. Jesus' words are all pregnant with meaning. They are quoted, or misquoted, a million different ways. As John the apostle said in the last verse of the gospel that bears his name, if all the words and deeds of Jesus were recorded, "the whole world would not have room for the books that would be written." Listen to some of his familiar sayings that are with us daily:

As ye would that men should do to you, do ye also to them likewise.[15]
Get thee behind me, Satan.[16]
Why do you look at the speck that is in your brother's eye, but do not notice the log that is in your own eye?[17]
Man shall not live by bread alone.[18]
Love thy neighbor as thyself.[19]
He that is without sin, . . . let him first cast a stone.[20]

You of little faith.[21]
Seek, and ye shall find.[22]

Furthermore, in today's world, people popularly are measured in relation to his words in one way or the other. Great individuals "walk on water." Traitors are "Judases." Befrienders are "good Samaritans." Events in his life are indirectly referred to thousands of times a day, every time such common words as savior, salvation, conversion, redemption, and crucified are spoken. In word and in deed, he made a profound effect as a teacher. One common reference point for history is his life, as shown in the terms "before Christ" [B.C.] or "anno domine, in the year of the Lord" [A.D.].

Reflecting further on the teacher's personality, it was apparent how much Jesus loved to interact with his fellow human beings, whomever and wherever they were. Constantly, he was teaching someone: from a "foreign" lady at a well to a Jewish scholar one night, from a group of children to a hated tax collector. He spoke to individuals and to crowds. Everywhere he went, Jesus looked for the opportunity to teach, to give himself to the world.

He had such great compassion for the lost. Day after day, late into the night, he healed people because he loved them. He also healed to draw a crowd so that he could teach them about the things of his father's world. He traveled from town to town going to synagogues, accepting invitations to the homes of Pharisees or tax collectors, attending funerals, and speaking to large crowds in outdoor gatherings.

He never quit pushing his disciples to become the best teachers they could be, so that they could carry on his work after he was gone. He was always asking questions. "Peter, whom do men say that I am?" He was always challenging their lack of faith. Up until his last hour on earth, he remained the teacher, speaking nowhere more eloquently than he did with his life as he hung from the cross. He was the only teacher in history whose deeds completely matched his words.

His life was also an indication of the kind of student he had been himself. From an early age, he loved to learn, to ask questions, to engage in the delights of the intellect. His life testified to the fact that he had first been the good student. Beginning with the brilliant discussions he held with the scribes in the temple when he was twelve, he handled all the intellectual challenges that came his way. In his first major battle, Jesus outwitted the most deceptive personality in the world, the "angel of light," Satan himself, in a face-to-face meeting. Consistently, Jesus turned the tables on opponents who tried to trick him with questions like, "Do you worship Caesar or God?" or "What do you say to this adulteress we've thrown at your feet?"

He was equally adept at meeting force with force when the occasion arose. A Pharisee approached Jesus, complaining because Jesus had called the Pharisees fools. Jesus replied by telling the man that they also were murderers. At moments he was so bold he personally threw people out of the temple. He was always a step ahead of the brightest minds of his day, constantly out-thinking the thinkers, always with the goal in mind of teaching, of reaching the lost.

As I listened to him teach, I also thought of how the people in his day reacted to him. They recognized him as one who had tremendous authority, unlike all the other teachers of his day, except for John the Baptist. Jesus was making the same impression upon me. He was so sure of who he was. He had taken the Scriptures and made them his, day after day incorporating them until he was the Scripture. He had reached a point as a man where he was certain that every word he spoke was true.

Long before he told us he was the truth, he had discovered that truth himself. His certainty was elegant and overpowering in itself, and within the bounds of humanity, it was a testimony that he was God. Through this "man," God was saying to all of humankind, "You want to know how great I am? Except for being sinless, I will limit myself just as you are limited. I will subject myself to those same conditions, face the same stresses, and even then I will shine so brightly you will know that I am God."

Back to the Narrative

After the transfiguration, you remained almost entirely in Galilee, going from village to village, teaching in synagogues, and, as the apostle John reported, staying away from Judea and Jerusalem where the Jewish leaders were plotting your death.

Before the last week of my life and my grand entry, I made two brief trips to Jerusalem, both for ceremonies on religious holidays. The first was in the early fall of my last year on earth for the Feast of Tabernacles, one of the three yearly ceremonies all adult male Israelites were required to attend.

My own brothers, including James and Jude, had urged me to attend this feast, knowing well that the Pharisees in Jerusalem felt that I was a phony even more strongly than did they. Secretly, my brothers wished the Pharisees would judge me, stone me, and end the embarrassment to the family. My brothers made no effort to hide their contempt, sarcastically telling me, "Go where more people can see your miracles! . . . You can't be famous when you hide like this! If you're so great, prove it to the world!"[23]

I told them their visit to Jerusalem made no difference, because they weren't being attacked for telling the world the truth. I was the hated one, not they.

They went on ahead of me to the feast, and I made a secret trip to Jerusalem. The Pharisees were desperately searching for me, and I enjoyed frustrating them. The people were being increasingly stirred up by the Pharisees' constant questioning of anyone who might have seen me. Typically, some of the people thought I was wonderful, some thought I was a deceiver, and some were afraid to say anything.

In mid-week, halfway through the festival, I went to the temple and began preaching. The Jewish leaders wondered how I could know so much, not having been to their school. I told them I was not presenting my ideas, but God's. I asked them what law I had broken. If I had done so, this would explain why they were trying to kill me.

I told them I healed a man on the Sabbath and was condemned, and yet they circumcised infants on the Sabbath. Wasn't it just as right to heal a person on the Sabbath as to circumcise him? Many of the people there, mostly those from out of Jerusalem who had seen and heard about my miracles and heard me teach, believed I was the Messiah. Most natives of Jerusalem didn't believe in me because they looked to their leaders to tell them what to believe. As a result of their dependence upon the Pharisees, the people didn't know the Scriptures at all and knew little about the facts of the Messiah.

You were getting more and more outspoken at this point in your career. Did the Feast of Tabernacles have anything to do with it?

The Feast of Tabernacles was the third and last required holiday of the Jewish year. It was the most joyous. The crops were harvested. The work was done. It was a time for giving thanks to the Lord for present blessings and for the deliverance of our nation out of Egypt. We thanked him for giving us the land. Also, as emphasized at crucial times in the feast, the Jews looked forward to the future, when God's goal would be accomplished and he would reign over the world.

Besides Passover, this feast contained the ceremonies richest in symbols. At the end of the first day after the evening service, there was a special time of rejoicing. People filled the temple, and the central element of this first night was light, symbolic of God's light that one day would penetrate the surrounding pagan darkness and light the whole world. On this night, light was everywhere in the temple. There was so much light that every court in the city of Jerusalem was lighted. Men and women danced in the temple before the Lord with torches in their hands. Harps, lutes, cymbals, and trumpets were played by the Levites as they stood overlooking the people on the fifteen steps that led to the court of the altars. The people sang with jubilation. Israel's choir at the temple in Jerusalem was famous all over the world.

The seventh and last day of that feast was called "the great day." On that day, the priests and a large number of the people went down to the nearby Pool of Siloam outside the temple to fill a golden pitcher with water and return to the temple to pour it out over the altar at the height of the feast. The water being poured out was symbolic of God's blessing and provision of water for Israel's crops. More important, it was a symbol of the future outpouring of the Holy Spirit, and, most important, it was a symbol of the day God would pour out salvation on Israel, the day he would send the Messiah, the son of David, to reign.

At that point in the ceremony, after the priest poured out the water, he would hold the empty golden vessel upside down for everyone to see that it was empty. Then the people would respond with "*hallels.*" Three trumpet blasts would sound, and all the people would wave palm branches symbolic of God's deliverance from their wilderness journey and his promised future deliverance. At this moment, as the priest had held out the pitcher at the altar and the people had chanted the last words of Psalm 118, I stood and shouted for all to hear, "If anyone is thirsty, let him come to Me and drink."[24] The temple guards were supposed to arrest anyone out of order, but they were too shocked. They had never heard anyone speak with such authority, and they didn't lay a hand on me.

The people argued back and forth, and some of the people, mostly those not from Jerusalem, began speaking up for me. The Pharisees mocked them. "Is there anyone among your leaders who believes in him?" Suddenly, for the first time, Nicodemus spoke up. He wanted to know if a man could be convicted without a trial. This was the first crack in the Pharisees' armor. Many of them began to believe in me, though they kept silent.

Caught in the Act

What happened then?

The Pharisees openly rebuked me and were determined to arrest me, but the crowd's reaction alarmed them, and they held off. I spent that night on the Mount of Olives. By the time I returned to the temple the next day, the Pharisees had a trap planned to turn the crowd against me. That's when they brought the woman "caught in adultery." They had set up the whole scene by arranging for a man to pay a visit to this promiscuous woman, and then they piously caught her in the act. They rushed her to me, threw her at my feet, and tried to trap me into judging her, hoping to deflate my popularity. These vicious, judgmental men had never heard of mercy. They knew I was quite aware of the Law. Adultery was a capital offense.

Somehow they must have sensed that you didn't want to judge her.

See how controlling they were? They wanted to tell me and everyone else how to act and when. Secretly, they wanted to be God. I looked at those self-righteous men in their long robes, men who had just thrown this woman on the ground. The crowd had moved back, and you could see the tension in their eyes. Again I asked my father for special knowledge, and he answered. I reached over and borrowed Philip's staff.

In the dirt, next to the girl, I began writing the names of each of the Pharisees and a particular sin of which he was ashamed. For example, I wrote, "Jacob bar Shanda—stealing, age fifteen. Joshua bar Samuel—lying, age thirteen." Some of them had sinned sexually earlier in their lives, and next to their names I would write the name of the person with whom they had sinned. I hadn't said anything to the Pharisees until I had finished the first six names. I pointed out each name and looked at each man directly. I said, "The law regarding adultery says that if this woman is found guilty, she is to be stoned to death. He who is without sin, let him cast the first stone."

No one moved, and I continued writing the names. Each time I finished one, I would look up for just a moment and stare at that man. You should have seen the looks on their faces, a mixture of shock and embarrassment. "How did you know?" I'd put down another name. Very quietly, the crowd began to thin out. Finally, I looked around, and they were all gone. Some didn't wait for their names to be written.

I looked down at the shamed woman who was just beginning to come out of her fetal-like crouch. She had been expecting a hailstorm of stones and, to her amazement, not one stone had been thrown. As she raised her head and glanced around there was surprise and relief on her face, for none of her accusers were there. I said to her, "Well, they're all gone. Neither do I condemn you. Go and sin no more."[25]

I will never forget the expression on her face when she heard those words. She was so grateful. It was another reminder of what I took with me to the cross. She was one I thought about when I lay in the dirt at the feet of the Roman soldiers, beneath the Roman cross. She was one of the reasons I was going through all of this.

Some people look at that adulteress and say you condoned adultery and sexual sins in the way you handled the situation.

I didn't condone them. I justified the woman. I meant what I said, that I came to fulfill every jot and tittle of the Law. I judged that woman, too, and I paid the price for her sins.

Justification means you took the stones in her place. So on the cross, you agreed with your own death.

Absolutely. I preached a sermon on the cross just by hanging there. And, if taken in the right way, every cross you see is a sermon. I'm saying to every man, "See who you are. See what you deserve." As much as I dreaded it and as much as I hated it when I was going through it, I definitely had a great sense of justice being done.

We all know the feeling when justice wins out. In heaven, that's what will bond me to every man. I will know each one's sins have been paid for by me personally, and we will share that tremendous feeling that justice has finally prevailed. Never think for one minute that justice won't prevail in heaven.

Maybe that will keep us humble and grateful throughout eternity.

It just might. It's going to feel so incredibly new for everyone to feel totally justified. By faith, many people today know they are justified, but they often don't feel it because they still have their evil nature with them that's constantly letting them down. What they have to take on faith is that they will one day experience firsthand what it means to be totally pure. I ought to know. I've felt this way for years.

Did your encounter with the Pharisees over the woman relieve you of harassment for a time?

The Pharisees left that confrontation with their hats in their hands, unable to utter a word. A few hours later, I was still teaching in the temple when another group of Pharisees gathered. I repeated the statement, "I am the light of the world."[26] The Pharisees were furious, called me a liar, and then made a sarcastic comment questioning my ancestry, "Do you know where your father is?" I replied, "You don't know me, and you don't know my father." I warned them that unless they believed in me they would die in their sins. I was from the father above; they were from below. I was going where they could not come. I also gave them another chance at the truth. "If you believe in me, you will know the truth and the truth will set you free."[27]

They informed me they were Abraham's descendants and nobody's slaves: "Our father is Abraham."[28]

"No," I told them, "your father is Satan. Abraham wouldn't try to kill me."

"We were not the ones born out of wedlock. Our father is God himself. You Samaritan devil—you are demon-possessed."

"I have no demon in me. It's the father who wants me to be great, not me. In all honesty I tell you, anyone who obeys me shall never die. Abraham and the other prophets never even claimed they could do anything like that. You think you're greater than Abraham and the other prophets? If I am just boasting, what I am saying is nothing, but I know the father, and you don't. I always obey him. 'Your father' Abraham rejoiced to see my day."

"You couldn't have seen Abraham. You're not fifty years of age."

"I existed before Abraham was born." That was the final straw. They tried to stone me, but miraculously they couldn't see me, and I walked past them and left the temple. Not far away, I came across a blind man who had been that way since birth. My father prepared the way again. He set the stage, and I carried out the plan.

To prove my words to the Pharisees, I healed this man, so that they would know who had the light. Once again I was telling them, "If you can't believe my words, believe my deeds." I was also saying to them "You're blind and need healing in order to see."

The man who had formerly been blind gave the Pharisees a hard time. His friends who had known him all his life were so frightened at what had happened that they immediately took him to the Pharisees, who tried to use him to attack me. Of course, the Pharisees' first accusation was again that I was working on the Sabbath. They started pressuring the man. "Who do you say this man is who healed you?" The former blind man said he thought I was a prophet. The Pharisees wouldn't even believe the man had really been blind until they sent for his parents, who came and established the fact that their son had been blind from birth. The Pharisees then pressured them. "Why can your son now see?" The parents wanted nothing to do with the situation. The Pharisees had threatened to excommunicate anyone who claimed that I was the Messiah, so the parents told the Pharisees they had no idea what had happened. "He's old enough to speak for himself,"[29] they said, referring to their son.

So the Pharisees turned back to the little man who was busy seeing for the first time, putting pictures with the mental images he had formed all his life. They began pressuring him to give the glory to God and not to Jesus, because Jesus was evil.

The man told them he wasn't sure if I was good or bad, but he knew one thing: "I was blind and now I see."[30]

The Pharisees kept asking him exactly how I had healed him. This man was no theologian, but he was having no trouble seeing through the Pharisees' theology. He was beginning to make up his mind as to who was good. He said to them, "I've already told you once. Didn't you hear me, or do you want to hear it again and become one of Jesus' disciples, too?"

The Pharisees cursed him, accusing him of being my disciple and proudly stating they were disciples of Moses. They shouldn't have pressed the issue with a grateful man, because now he wasn't backing off an inch. "You know, it's strange that he can do such good deeds, heal blind people, and you don't know anything about him. There's never been anyone like him, and if he weren't from God, he couldn't do it."

"You illegitimate bastard, you!" they shouted. "Are you trying to teach us?" And they threw him out.[31]

I found the man and asked him, "Do you believe in the Messiah?" The man said, "Who is he, sir? For I want to." I said to him, "You have seen him and he is speaking to you." All he said was, "Yes, Lord, I believe!"[32] and fell to his knees. As he would later tell his friends about this event, "My eyes worked for the first time in forty years, and the first person I saw was the Messiah. It was not a bad day!"

As I left, I told the crowds,

> I am the Good Shepherd. The Good Shepherd lays down his life for the sheep. . . . [I] know my own sheep, and they know me. . . . The Father loves me because I lay down my life that I may have it back again. No one can kill me without my consent—I lay down my life voluntarily. For I have the right and power to lay it down when I want to and also the right and power to take it again.[33]

Some said I was crazy or demon possessed. Others believed.

Final Months . . . Great Faith

When did you next return to Jerusalem?

Three months later, in December of that year, I was back in Jerusalem. As I was walking through the temple, in the part known as Solomon's Hall, the Pharisees again gathered around and said to me, "If you are the Messiah, tell us plainly."[34]

So I obliged them and told them I had already said who I was and that the miracles I performed in the name of my father were my proof.

I knew, of course, that they couldn't believe in me because they weren't part of my flock. I knew exactly who was, and no one would be able to take my followers away from me. My father had given them to me. No one was stronger than he. Finally, so they could hear it straight from the source—a fact I will remind them of one day—I told them, "I and the father are one."[35]

While they were still confused, I tried to reason with them. One last time I reminded them, "Don't believe me unless I do miracles of God. But if I do, believe them even if you don't believe me. Then you will become convinced that the Father is in me, and I in the Father."[36]

The Pharisees again had received an earful, more than they expected. And, at the same time, they didn't hear a word of it. Immediately they tried to arrest me, but I just walked through the middle of them just as I had done with another crowd in my hometown. When your time is not yet come, you can be as bold as you want to be. My father was the timekeeper, and it was his clock we were going by.

Previously, I had also gone back to Nazareth just to send them that message, too. I taught in the synagogue there and could only perform a few miracles because of their unbelief. Finally, I told them that a prophet is honored anywhere but in his own country, and I left. I wasn't afraid of anything except that last day.

There were now about four months left before the crucifixion. How did you spend your time?

Often I was alone with my father. I also visited a number of small towns in Galilee. I wanted to visit as many towns as I could. I came to all the people, and I wanted to spend a lot of time with my disciples, something the traveling enabled me to do.

Frequently I tried to teach them that my death was near, but they would have none of that. They "knew" the Scriptures. They knew the Messiah was to sit on David's throne. Death was an impossibility. Of course, John the Baptist had died, but they pushed that out of their minds. The Baptist wasn't talked about much after he was gone.

Every time I mentioned my death, my disciples always thought I was talking in parables. Surely, they thought, I meant my movement was to die in the way it presently was, an obscurity of sorts, and "rise again" into a grand and glorious kingdom. Even when I pressed them with the details of my death, my men couldn't take it. They just argued endlessly as to which one would be first in the kingdom which they were sure was imminent. As I said, James and John even put their mother up to making certain suggestions about whom should help me rule the kingdom.

Toward the end, I sent out seventy disciples in pairs for two weeks by themselves to do miracles in my name and to prepare the way. I continued to heal the sick. The response was great at times, but I knew the end result. I had already been to Jerusalem and had seen my father's words coming true.

Still, wherever I went there were crowds, however fickle and uncertain they might be. I knew all of them were going to be at Passover, and, if Jerusalem wouldn't accept me, I would bring my own crowd. Word was out that anyone who believed I was the Messiah would be excommunicated. Word was out that I would be arrested when I came to Jerusalem. Oppression, however, never ultimately stops people. Besides, I had already been to Jerusalem twice, and nothing had happened. Nor would anything happen until I allowed it.

My burden became increasingly heavy. Don't think for one minute I didn't feel it every step of the way. My father knew that, too, and always arranged circumstances to lift my spirits as he had done with the blind man at the Feast of Tabernacles.

Take Zacchaeus. One day I was walking through Jericho with great crowds surrounding me, following me everywhere I went, lining the roads I walked. As I was coming down a hill, I saw ahead of me one little man in a sycamore tree. Obviously he was there because he couldn't see me from the side of the road. He was very small, but more of a handicap than his size was his beautiful robe, more expensive than that of almost anyone in the crowd. He was a tax collector.

I knew the crowd wouldn't have dared let a tax collector through to the front to see me, and I felt for this helpless, rich outcast who cared enough to climb up in a tree, robe and all. That told me something about him. He wasn't too proud to get up where everybody could see and mock him. I knew he was determined. As I walked toward him, I asked my father to tell me his name.

When that answer came, I thought of how many times he had answered me. That was why at the last supper I could tell my men to ask my father for things if they wanted to have my joy. My father constantly thrilled me with his answers to my prayers, often after he had created the very situation that prompted the prayer. Joy is one of the gifts he creatively built into prayer. I was a man like all men and women who didn't always know what was going to happen. I had to wait for his answers as you do. That's why prayer gave me so much joy. That is how I heard my father. Many times I had to wait for his answers, but thousands of times he answered me immediately. Because he heard me, joy was mine in abundance. C. S. Lewis was right. My father wants to give.

I reflected on these thoughts until I was almost under the tree where this brave little man was. With the crowd surrounding me, I stopped and looked up at the man. There was first surprise and shock on his face, and then fear. He wondered what I was going to say to him. He thought that perhaps I would judge him. As he later told me, he had already heard about my physically throwing some greedy people out of the temple. Then I called him by name, "Zacchaeus, come down here with me. Do you have anything to eat at your house?"

You've never seen a man come down a tree more quickly. He walked beside me for about another mile with a crowd following. There were sarcastic comments about my daring to associate with a tax collector, particularly the infamous Zacchaeus. I had to ask him where he lived, because he was too excited to say a word. Tears filled his eyes. All the poor man really wanted was for someone to love him, to recognize him. I had.

By the time we got to his house, he was a new man, gentle, repentant, and sensitive. I didn't have to say anything about his sins. He knew. By the time the meal was over, he had confirmed my initial impression. He had responded to my compassion with enormous repentance and a generosity I rarely had seen. After the meal he announced publicly that he would give half his wealth to the poor, and promised to repay four times over those whom he had cheated on their taxes.

Some people don't respond like Zacchaeus. Why do you think that is?

As I was to say later to a Pharisee in his home, "He who has been forgiven much, loves much." People who have been the most overtly evil and then have a fresh chance at a new life often are the most ready to take advantage of it. Sometimes it's because of their situations. These are the people who deep down see themselves most clearly. Other people have to be convinced over the years that their "little" sins are really just as bad.

We all are in great need of forgiveness. It seems to me, though, that the central truth in the story of Zacchaeus is the same as it was in the conversion of Matthew: No matter how evil people are, potentially they are not far from the kingdom of God.

Many people are much closer than you think. No matter who they were, I saw every person as potentially one of my followers. Remember, whenever you talk to a man about God, his conscience is on your side. Everyone you will ever meet is made in the image of God, and we must encourage people to believe that, to have faith in whom they really are.

Faith is such a delicate thing. We have to be careful with it, nourish it. It's at the same time both the easiest and the hardest thing to have.

Even if we've had a clear look at another reality, God's reality, we forget so quickly. My disciples saw me feed about twelve thousand people* with two fish and five loaves of bread, but a few weeks later when we were surrounded by four thousand men and their families who didn't have any food, my disciples asked, "What do we do now?" They saw me raise the dead. They themselves performed many

---

* Only the men were counted in the crowds the Scriptures record. Estimates vary, but actual crowd size was significantly higher.

miracles. They healed the lame, made the blind to see. Still they tended to panic. When I was crucified, they all ran.

The day I was resurrected, I appeared in a disguised form to two of the disciples and walked with them for miles on the way to Emmaus. I asked them all about this Jesus they had followed, and they said, "We thought he was the Messiah." They weren't sure, but they thought I was the Messiah. What faith! This was after I had told them exactly what would happen—that I would be killed, but I would return. It's not easy to have faith. That's why there are great rewards for those who do.

Life That Springs Eternal

What did you do after leaving Zacchaeus?

I left his house before sunrise the next morning and began walking toward my goal—Jerusalem. The sun began to shine on a countryside carpeted with flowers. Spring was in all its beauty in Israel. What a sight it was!

Suddenly, I realized that my father had done something else for me. He had given me spring as an eternal picture of my resurrection. Not only that, but he had set the stage for my death to occur in the early spring. Would it do for the savior of the world who was coming back from the dead to die at any other time? When God had initiated the exodus and passover centuries before, was it any accident that he planned it in the spring so that Passover would be celebrated then? He was telling me, "Even the seasons of the year are yours." I was moved to tears as I looked up at the beautiful sun coming over the horizon. It was yet another present for me. I had noticed that the sun had my name, and now I saw that it was the rising sun. All of nature was mine, too. My father was saying to me at just the moment I needed to hear it, "Look around. See the flowers, the light, the sun. You, too, will be back in unbelievable glory." He has been reminding people every spring and every day since of the same thing.

Martin Luther said that every spring is a testimony to the resurrection.

The same is true every time someone awakens from sleep. My father and I left many pictures to remind humanity of our great gift.

You knew that you were moving toward your death at Jerusalem, yet the Pharisees didn't. What finally made the Pharisees decide to murder you?

I'd saved the best for the last. The Pharisees couldn't stand the power that I was demonstrating for the glory of my father when I came to the aid of my friend Lazarus.

A few weeks before the third Passover in my public ministry, I got a message from the sisters Mary and Martha. Their brother, Lazarus, who lived with them in Bethany was very ill. Immediately, a vision of Lazarus lying dead came into my mind. I knew it was "a special vision" from my father. I wondered for a minute why he would be showing me that now. Then I understood and saw what I was going to do.

I waited in Bethabara on the other side of the Jordan River for two days, just as they would wait for me in that grave two days. The third day was the day for action. That morning I told my men, "Let's go to Bethany." Only two miles down the road from Bethany was Jerusalem, where the Jewish leaders had tried to stone me. My men became anxious about going there, and I told them not to worry. Nothing would happen in the daytime. I always thought that when the authorities came to get me, it would be at night, and, as it turned out, I was right. Thomas was the only one ready to go with me to Bethany.

I had waited until Lazarus had died. On the way to Bethany, I told my men what had happened to Lazarus, but said for them not to worry, that I would go and awaken him and give them another chance to believe in me. I told them this was happening for my glory. I saw what my father was doing. He was getting me ready, encouraging me every step of the way.

Apparently your disciples still did not understand. Didn't they think you'd somehow been telling them another parable and using the word "death" symbolically?

Death is a blinding word. When we got to Bethany, Martha heard I was coming and ran to greet me. She told them that if I'd been there her brother wouldn't have died. I promised her that her brother would come back to life. I said, "I am the one who raises the dead and gives them life again. Anyone who believes in me shall live again."

Then I asked her if she believed, and Martha amazingly replied, "I believe you are the Messiah, the Son of God."*[37] She was the only one besides Peter and Thomas who had ever called me that, and, with them, many have ridiculed Martha. But how she had learned. Before it would have been her sister, Mary, who ran to greet me. After I had rebuked Martha, though, she was a different person. What faith she had!

Immediately Martha ran to get Mary. She came at once. Her house was filled with people who had come to comfort her. Thinking she was going to the grave to mourn, they followed her. When Mary finally saw me, she said, "Sir, if you had been here, my brother would still be alive."[38] She fell at my feet, clutched me around my legs, and started sobbing. Following close behind her were friends who began to weep with her.

Again, I felt the sting of death. I was reminded of my father Joseph's death. I still missed him. Then the utter finality of death swept over me. There's nothing like it to convince you that sin costs everything, that evil is not to be taken lightly. In a moment, all my hatred of death came storming back. Then a strange thought went through my mind. I understood more clearly why hell would exist. My father hated death so much that he would let everyone live forever, only in different places. Even those who refuse my father's offer of life with him will still "live" with the consequence of that choice.

---

* Once when visiting their house, Jesus was teaching people in the "living room" when Martha began complaining about her sister, Mary, who was listening to Jesus instead of helping her in the kitchen. Jesus said, "Martha, why do you worry and get upset about many things, but only one thing is needed? Mary has chosen what is better" (cf. Luke 10:38–42).

I looked down at Mary and Martha. I was indignant, and said, "Show me where he is buried." I started walking to Lazarus's tomb with one arm around Mary and one arm around Martha as they each cried on my shoulder. It reminded me of another funeral I had walked to, listening to the sobs of another Mary crying on my shoulder, my mother Mary crying at the loss of Joseph. That moment with Mary and Martha was so powerful I couldn't contain my emotions any longer. As we walked down that road, I wept for my friend Lazarus, for my father, and for my impending death. Everyone surrounding me would go through that shattering experience.

As we came to the tomb I was still crying, and I heard one person say, "They were close friends. See how much he loved him." I heard some other people say, "He healed a blind man; why couldn't he have healed his friend?"[39] The whole situation made me angry. Death was so senseless. Their faith was so weak.

I walked up to the tomb. A large stone was in front of the entrance. I told them to roll it away, but Martha's faith wavered. She was worried about the odor because Lazarus had been dead for four days. I reminded her that I told her she would see a tremendous miracle if only she would believe. I looked at the heavens and thanked my father for hearing. This was for the people's benefit, not for mine, because I knew my father always heard me. With much uncertainty, several men rolled the stone back. I could see a look of fear on all their faces, with just a tinge of hope trying to break through. My last thought before I said anything was, "Three weeks from now I will be in a tomb, and the third day after that I will walk out of it." Then I commanded in a loud voice "Lazarus, come forth!"[40]

Out of the tomb walked Lazarus, looking like a mummy, wrapped from head to foot in the white grave cloths. The wrappings were so tight he couldn't talk, but you could hear him mumbling. His mumblings scared everybody until they could unwrap him.

Imagine waking up from an illness to find yourself dressed in a shroud surrounded by dozens of people.

Two weeks later, six days before Passover, I had dinner at his house, and we laughed about that. I knew, though, that the miracle with Lazarus was more truth than the Pharisees could stand. That's when they set about destroying me.

Palm Sunday

Tell me about Palm Sunday.

I was staying at Lazarus's house, a thirty-minute walk from Jerusalem, just on the other side of the Mount of Olives. I knew the time had come. Early Sunday morning we began walking toward Jerusalem. I sent my disciples on ahead to Bethphage where I told them they would find a donkey they were to bring to me.

How did you know where the donkey would be?

I knew this was the day for my announcement. The Scriptures had told me, as Psalm 118 said, "This is the day the Lord has made."[41]

This was the day promised to me for over four hundred years by the prophet Zechariah, the day the Messiah would ride into Jerusalem "righteous and having salvation, gentle and riding on a donkey."[42]

This was the day for which the Jews had waited for centuries, and since my father had set the stage, I knew he would have a donkey waiting for me. I just asked him to leave it in a certain place.

Why did you want a donkey?

All of God's kings ride donkeys, at least at first. The world's kings, men of war and fame, ride great white stallions to denote power. God's kings rode donkeys of humility and peace. It was the same way I came into the world. My first bed was a donkey's trough, and I never quit identifying with the common person. That was who I came to save. My disciples had no understanding of why I was riding a donkey, though. Only later did they understand that it also had been prophesied.

My father had done his part. There were great crowds, and they were ready. Several hundred thousand people from all over the world, from wherever Abraham's seed had gone, were coming to the "holy city" for Passover. My fame, on the wings of my greatest miracle—raising Lazarus from the dead—had reached its peak, and the crowd, hearing that I was coming into Jerusalem, couldn't contain itself.

They had been promised a Messiah by Jehovah, and surely I was the one with the power to overthrow the Romans. It was only a matter of time, they thought, until I would bring my angels with me to overthrow Rome and the rest of the world. They knew I could do it, and they were right. There was no question about that. Anyone who could raise the dead and heal the sick and feed thousands could take on the Romans. So the crowd rushed to get their hosannas. A hosanna was a palm branch signifying not only peace, but peace following a great conquest. Traditionally, leaders would ride through the towns they had conquered surrounded by palm branches. Now the thousands of people, anticipating my conquest of the Romans, began waving palms and shouting "hosanna."

Although they had my method backward—I would conquer through peace, not war—it was tremendously moving to be in the midst of this huge throng of people, hearing them shout over and over that verse in Psalm 118 which I had anticipated hearing for years, "Hosanna! 'Blessed is he who comes in the name of the Lord.'"[43]

The Pharisees came running up and said, "Tell your disciples and followers to stop shouting." They wanted me to refrain from giving the impression I was the Messiah. What a perceptive lot they were! I told the Pharisees that if the people stopped shouting the very stones around me would cry out. Scripture had proclaimed that my father had planned this specific day for centuries, and the Pharisees were not going to be able to stop it. Is it any wonder that I accused them of being related to Satan?

This day in one sense was the centerpiece of our history, before and since. I'm the only prince of peace who's ever come to this world. I had thought about this moment for years, but this was my official announcement. The prince of peace was here, bringing peace to

Jerusalem and to the world. This was my coronation day, although five days later I would get a very ugly "crown."

As I rode on and on into the growing multitude, with everyone crying out and my disciples parting the throng, I realized they didn't understand who I was. They were lost. I looked up at the beautiful city Jerusalem standing majestically on that hill, a view that was always awe inspiring every time I came into the city, but particularly at Passover.

I was reminded of what really lay ahead for me and for this elated crowd. I knew the prophecy awaiting them. Soon they would be utterly destroyed, along with their children, within their own walls. Holy Jerusalem would be leveled. Not one brick would be left upon another. In the midst of all the shouting, I was thinking, "O Jerusalem, isn't eight hundred years of suffering enough? Since the days of David and Solomon, you have been constantly persecuted. Rulers have made war on you time and time again, destroying your families and taking your children captive. What's it going to take? Can't you hear the prophets?

"Even though you've ignored them before, listen to them now. You have another opportunity to listen to whom the prophets say I am—the prince of peace. This is the day set aside for you to receive your Messiah. I am your king. My father is your God. You are my people. Do you know what I'm offering you, what peace I bring to every one of you? Do you understand what kind of nation we could build?

"Instead, you are lost. You can't receive me because you can't really see me. Some of you may wave at me from a crowd today, but next week some of you will be in a crowd that condemns me. Look at what your blindness is costing. After you kill me, they will kill you."

I wept for them and for all humankind at that moment. The curse had made them blind fools. They were like an old miser who buries a fortune and then starves to death. I knew it couldn't be any different. Jerusalem, the "city of peace," would continue to be a city of war until I returned.

Were you so consumed by your sadness that you couldn't respond to the crowd?

Hope is a marvelous thing. After I wept, I thought, "Now I know again why I'm going to the cross. I'm going to take away your blindness so that one day you will be able to see, and then we will have a reception that will surpass all others."

I had waited for this moment at Passover for twenty years. As I rode into Jerusalem on the back of that donkey, the crowd became larger and larger, and louder and louder. They began to chant until they reached a tremendous roar, singing at the same time, "Hooosaaanna! Hooosaaanna!" People were crying out, "Blessed is he who comes in the name of the Lord! Blessed is the King of Israel!"[44]

Many were waving palm branches. Others began throwing the branches they were carrying on the road in front of me. With each branch came the message, "You are the prince of peace." Finally palms covered the ground until the road in front of me, which was usually a dusty brown, became a sea of green. From brown to green, dust to life, my father had thought of everything. As I came up the final hill to the magnificent city gates surrounded by the tremendous walls six stories high, thousands of people stood along the walls, waiting to see me.

During all of Jerusalem's years, the Jews had seen many a king and ruler ride through those gates in triumph. I thought particularly of Alexander the Great, by whom all conquerors were measured then and now, who three hundred years earlier had ridden down this same road on his great stallion as he conquered the world for Greece. I thought to myself, "Move over, Alexander. A carpenter from the little town of Nazareth riding on a donkey is the true king. This is the kind of kingdom he and his father are bringing in. See what his father calls him. Prince of peace, prince of life."

I also thought about all those times people from Nazareth had been laughed at and ridiculed. In front of me, busily parting the crowds, were several of my disciples, one of whom was Nathaniel. As I looked at him I remembered the first words I had ever heard from his mouth: "What good can come out of Nazareth?"[45]

"Well, here's your answer, Nathaniel. Look around. Nazareth

produces kings. Take heart, Nathaniel, and the rest of you who are my followers, for one day you will be as royal as a king's brother."

It's strange the thoughts that occur to you at those moments, which stand still in your mind forever.

The nearer I got to the walls, the greater the crowd. The people began to sing in unison Psalm 24, which David had written, announcing the Messiah's entrance into Jerusalem. "Who shall ascend into the hill of the Lord? or who shall stand in his holy place?" The crowd surrounding me answered, singing, "He who has clean hands and a pure heart."

The whole crowd, as they had done for hundreds of years at Passover, sang, "Lift up your heads, O ye gates, be ye lifted up, ye everlasting doors, and the King of glory shall come in."

Then all of the women sang, "Who is the King of glory?" The men answered in unison, "The Lord, strong and mighty, the Lord mighty in battle." Together they again sang the chorus, "Lift up your heads, O ye gates; even lift them up ye everlasting doors; and the King of glory shall come in."[46]

Now I knew firsthand what David felt when he danced alone before his people along this road and stood symbolically in my place as he came into Jerusalem, returning the ark to the city. The whole scene that particular Passover day was for me just as the Scriptures said it would be. It was one of the most moving experiences of my life. From studying the Scriptures, I had always thought my father was telling me people would sing that psalm to me before my crucifixion. I knew that it would be an incredible experience. It was beyond anything I had imagined. That's the kind of gift my father gives.

Using that great twenty-fourth Psalm, the composer Handel wrote his most famous work, "The Messiah," which is sung by choirs all over the world. It must have been a tremendous thrill to hear that psalm sung to you.

As Hebrew poetry often does, verses are repeated in a slightly different way for emphasis. The last verse of that psalm goes, "Who is this King of glory? The Lord of hosts, he is the King of glory."[47] As I was riding into Jerusalem that day, my father had literally taken a scene from the Scriptures, cast it, directed it, and made it come alive in the theater of reality. I came as "Lord of hosts," the commander of all of heaven's armies. The scene had never been played before, except by David in a "dress rehearsal." My father was telling me as I was going to my death: "You are the prince of peace." I kept thinking, "Now I know what a king feels like." It was a taste of the future, and I was overwhelmed.

It went through my mind, "This is what I am working for. One day I will be back. I will have all my glory, all my heavenly hosts, and they will see me mighty in battle. But for now I am come to give my life on a cross." I savored every minute of that experience, and thought about it the whole week before my death. It was an experience that would enable me to get through the tremendous shame just ahead.

The reception my father planned for me brought all the leaders in Jerusalem to their knees. The Pharisees and the Sadducees knew Jerusalem was mine that day if I wanted it. The people had revolted before. They had killed oppressors and fought for years, making life miserable for the Romans. If the people rioted, the Pharisees and Sadducees would lose their power. The Romans would strip them of their authority because they had lost control of the people. The authorities were relieved that I made no effort to take over. They didn't realize I had much greater plans in Jerusalem, much larger than those of Alexander the Great. I had the whole world in mind. My plan wasn't to oppress the world, but to free it.

The Jewish leaders, however, missed my final offer to accept their king. That reception made the Pharisees move more quickly than they had wanted to with their plan. The usually uninvolved Sadducees became so frightened that they formed an alliance with the Pharisees to get rid of me. The Pharisees didn't want to kill me at Passover, but once again I was forcing their hand. We were still going by my father's calendar, not theirs.

How could this great crowd, so totally enthralled with you, cry out five days later for your execution?

First of all, they were manipulated by the Pharisees into betraying me. They got into that position because they were all naturally traitors. Like Judas, they wanted a certain kind of messiah, who would rule in the way they wanted. They wanted me to conquer the Romans. When they saw that I wasn't going to do that, they became bitter and didn't want me anymore. I died for many Judases.

Choosing to Die

How did you know when you were going to die?

I was more of a threat to the Pharisees. They were becoming more vicious in their attacks. My disciples were as ready as they would ever be. I always knew that I must die during Passover, because I was the Passover lamb. My father was too good a communicator for me not to die then. You know the story.

Years before, when the Jews were in captivity in Egypt, God acted to free his people. He judged the Egyptians with an angel of death who took the lives of all their first-born sons. However, the angel passed over the Israelites' homes because they had put the blood of a lamb on the door according to God's instructions. Symbolically, the Israelites' sins had been covered. Interestingly, the blood was placed over the top of the door and in the middle of each side so that if two lines were drawn from top to bottom and side-to-side, they would form the sign of a cross.

My father showed me in many different ways at which Passover I should die. Moses, Elijah, and I had said at the transfiguration that the end wasn't far off. The Scriptures led me to see precisely at which Passover I would ride into Jerusalem as the Messiah on Palm Sunday. That would be when I was thirty-three.* I knew if I made my historic entrance on that specific Palm Sunday, the Pharisees would immediately try to kill me, because they couldn't tolerate my popularity. No

---

* Detailed studies of the book of Daniel and the Jewish calendar reveal that Palm Sunday had been prophesied to the day for over 490 years.

one could take my life. I chose the Passover at which to die. I gave my life. I was the king. I had power over all of nature—the wind, the water, the land, and the body. I had power even over life and death. I had always given life, and never once used my power to take a life. Now I would allow death. In sending for the donkey, I dropped the gauntlet.

Did your father give you any other signs that it was to be this specific time?

Every interaction with my father had also confirmed his will that this was *the* Passover. Six days before my final Passover, my father sent me a sign that the time was very near. It was one of the nicest things anyone ever did for me. It was on the Friday night before Palm Sunday.

My death was very much on my mind. It was a very hot day. All of us were tired and needed a bath. We all smelled a little back then. *(He roared with laughter.)* Lazarus, his sisters, the disciples, and I were having supper nearby in the home of a man I had healed known as Simon the leper. At the end of the meal, Lazarus's sister Mary got up and walked over to me carrying a large bottle of perfume. She began to pour it over my head. It was tremendously refreshing, like a cool sponge bath. I knew that it was an enormous sacrifice for her financially. It was worth a year's wages. It was also an encouraging message from my father. Through Mary and her deed, he was saying, "I know the cost, and I honor you." It was a symbolic anointing for my impending burial.

At the same time the cool oil was covering me, I looked at Lazarus, the man I'd raised from the dead. My father was also saying to me, "You will be back from the grave. Look in the mirror. See Lazarus." I looked at the other end of the table, and there was Simon, one of the most deformed lepers I had ever seen. Simon's face had at one time been so offensive most people couldn't look at him. From Isaiah, I knew my face would be so distorted by my persecutors that no one would be able to look at me.[48] Once again my father was telling me, "Look in the mirror. See Simon's face now. Your face soon will be healed. The damage won't last long." My father was telling me I could handle my two biggest obstacles—bodily damage and death. He always found the most touching ways of reaching me.

When Mary anointed me with the perfume, Judas berated her for wasting money. I stopped him immediately and told him that the poor would always be with them, but this anointing was for my burial. You should have seen the shock on Judas's face. Every time I revealed that I knew my death was imminent, he became frightened. I told them that, wherever the gospel went, wherever my story went, people would know what Mary had done because her deed would be included in the story.

It has been through all these years.

She gave everything she had. When you do that, honor will follow you. God will make sure of that.

The incident also reminded me of the time I was eating dinner at a Pharisee's home and a prostitute washed my dirty feet with her tears and dried them with her hair. I was moved by the love of both those women. Three days later, when I was alone with my disciples preparing to leave them and wanting to do something that would leave a lasting impression on them, I thought of those two women. I washed my disciples' feet.

How did you cope with your impending death?

I handled it the same way I coped with everything. I looked to my father. The Lord is my shepherd. He always knew what I needed.

What other events about that last week stand out to you?

I thought I should clean out the temple one last time. It had been two years since I'd straightened out the matter of whose house the temple was. Although the moneychangers still had a sharp recollection of what had happened then, they continued to ply their trade in the temple. At each of the three annual feasts they became a little uneasy as they continued to hear of my deeds. Nevertheless, they were no less corrupt and as raucous.

The day after Palm Sunday, I walked into the temple. As the moneychanger at the table closest to the eastern wall saw me and the familiar look in my eye, he called out, "He's here again!" I didn't want to disappoint him. So his table was the first to go. After I turned it over he reached down to try to save some of his money. I kicked it away and literally threw him out with my hands. Once again, greedy moneychangers ran in panic, their pockets jingling as they tried to hold on to as much money as possible.

I thought of Judgment Day, when they were going to wish they had never seen the money that weighed them down. There were merchants selling their animals, and I overturned their benches and drove them out, too. When I got to the entrance, another group of merchants was about to bring in fresh merchandise, but I forbade them from entering the temple courtyard. As usual, they had to be convinced, because they hadn't seen what I had done inside. One person tried to test me. He thought he would overpower me, but suddenly his friends were picking him up off the ground. Then I looked at the crowd and asked, "Is it not written: 'My house will be called a house of prayer for all nations'? But you have made it 'a den of robbers.'"[49]

Word quickly spread about what had happened. Many were hesitant to enter the temple with the courtyard in chaos, but those with needs did not hesitate, nor did the children. First the blind and the lame heard I was there. They came in droves, and I healed them. Groups of children came. Some of them had seen me come into the city. When they saw me standing there teaching, they began to shout again, "Hosanna, Hosanna, to the son of David."

Some of the scribes and the priests who were watching all this once again became vocally upset with my supporters. They asked me if I heard what the children were saying. I reminded the Pharisees of another prophecy to let them know that nothing they could do would stop me or my father. "Have you never read, 'From the lips of children and infants you have ordained praise'?"[50]

I left the temple and returned to Bethany.

Four Days

What do you most vividly recall about those four days between Palm Sunday and the last supper?

In spite of the Pharisees' threats to arrest me, I continued to go to the temple daily to teach. They were afraid of the people now. My parables were intentionally directed at the Pharisees. I repeated stories about ungrateful servants who didn't listen, who killed their masters' favorite son. Like a good prophet, I proclaimed the judgment awaiting those teachers. The other focus of my parables was the last days at the end of the world. I tried to heighten the people's awareness of the fact that the end was coming.

Every time the Pharisees saw me teaching the people, they became incensed and tried to discredit me. This time they brought me a coin and tried to trick me into taking a stand against Rome for which I could be arrested. "Sir"—it was the most respect I had received in three years from them—"You are an honest man, and tell us the truth. Is it right to pay taxes to the Roman government or not?" I told them that I certainly thought Caesar should have his due: "Render therefore unto Caesar the things which are Caesar's; and unto God the things that are God's."[51]

Once again the Pharisees failed in their mission. Not only did I embarrass them in front of the people. Shortly thereafter I confronted them with the question about how the Messiah could be David's son and yet exist before David had. As usual, a big crowd surrounded us and awaited their answer. Again not one of the Pharisees could answer the question, and they had to walk away. The Pharisees didn't understand that I had already been challenged by their best and had won.

Not only did I embarrass them in front of the people at every encounter. I directly and rather loudly told the people what the Pharisees were—hypocrites. "You hypocrites. You pray long prayers in public and kick widows out of their homes. Hypocrites! You tithed to your last nickel and ignored justice. Hypocrites! Everything you do is for show. You load the people down with rules you don't even try to keep. Hypocrites! You are so concerned with appearances, with the outside, while inside you exploit your neighbor and are filled with greed. You say you wouldn't dare kill a prophet like your fathers did, and yet you are following in the same steps. You snakes, sons of vipers, hypocrites, do you think you will escape the judgment of hell? You won't ever enter heaven."[52]

They had to get rid of me. I had humiliated them in every way, but I was also giving them a chance to see their true need to repent.

On Wednesday of that week some Greeks who had traveled a long way for Passover asked to speak to you privately. You refused to see them. In the past you had been more than receptive to foreigners, to people Jews disdained, like the Samaritan woman at the well and the Roman soldier. You had even spent time with tax collectors. Why didn't you talk with these Greeks?

I was comforted by their request, but I left the work with the Greeks for my men to do. I did speak to those Greeks and the rest of the world. I told them that I had to be like the kernel of wheat that dies and falls into its grave in the earth. If I didn't, I would produce no harvest. It was my last public statement. One last time I wanted to say, "If you love your life foremost, you will lose it."

I told the Greeks, and everyone else listening, that if they wanted to follow me, they should come and be where I am. If they did, my father would honor them. Was I to back off from my death because it was a terrible burden? No, I answered, this was the reason I came. I stopped and prayed, "Father, bring glory and honor to your name." Immediately a voice from heaven declared, "I have already done this, and I will do it again."[53]

I heard that beautiful voice again. My father knew the cost of living. I had to tell the world again that living is losing your life. It is sacrifice and love. That was the best thing I could do for these Greeks.

I wanted to see those Greeks, but I had to put aside my wishes. My time was up. I had to stop my work and die. Years later, Paul did the same thing when confined to a jail in Rome. When you lose your life you multiply it. Paul was a living laboratory, testifying to people forever that there is a way for men and women to rise above their circumstances. The death of my own dreams had its reward. My last days were not in vain.

Jesus came in, and he went out like a king. In the two weeks before his death, he performed his most famous miracle. He raised a man from death to life, a deed that had caused the crowds in Jerusalem to swell to enormous proportions in the week before Passover as they anticipated Jesus' presence there. Not to disappoint them, he had made an unforgettable entry into Jerusalem on the Sunday before his last Passover. He made that entry in daylight; humble, unarmed, cheered by the masses, and knowing full well he was headed toward his death.

He was keeping his promise to the Pharisees who once had tried to intimidate him into leaving Jerusalem by telling Jesus that Herod would kill him for causing trouble. Jesus had replied, calling Herod a name. "You tell that fox, Herod, I will keep on healing and casting out demons until I reach my destination."

Now he had reached his destination. Shortly before he had been anointed by his friend, Mary.

In a way so radical it was almost beyond comprehension, in the last week of his life Jesus confronted the authorities of his day. He made them the villains of his parables. He publicly denounced them. He out-taught them, outwitted them, and continually demonstrated greater authority even to the point of taking control of "their" temple again. At the end of his life, Jesus was at the height of his popularity and his authority, and the Pharisees were afraid of him. They were sure the people were going to make Jesus king, and then they would lose their "positions of honor." As they put it, "The whole world has gone after him!"[54]

He would have been king had he allowed it. However, he knew that wasn't his father's plan, so he permitted them to manipulate the scene to bring about his death. Jesus was so popular, however, that the Pharisees didn't dare try to challenge him in daylight in front of the people. In order to apprehend him, they had to contrive a devious plan to capture and try him at night, away from the people. Every step of the way his power testified that he was the king from Nazareth and from above.

The Last Supper

Four days after Palm Sunday, on Thursday night, you had your last meal before your death. Tell us about the last supper.

After three years of constant companionship, the disciples and I gathered together in a room on the evening before my death for our last meal together. This was also the famous Passover meal of the bitter herbs, the unleavened bread, and the paschal lamb, along with the ceremony of the great deliverance.* My disciples and I had usually been surrounded by hundreds, sometimes thousands, of people. We tried to keep mealtimes just for ourselves, though.

As I was preparing for the meal, knowing this was the last meal I would eat before I died, memories of my men came flooding back. I thought of the first time we had met, of their courage in dropping what they were doing to follow me. There were the talks, the laughs, the good-natured kidding that goes around the dinner table. I thought about their struggle to believe, about their unique personalities. I remembered Peter's exuberance, John's devotion, Matthew's gratitude, James's determination, Thomas's intellect, and Philip's humor. I remembered all the different places we had stayed, each with its own special set of memories.

I saw how much I was going to miss them. I thought about what I was asking of them—things they didn't even know yet. They would have to carry on. Most of them would be killed for being my followers.

---

* The bitter herbs signified the bitterness of the Jews' oppression by the Egyptians. The unleavened bread was the type of bread eaten on the road as the Jews scurried to leave Egypt. The paschal lamb signified the lamb that took away the sins of the Israelites, causing the angel of death to pass over their homes.

All would be martyrs. I had to prepare them for what was to follow one more time.

It was the last time I would teach them "in person" before my death and resurrection. I wanted them to know how much I loved them. I wanted to say good-bye. Because I wanted it to be a special time we would always remember, I saved the best secrets until last.

Earlier in the evening, I'd been thinking of what I could do that night that would stay with them, that would remind them of the kind of persons to be. When we came to the banquet room prepared for us in the upper room of a friend's house, everything was so elaborate that one of the disciples, in jest, said, "Everything's here but the servant to wash our feet." I got up, took off my robe, wrapped a towel around my waist, and washed each disciple's feet. They were shocked, but I wanted them to know that in my father's house they were servants and not masters. What a picture it was of my task and of theirs. I thought of those women who had comforted me, who had anointed me.

Judas was there?

He was. When I washed the disciples' feet, I looked at each one of them directly while I was doing it to let them know how much I cared. Judas, who was going to betray me within the hour, wouldn't look at me. He was uncomfortable, and as I was washing his feet, he said several times, "That's enough, Lord."

Did you try to convince him not to go?

Before he left, I quoted the Old Testament prophecy that the Messiah would be betrayed by one of his own to show Judas that he was Satan's puppet.

You knew, though, your father's prophecies were never wrong.

My human emotions hoped that he wouldn't go through with it, just as later that night in the garden I wanted out of the terrible situation

I knew I had to endure. I knew from the Scriptures what was to happen, but that didn't stop me from being human. I didn't want either event to happen, and I tried to change them to the degree that I could. Even after Judas had completely betrayed me, as we stood there in the garden surrounded by the guards who had come to get me, I looked at him and thought, "I know what you have done. You can still return to me." I also knew that his heart had grown too hard.

Obviously, on the eve of his death, serving was very much on the mind of Jesus. How typical of this man it was to wash his disciples' feet with his own hands less than twelve hours before his crucifixion. How fitting it was. For he was getting ready to wash the feet of the whole world. If one act apart from his crucifixion portrayed above all others the essence of his life, his central message, this was it. The Lord of the universe, intrinsic to his regal nature, came to serve. He was a king unlike any other.

What happened then?

After washing their feet, I sat down, said another blessing of praise, and passed around the second cup. Then, according to ceremony, we each prepared the unleavened bread with the herbs to give to our neighbors. This is when I told them I was not speaking to all of them, for one of them was about to betray me. I wanted Judas to know how bitter his betrayal was for me, and ultimately for him. I wanted the others to know I knew about the betrayal in advance, so that when I was on the cross they would know I had gone willingly. I wanted them to know I was still God, even when I appeared helpless.

When I told them about the betrayal, their anxiety immediately became apparent. You could see the self-doubt in their eyes. "Betrayal?"

As I recall, most of the disciples didn't know who would betray you until after the deed was done.

It didn't take them long to block my uncomfortable comment out of their minds, but you should have seen the look on their faces when each of them started wondering who it might be. If you had taken a survey, Matthew would have immediately been at the top of the list—"of course, Matthew. He was a conniving deceitful tax collector, and I've always wondered about him. He's always been an outsider. Most likely he's had enough of our transient lifestyle and lack of luxury, and he's ready to go back to his mansion and all his wealth. All along I suspected he would never last. Old dogs as they say, can't learn new tricks." Most of them would have immediately suspected Matthew.

Thomas would have been a solid second choice. "After all, he never seems to have any faith and always seems to be challenging Jesus with 'why this and why that.' He always wants something proven to him. If anybody in this group marches to his own drum it's Thomas. I'll bet he's the one, and the person Jesus had mostly in mind when he chastised us 'Oh, Ye of little faith.'"

They would have gone through most of the list. Others would have focused on yet another disciple: "Peter's so impulsive and headstrong, he could easily be the culprit. You never know what outrageous act he's going to do next, and he's the only one Jesus himself told to 'Get thee behind me Satan,' comparing him to the king of evil. That really hurt Peter, and with that huge temper of his, he probably wants to repay Jesus, and I'll bet he'd do something like that before you even knew it."

Nathaniel would have been another possibility—"Remember he's the one that wondered what good can come out of Nazareth when he first heard about Jesus. He's always had a snobbish attitude about being from Bethsaida and from a family with more money than the majority of us. I'll bet he's had enough of the tough life out on the road and enough of being a servant like Jesus teaches and wants to go back to his old life. I never really trusted Nathaniel who always thought he was a little bit better than others."

Some would have even wondered—"What about the Sons of Thunder, the two hot-headed brothers James and John? They're so pushy—the gall, getting their mother to ask Jesus if her two boys could sit on his right and left when he comes into his kingdom. They had that family fishing business and are just a little spoiled, too used to having their way. Remember the time they wanted to kill a whole town full of people for not embracing Jesus, wanted him to call down fire and rain on them. We've all heard them talk about how they are going to be favored above the rest of us in Jesus' kingdom. Well, I'll bet it's finally dawning on them that it's not going to happen. Maybe bitterness got to either one of them—they've certainly got the potential."

Even the quieter disciples who never spoke up much, like James Alphaeus, would have been suspects—"You never know what they're thinking. I wouldn't put it past them. You never knew if they were passionate about what Jesus was doing, and Simon is such a complainer."

Judas would have been at the last on almost everybody's list. He could be so devoted, and everyone respected him for his passion. When he believed in something he threw himself into it as his being a zealot revealed. All the disciples could tell he and I really hit it off from the beginning—we enjoyed lively discussions about the spiritual life, and he was the one above all who loved to go to the synagogue with me, particularly to interact with the teachers. From the beginning his demeanor had gained the group's respect, and they had spontaneously made him the treasurer. This is why they all paid no attention at first when later Judas left our last meal together, as they thought once again he was going on another responsible mission. Only John knew. I told John when he found the courage to ask me.

The disciples saw the awful truth. Any one of them could have betrayed me, given the right twist in circumstances. But God had reined each in to protect him from himself, all except Judas.

Following my announcement of a betrayal by one from my inner circle, the disciples sat in silence awhile until Peter, who faced everything head-on, whispered to John, who was sitting next to me, "Ask the master which one will betray him." So John leaned toward me and said, "Lord, who is it?"[55]

Just as the Scriptures had prophesied in Psalm 41, "Even my close friend, whom I trusted, he who shared my bread, has lifted up his heel against me."[56]

I picked up a piece of bread and dipped it in the sauce on the table. There was a custom in my day that if you wanted to honor someone at a feast you would offer him the sop. As I did that I answered John by telling him it was the one to whom I gave this piece of bread.

Were you, when you gave him the bread, fulfilling that prophecy you quoted?

I didn't give Judas the bread. I offered it to him. I offered him a chance to refuse me, after I had quoted the Old Testament to warn him. It was bitter bread, and he knew it. In effect I was asking him, "Judas, do you really want this bitterness? Do you really want to be the bitter herb? Do you really want to be the one who punishes God's chosen?"

As I held that bread out to him, his eyes were like a kaleidoscope, showing a hundred different things at the same time. There was fear, sadness, guilt, anger, and most of all, confusion. I'll never forget the uncertainty. It was an uncertainty on which he was basing his whole life. Then there was a fleeting look of hope when he hesitated, and, finally, for one second, his face was the saddest face I had ever seen. Then he grabbed the bread. I told him to go quickly and do what he had to do. He immediately left, and I knew it had begun.

The Scriptures record that you were in great anguish as you talked about one of your disciples betraying you. Even though you knew it was going to happen, it hurt when Judas left.

Even at the last supper, when I was so confident about whom I was and what was to come, I was vulnerable. I couldn't escape the grief Judas caused me. Even though I knew it was coming, even though I had prepared myself, even though I was God, Judas could still hurt me because I was a human being. I never once in my entire life gave up that vulnerability.

Was your reaction similar to the way God reacts? Even though God knows some are going to reject him, he's still offended and hurt by that rejection?

God never made us immune to pain, because he's not immune. The only kind of relationship worth having is one where you are sensitive to the other person. All of life has always been, and always will be personal to the core.

At first Judas had such a tremendous view of my father, and he understood things about God that the others didn't. He often answered their questions before I did. It was sad. He was so gifted. We could have had so much together.

Jesus paused here for a few moments with a look of deep grief on his face. He still felt the pain from Judas's betrayal, so poignantly expressed in the way he said the one word, "sad." Yet, he was more concerned about someone other than himself. He grieved for what his friend, Judas, had lost. It was also striking how freely he expressed his emotions and his vulnerability. These powerful feelings did not detract in any way from his strength. Perhaps his father has similar emotions. That's what Jesus told me.

Judas

You seem to have been closer to Judas than many people think.

I shared everything with Judas—my trials, my blessings, even my power. The time I sent my men out with my power, Judas performed miracles in my name. He healed the sick and made the blind see. For two weeks he performed hundreds of miracles, yet he still didn't believe in me. He used me, but he never worshiped me. He never deeply honored me. He saw me walk on water, calm the sea, and raise the dead, yet he still thought he was wiser than I.

There were three and one-half years of living together and often comforting him or being comforted by him. He was the only disciple besides Thomas who at moments understood total sacrifice to the point of death. He was the one disciple who would make sure I had time to be alone because he knew the importance of it. Many times he would keep the others from interrupting my prayer time. He would never bother me. Judas always waited for me to approach him.

Only once do I recall his interrupting me or challenging me directly, and that was at the end of my life when, in Judas's eyes, Mary wasted the expensive perfume on me. He hated materialism and thought the money could be used for better purposes. He was the disciple who was the least concerned about "things of this world."

When I started my public ministry, he wasn't working like the rest of the disciples. He had already given up the security of a regular job to "do God's will." Even though toward the end of my ministry he began to take money from our treasury, it was because he thought he knew how to use the money better. He was giving it to the zealots. Contrary to what he said, Judas cared more for power than for the poor. When he saw me allow Mary to pour costly perfume on me, he became incensed because the money could have been used for "the true cause."

Sadly, he was secretly proud of his brilliance. As so often happens when one trusts his own vision completely, he took the next fatal step of deviousness.

My anointing was the final straw that made Judas decide to betray me. Not only was I "passive and lacking a vision" but I was simply "extravagant." When he took the thirty pieces of silver from the Pharisees to betray me, he did that only to have some friends continue "the movement" to restore Israel to the Jews, which he was certain was God's will. Judas could have cared less about gold or silver in and of itself.

It must have hurt deeply to have a person in the inner circle betray you.

I would not have hurt nearly so much had an enemy found out where we were and led the soldiers to me. For a friend to do it, hurt deeply. He was not just a friend, but the first close friend I had had after being alone for so long prior to disclosing my identity. Before I announced that I was the Messiah, you can imagine that I was keeping much hidden. I hadn't been able to tell anyone except my mother who I was. I could share with no one my visions, my struggles. When Judas came into my life, he was like a breath of fresh air. All the other disciples I had gone looking for, but Judas came looking for me. He was the one who looked forward to the Messiah the most, so naturally I could talk to him about things I had never talked about before. He was a true friend.

He was the one I could leave in charge if I went off by myself or with a few of the others such as the time I spent with Peter, James, and John. I could count on Judas. That was who he was to me. After all I had shared with him, all of myself that I revealed to him, he was the one who betrayed me. Though I had known for some time before the actual betrayal itself that it would be by Judas, I could always see his good side.

Because I knew he would be the one, it made me try harder to keep him from doing it. I would take special pains to let Judas know I loved him. I'd praise him, acknowledge his wisdom, pray with him, share his burdens, reveal myself to him, and give him authority. I tried to honor him in every way I could think of, even at the last supper when I gave him that piece of bread dipped in the sauce. That was done for the guest of honor at parties.

The moment Judas left to betray me, he did so on the wings of honor, in the midst of tremendous acclaim. He had just had his dirty feet washed by the son of God's own hands. He had just been the honored member at the banquet given by the son of God. It will be the same for anyone who chooses hell. Every step of the way will be on roads where I have laid out the royal carpet, stained red with my blood, just for him or her.

When Judas left to betray me, I had a tremendous personal investment in him. When I saw him leave that night, I understood more clearly what my father felt when Satan betrayed him. Satan was great, just as Judas was, but pride destroyed both of them. Satan was once the most gifted angel in heaven. He had been given the distinction of being the most brilliant creature in existence. Outside the trinity, no one compared to him. He was so like us. So close to us in his ways because he had been given beauty, magnificence, intelligence, and power. He had so much power that he was God-like, so much power that he forgot he was a created being.

Judas forgot the same thing. He wanted to take over "our movement." He had plans to take my place. Upon my death, he would mobilize the movement we had begun in the direction it should go. He wanted more power and immediate social changes. Jerusalem was ours. Judas saw the weakness in the other men. He saw the strength in himself, but he underestimated me. He never comprehended that I was God. Envy colored his vision.

One wonders how he, one of the inner circle, could really miss the fact that you were the Messiah. What went through his mind?

He heard me say I was the Messiah, but he never believed it because I wasn't what he wanted me to be. He thought to himself: "Jesus is deluded. He says he is the Messiah, but look at him. All he is doing is healing people with some kind of mystical power. He won't take over. He just sits back.

"Oh! He'll tell the Pharisees what he thinks of them, but he will never really do anything about them or about the Romans. Jesus has no plan. All I've ever heard him say is some high-sounding nebulous business about humility, 'a seed must die before it produces fruit.' Does he think I don't know about humility? I gave up all I had in a lucrative business to follow someone who could turn the country around. Someone has to lead if we're going to fulfill our destiny. If that somebody has to be me, at least they can't say I don't have a plan. They're just going to kill Jesus, and where is that going to leave the rest of us? I believe in being humble, but not stupid.

"I thought Jesus was on a mission. He understood so much, but he's making no effort to start a real movement. Most of the people just use him and forget about him, but that's his own fault because he hasn't given them a vision. As a man, he's kind. As a leader, he's failed. Look at the people. There are thousands of them, and he is doing nothing but giving platitudes such as, 'Blessed are the peacemakers.'[57]

"Well, these bloodthirsty pagan Romans have God's country in a stronghold. Has he forgotten that? I will not rest until Jerusalem, Zion, God's holy hill, is once again God's and not Rome's. Has Jesus forgotten whom his father loves, and who formed this nation? You can't tell me God did that just so some pagan Roman could take over. No, Jesus doesn't see far enough. He just thinks he's the Messiah. The real Messiah would deliver us. At least the Pharisees see this, even if they're cowards. Die for God. For Zion. Don't be a doormat to Rome. It will be Jerusalem or death.

"There are not many brave ones around. Look at all these disciples trying to prove which one's the greatest. They'd all probably run if it came down to taking on the Romans. What about Peter and his big mouth? James and John with their great tempers? Even if Jesus does spend more time with them, it won't do any good, because he's not teaching them anything.

"Just because they're fishermen they think they're so bold, those Galileans! They were just as scared as the rest of us in that storm. I have to give Jesus credit. He doesn't panic, and he does have incredible power, but if his goal is to die, I'll help him do it. He knows it's going to happen anyway. He's always talking about how Scripture says this and Scripture say that, all to justify this passive position. He twists the Scriptures. Hasn't he read the parts about the Messiah reigning, putting his boot on the enemies' necks, and treading them down?

"I'll tell you what I think. I think Jesus never got over the loss of his father, Joseph, at an early age, and he never had a father to teach him how to be truly assertive. He and his followers don't really have a heart for Zion because they're not from Judea. Jesus is a nice man, but somebody has to take advantage of the people in their present rebellious state. Jesus and John the Baptist got them fired up, and we may never get another chance this good in my lifetime. I know what I have to do. Somebody has to see the light. After all, I'm not going to do anything but lead them to him. They would have found him sooner or later, anyway. He'd just as well get it over with. I'll be doing every one of them, even Jesus, a favor."

Talent can be a temptation to worship yourself. Judas was brilliant and perceptive, but he couldn't see far enough by himself. He thought he was the light, didn't he?

He was, over all, the most gifted person I ever knew on this earth, except for one thing: he had a bad heart. He could have been a Paul. In fact, Paul in a way took Judas's place. What Paul did might have been done by Judas, if he had trusted. He placed himself among the first who "shall be last."*[58]

Judas tried to give the money back after he betrayed you. Why?

He felt the guilt. When the Pharisees wouldn't take it, he threw the money away and went into a deep depression. God, who loved Judas, had prophesied the betrayal down to the specific amount of thirty pieces of silver and to the actual dissatisfaction that Judas would have with himself.[59] Judas's pride ruined him. Even after the betrayal, my father and I would have taken him back, had he repented, but he wouldn't. He was his own savior, who provided his own cross and had no use for my atonement. He found those lacking and committed suicide shortly after betraying me. There's a real danger in being a "good person." It tends to make you forget your own evil and forget who made you. Obviously, in the end Judas was a very foolish man. He had let his pride turn him into an evil man—into a son of Satan. One of the most talented men in history became one of the most evil, the

---

* After Judas's suicide and following Jesus' resurrection, the remaining eleven disciples cast sticks to decide upon the man to take Judas's place as a disciple. They knew there had to be twelve disciples to fulfill the prophecy that each would rule one of the twelve tribes of Israel upon Christ's return. Matthias was the man the disciples selected, and little was known or heard about him after that. However, shortly thereafter, Paul was selected by Jesus himself to be an apostle in the miraculous conversion on the road to Damascus.

greatest traitor in history by whom all others pale in comparison, the biggest fool humankind has ever produced.

Though Jesus here called Judas a fool, there was no vindictiveness in the way he said it; rather there was regret. It made me think of the grief God must bear in watching children to whom he has given life choose hell over him. God must understand well a mother who loses a child, and particularly one who loses a child by watching him turn into a drug addict or a monster like Hitler. He has lost millions of them forever, even after paying the ultimate price to save them.

You didn't reach Judas. Was that a failure for you personally?

No, that was the price of freedom, the same price that my father paid with Lucifer. Love can come only from freedom. I did all I could for Judas. I never quit holding out my hand to him even after I knew he had betrayed me. Four hours before he led the Roman soldiers to me, I washed his feet with my hands. Even when he brought the soldiers to capture me, I called him "friend."

It amazes me that you contained your feelings toward this man whom you knew was going to betray you. When you told the disciples that one of them was going to be a traitor, none of them knew who it was. They obviously didn't pick up any bitterness you had toward Judas.

I could not stop loving him until he totally refused my love and walked away. It was his only hope. After Judas had made his choice and left, I remember looking at the still uneaten paschal lamb in front of us, the last part of the Passover meal. This lamb was roasted over a fire, not allowed to touch anything, undefiled. It was eaten without breaking any of its bones, meaning the sacrifice was complete and unbroken. How could anyone miss the fact that the Messiah, the Lamb, was to suffer? Sacrifice was the heart of Passover, of worship. How appropriate it was that Judas had left before eating this sacrifice, because he didn't think he needed it. As I was mulling over the pain Judas had left me, I looked around the table at John, Peter, James, and the others. With all their faults, they had not betrayed me. I took great comfort in knowing that what I did, I did for the Johns, the Peters, the Jameses of the world; not the Judases. They didn't want it. They couldn't accept it.

Despite the pain, it was also a great time. That day was finally here. Now I was attaining my glory. As I told my disciples right after Judas left, "Now is the son of man glorified, and God is glorified in him." I was getting ready to do the most courageous thing a man had ever done. The fate of the whole world hinged on what I was going to do the next day. My deed was to be the centerpiece of history. I had waited a long time for the world to see my glory win out over pain. I was ready.

What unbelievable personal strength Jesus had as Judas left to set up the betrayal. Jesus met the challenge, in effect saying, "I'm waiting for you; bring me my glory." For centuries to come, Christ's strength would enable his martyrs to demonstrate an uncommon courage in the face of persecution. Jesus' deed was so great that his courage would permeate his church until his return. Interestingly, at the same last supper he demonstrated the tremendous range of his emotions and his unusual sensitivity by comforting his disciples, preparing them for the separation anxiety they would soon experience:

I will be with you only a little longer.[60]
Let not your heart be troubled. . . . In my Father's house are many mansions. . . . I go to prepare a place for you.[61]

Peter

When you told the disciples that one of them would betray you, didn't Peter vow that he wouldn't?

When I had made that prediction, Peter immediately vowed that under no circumstances would he deny me. He would die for me at a moment's notice. That's when I looked at him and said, "Peter, you will deny me not once, but three times before the sun comes up." I had to tell him, "No, Peter, there's only one man who would die for his neighbor at all times in all circumstances, and it's not you." Peter was the bravest of the lot, but I had to show him and humankind for centuries to come that there is none good but one.[62]

I wanted Peter and the rest of the world to know I suffered no illusions. I had to be firm and honest with Peter, despite his good intentions.

You obviously loved all your disciples, but you really liked Peter.

Peter was always Peter. Earlier that night when I washed the disciples' feet, he reacted to that, too. As usual, he had his own thoughts, which he freely shared. He insisted that he would not let me do something so low as to wash his feet. I informed him that, "Unless I wash you, you have no part with me."

Peter, as quick to admit a mistake as to volunteer an opinion, a man of extremes, but so honest, immediately said: "Well, Lord, wash all of me." It was all I could do to hold Peter down a little. I told him gently, "A person who is clean needs only his feet washed, and all of you are clean except one."[63]

Down through the centuries, Peter has often been laughed at, yet he is the one disciple we know the most about. Why did you choose him to be in your inner circle of three?

Peter had a contagious exuberance. He always expressed himself. Sometimes it was not with enough thought, but it was an honest, straightforward boldness. There was no guile in Peter.

Peter was not the one who asked behind everyone else's back to be favored like James and John did. When Peter wanted to be special, everybody knew it. If he wanted to walk on water, he asked in front of everybody. If he thought you were wrong, he told you, "Lord, you shouldn't wash my feet." His boldness was his greatest weakness, but also his greatest strength.

There was something comforting about being around Peter. You always knew where you stood with him, and there's nothing like having someone such as Peter on your side. At one point, when the rest of the disciples were confused, Peter was the one who understood most clearly who I was, and he declared it. Peter knew I wasn't Elijah or John the Baptist come back to life, as some said. I wasn't just another prophet. He said: "You are the Christ, the Son of the living God."[64]

You gave God credit for showing him that.

God did reveal it to him, but he picked a man who could think big. It took that kind of man to see how big I was. Yet, even though he knew my abilities to prophesy, he was so determined to insist that I was wrong when I told him, "Peter, you will deny me three times before the cock crows in the morning."

He took criticism well, however. After each failure, he came roaring back: "Teach me more, Lord." He never let his failures slow him down. "If I'm wrong, Lord, then wash my whole body." The time I was teaching the disciples that I had to die, Peter told me, "Lord, you're not going to die." I had to rebuke him with, "Get thee behind me Satan."

Undaunted, a few days later at the transfiguration, Peter wanted to build me a temple. He always wanted to learn, and he was bold.

People have laughed at Peter for his impulsiveness.

Some always laughed at Peter. He had faults, but Peter's indomitable spirit reflected what my father intended men and women to be when he created them. Peter was the only man other than myself to

walk on water. What potential for faith he had, and ultimately he fulfilled it.

The Gifts

*After Judas left the room, you taught your men some great truths that last
night.*

It was a bittersweet time. I had all the memories of my disciples,
and I knew I would miss them. At the same time, I was about to see
my father again. After all the years of waiting and wondering, now it
was almost here. That long-awaited reunion with my father was just
around the corner, and yet in front of me was the horrible battle I had
dreaded for years. I had just felt the pain of enormous rejection. I was
having to leave these men into whom I had poured my life. Even the
last time together couldn't be perfect, for it was obvious to me my
men did not understand, and I knew from the Scriptures that each of
them in his own way would deny me.

Still, you loved them.

There is no perfection on this earth. We all wait on heaven; even
the Messiah, even the father. All of my work came down to these eleven
men, and in just a few hours I would be gone. I would never be with
them again in the same way as a human being. I would never again
teach them face to face in this way.

Another teacher, the Holy Spirit, would be taking my place. It would
be better for them as he would continually teach them my words, and
I would indwell them spiritually. Still, it would never be like this again.
I wanted their calling to be clear in their minds, so before I told them I
was leaving, I reminded them of their duty to serve. I washed their
feet, and I was their Lord.

As soon as Judas left, I told the rest, my true disciples, that I would
be leaving, that this would be our last meal together. As soon as I said
it, the panic of abandonment was written all over their faces, as I knew

it would be. So I immediately told them I was going to prepare a place for them, and I promised them I would be back to get them so that "you also may be where I am."

> Where I am going, you cannot come.[65]
> I am going there to prepare a place for you. And if I go and prepare a place for you, I will come back and take you to be with me that you also may be where I am.[66]

I had nothing material to give them now, but I knew that at my return each of them would have a permanent mansion in my father's kingdom: "In my Father's house are many rooms."[67]

As far as the world was concerned, a poor man died on that cross, but I was a rich man, and everything I had I gave to them.

On the eve of his death, the greatest man the world has ever known had no material possessions except the clothes on his back. By the next day, even those would be taken from him. When he fed five thousand people, he had to borrow the bread to do it. When they asked him about his allegiance to Caesar, he had to borrow a coin to make his point. Even the last supper was held in a room that was loaned to him for the night. Jesus intentionally was saying to a world whose primary standard of worth was measured in material wealth, "There is more to being human than wealth. Living does not consist of the abundance of things that you possess." He was also making another statement: "My father looked after me, and he will look after you."

What did you tell them after that?

After I told them of their future inheritance, I gave them their earthly inheritance in the way they had longed for. For three and a half years, they had heard me refer to myself as the light of the world, the good shepherd, the bread of life, the son of man—but rarely directly as the Messiah. They had watched me heal people and tell them to keep it a secret. During the time they had observed my restraint, my disciples had wanted me to come out boldly announcing who I was. John the Baptist urged me to do the same thing. My disciples had wanted to hear me say who I was. Now they got their wish. I was going to say it to them clearly.

> Anyone who has seen me has seen the Father.[68]
> I am the way and the truth and the life. No one comes to the
> Father except through me.[69]

I told them, "I have glorified God on this earth," "I have power over all flesh," and "I was with God in all my glory before the world was created." I gave them my glory. In fact, that was the essence of their inheritance: "I have given them the glory that you gave me, that they may be one as we are one."[70]

First among the gifts I gave was service. Then I gave them my authority. If they were going out into a hostile world, they were going out armed. To make sure they were, I gave them my teacher, my guide, the spirit of truth to be with them forever.

> Because I have said these things, you are filled with grief. But
> I tell you the truth: It is for your good that I am going away.
> Unless I go away, the Counselor will not come to you; but if I
> go, I will send him to you.... But when he, the Spirit of truth,
> comes, he will guide you into all truth.... All that belongs to
> the Father is mine. That is why I said the Spirit will take from
> what is mine and make it known to you.[71]

Even though my disciples were temporarily about to abandon me, I was very confident in them because their teacher had been mine, too. I knew what kind of results he got. He never failed.

As I continued to "arm them," I gave them my power. It was the influence I had with my father, the influence that heals people, that raises people from the dead. I prayed that my followers could know how great their inheritance was. I told them that anyone who had faith in me could do the same things I had done, and even greater things because I was going to the father.

> And I will do whatever you ask in my name, so that the Son may bring glory to the Father. You may ask me for anything in my name, and I will do it.[72]

> The father will give you whatever you ask in my name.[73]

Never before had they had this much power, this much influence with my father. I told my disciples to use their power. Go ahead, ask. Ask for anything? Six times I told them, "Ask. . . . Ask. . . . Ask. . . . Ask. . . . Ask. . . . Ask." With their power, I gave them my confidence, my success. I gave them the guarantee my father had given me. I personally guaranteed them that their mission would succeed, just as my father had promised me mine would: "You did not choose me, but I chose you and appointed you to go and bear fruit—fruit that will last."[74]

So that they would know for sure that my father and I delighted in letting their lights shine, I pushed them to do great things. I told them that my father got much joy when they did great things, and so did I. Plan. Think. Ask us. We will help you. "I tell you the truth, anyone who has faith in me will do what I have been doing. He will do even greater things than these, because I am going to the Father."[75]

In addition to my power I gave them my peace, a different kind of peace than the world offers. It was immune to circumstances. It was peace over fear, over discouragement, and over death. Particularly it was over death: "Peace I leave with you; my peace I give you. I do not give to you as the world gives. Do not let your hearts be troubled and do not be afraid."[76]

Then I gave them another priceless gift that is really the essence of all gifts. It was my joy, the greatest joy that any person on this earth has ever experienced: "You love righteousness and hate wickedness;

therefore God, your God, has set you above your companions by anointing you with the oil of joy."[77]

This joy would come from their influence with the father and their importance to the father: "Ask and you will receive, and your joy will be complete."[78]

The one thing that had given me happiness beyond belief was that I knew how much I was loved. When I gave them my joy, I gave them my love. As I told them, "Greater love has no one than this, that he lay down his life for his friends"[79] and "As the father has loved me, so have I loved you."[80]

They were the most loved people in history. To show them exactly how much they were loved, I gave them my glory so that I could give them above all my father. They now had my righteousness so that they could have the one thing I treasured most—my oneness with my father: "I have given them the glory that you gave me, that they may be one as we are one."[81]

They were now a member of the family called trinity. I had given them a new identity, unique in human history. As C. S. Lewis later said, I had made them little gods.

When the great resurrection day would come in the future, I would live inside them. Just as my father had lived in me and I had spoken his words, they would speak my words. I had literally given them myself: "On that day you will realize that I am in my Father, and you are in me, and I am in you."[82]

Not only had they seen God when they had seen me, a privilege very few men in history have had, but now they were going to be a part of him, and he of them. The isolation that had existed for centuries was now broken. Now they had far more than Adam had possessed in Eden. They had been given my ability to love, and from that time on they were to love as they had been loved: "A new command I give you: Love one another. As I have loved you, so you must love one another."[83]

This was their heritage. Love was to be our power that would conquer the world, not might or material wealth or political strength or fear. A new day was dawning for all people, and my disciples were the first to know. Those who believed in me and my father were to be my brothers and sisters, and there would be a oneness that the world had never known.

Warnings at the Table

You also gave them some warnings.

At this point I gave them a warning. I talked to them about obedience and discipline. I said that there was a key to protecting the gifts they had been given. The key they would need to use was the same key I had had to use—obedience and discipline: "If you obey my commands, you will remain in my love, just as I have obeyed my Father's commands and remain in his love."[84]

Now I had shared my secrets, things no one else in history had learned. I shared all my blessings, all the treasures of my heart, even my own inheritance I was about to receive. Everything. Only then could I give them the other part of their heritage—my cross. If they were to live out the truth, pain would come. Pain always follows truth. They would be martyred, just as I was to be.

> If the world hates you, keep in mind that it hated me first. If you belonged to the world, it would love you as its own. As it is, you do not belong to the world, but I have chosen you out of the world. That is why the world hates you. Remember the words I spoke to you: "No servant is greater than his master." If they persecuted me, they will persecute you also.[85]

I told them so they would be sure to know my persecution was no surprise to me. The Scriptures had predicted this moment, and all of them must be fulfilled: "Those who hate me without reason outnumber the hairs of my head; many are my enemies without cause."*[86]

---

* In the New Testament, the most quoted Old Testament book is Psalms, and among the Psalms, only 22 is quoted more frequently than 69. These are the two great prophetic psalms about messianic suffering.

Psalm 69, the psalm that had comforted me, would comfort them. One of the tremendous things the Scripture did for me was to say, "See, this is happening just as it's supposed to." When you know what to expect, it certainly helps you to be prepared. The promise of persecution was a difficult gift to give. This gift brought us closer together, though. At the same time I gave them my cross, I also gave them my courage: "I have told you these things, so that in me you may have peace. In this world you will have trouble. But take heart! I have overcome the world."[87]

Finally, I prayed with them. I asked God to protect them and to teach them so that the world could see this oneness and believe that he sent me. I asked God to give me glory for what I was about to do.

Right after this, didn't some of your disciples start arguing about who would betray you and which one of them would be the greatest in your kingdom? Wasn't that somewhat discouraging?

They did, and it was. They were still connected to this world. Even the oneness of the last supper was tainted with envy. That is why I had to go through the crucifixion for them. That is when I told them that Gentile kings lorded it over their servants but they were not to imitate them. The one who ruled should be a servant. I told them not to worry about their rank. All one day would eat at my table. Each of them would rule over the twelve tribes of Israel.

Why, at the moment they least deserved it, did you give them their blessing?

For the same reason that, after I washed their feet, I assured them that they were clean. I was preparing them for their failure so that they could teach the rest of the world how to respond to failure by witnessing God's mercy and forgiveness. After I was gone, I wanted my disciples to treat the people of this world in the same way. In the face of abuse, they were to respond with kindness. That's the type of love that overwhelms people, the kind they don't understand.

After my gifts to them, we completed the Passover ceremony. We finished by passing the traditional cup around seven times. When it came to me the last time I did not drink, but told them: "I will not drink this cup with you until we drink it together in heaven." I would drink the final cup later that evening and the next morning by myself. It was to be the most bitter cup of my life on earth. Finally, we sang one of the great messianic psalms, Psalm 118, the way we traditionally ended the Passover meal. Afterward, we left the room and set out for the Mount of Olives where I would prepare myself to make my final entrance into Jerusalem, this time not as a prince, but as a prisoner. I had to resist one last temptation to turn away from my father. It was a strong one. You can't imagine how strong it was.

In what was the most moving and most important speech in history, and perhaps the most overlooked, Jesus the Messiah was ending his life on earth in a blaze of glory.

On the eve of his death, he was able to give those closest to him his joy and his peace. To have any joy or peace six hours before undergoing the most horrible persecution in the history of the world, you must have overcome the world. Only a great man could face his impending death with courage, and at the same time be concerned with alleviating the fears of others. He made incredible promises to his disciples, concerned that they might overlook the tremendous power they now had if they would but ask. Jesus not only dominated life then but does even now. He made it plain that his involvement with his men was to be far from inactive, even though he was "stepping up" to a new role. He would be busy answering their many requests in which his father would take great delight: "And whatsoever ye shall ask in my name, that will I do, that the Father may be glorified in the Son."[88]

The book of Hebrews records that Jesus is our high priest in heaven, never ceasing to make intercessions for his people before God.

It also struck me how Jesus went out as he came into the world, most humbly. While those in the world secretly, and sometimes not so secretly, wish to do greater deeds than their neighbors, Jesus, the Lord of the universe, left his men saying: "Greater things will you do than I have done."

For centuries to come he gave his servants hope as he directly connected their service to him. Not only were they to serve as he did, but also
they were to serve him. As Paul taught, "Whatever you do, do it as unto
Christ and he will reward you accordingly."89 Jesus brought dignity to
every moment of life, whether it was the life of a king or a servant.

After my talk with him, I was utterly convinced that the key to life is in
seeing God and his son for who they really are. Many times since my talk
with Jesus, my thoughts have taken me back to the last supper, and I have
gone over his words to his disciples more times than I can count. Each
time, it's like viewing a masterpiece of art from another angle. I discover
something I had never seen before.

Nowhere else in the Scriptures than at this last meal with his men, as
John recorded it, is there a more intimate conversation. Of all the parts of
Scripture that inspire, this is my favorite. It's how I imagine he will talk to
me in heaven, for it's how he talks to me now.

I have often been struck by how frequently he used the word "I," and
how plain, almost primitive, his phrases were:

> I will be with you only a little longer.[90]
> I am going there to prepare a place for you.[91]
> A new command I give you.[92]
> I am the way and the truth and the life.[93]

They had a familiar, comforting quality to them. The universal "mother
tongue," telling us "everything will be all right."

How much I loved those words, "My peace I give you"[94] and "I am the
vine; you are the branches."[95]

These particular words of the last supper make me realize how desperately
I want to hear God talk to me, to hear him say, "This is how I feel about you,"
and "This is what I will do for you." It's a personal universe to the core.

With each successive reviewing of his last talk before his death, I am
more and more amazed at Jesus' authority and confidence. If indeed he
had to grow in "wisdom and stature, and in favor with God and man,"
then certainly on his last night as "just a man," he was in full bloom:
"Anyone who has seen me has seen the Father."[96]

He had become all of what man was meant to be—the perfect blend between a man of faith and a man of authority. He was the only true man.

At other moments of reflection, I am again impressed by Jesus' brilliance as a teacher. Imagine that you, the son of God, have to tell the world who you are, who they are, who God is, and what the relationship between all of you can be, and to do this in a way that all will understand. These words have stood the test of time, and down through the ages have spoken with the same impact to both the scholar and the unlearned.

The focus of his brilliance was always the father. All the gifts that Jesus gave to his disciples and to us at the last supper were because the father had first given them to him. Only then would he say that the spirit could take what was his and give it to us. Always it was what the father wanted, "I only do what I see the father doing. What I say are not my words but my father's."

His was not a submission based on weakness and dependency, but on love.

Random Reflections from the Master

Here you were—God with no flaws—even in your humanity. Here were your men with all their shortcomings. How did you really feel about your disciples?

I wanted to take them with me to spend eternity together. I could have had anybody in heaven with me, and I chose them. I took care of their failings. They won't have them when they're with me.

The book of Hebrews says that you endured the cross for the joy set before you, despising the shame.[97] At the last supper, at the end when you prayed with your men what many people have called the true "Lord's prayer," you asked your father to restore the glory that was once yours before the world was created. Were you looking forward to heaven?

I really wanted to see my father. I understood how people look forward to heaven, because I did. Heaven for me was receiving and being received by my father in all his glory. All the memories of times past with my father that I had laid aside along with my own glory would be clear to me again.

Why did you choose the symbols of bread and wine?

My father taught me to use those. The first priest mentioned in the Scriptures, Melchizedek, was a prototype of me. In the Scriptures he came from nowhere to be a priest to Abraham. He also was the king (of Salem). Abraham, after his first great military victory, offered his tithes to God through his priest, Melchizedek, then sealed his pledge with bread and wine at Melchizedek's instructions.

In one way, communion is a picture of the basic sustenance we need for life—bread and water. Now, however, the water has been changed to wine, symbolic of the new covenant. You must depend upon and take into your very being my sacrifice. In one sense, there is something desperate in communion, just as I told people that they had to "eat my flesh" and "drink my blood" to gain eternal life. Communion says, "Now you eat what you killed if you want to live." It's a jarring image that conveys the high cost of my love.

You told your men that after you were physically gone, your spirit would be in them, and your teacher would be, too. How did you know that?

It's talked about all through the Old Testament. It says, "I will put my law in their minds and write it on their hearts. I will be their God, and they will be my people."[98] That's clearly saying, "I in him and he in me." Never forget the old saying, "The new is in the old concealed. The old is in the new revealed." The New Testament is in the old and vice versa. There is a unity to Scripture. Once you look, it's obvious.

Notes

1. Isaiah 9:6
2. Isaiah 40:11
3. Isaiah 53:6
4. John 10:11, 14b NIV
5. John 10:16 NIV
6. John 15:5a NASB
7. Isaiah 9:2a NIV
8. John 8:12a NIV
9. Matthew 5:16b
10. Matthew 22:39
11. John 10:30 NASB
12. John 14:24b NIV
13. John 1:1, 14a
14. Matthew 24:35
15. Luke 6:31
16. Luke 4:8a
17. Luke 6:41 NASB
18. Matthew 4:4a
19. Matthew 22:39b
20. John 8:7b
21. Matthew 14:31b NASB
22. Matthew 7:7b
23. John 7:3b–4 TLB
24. John 7:37 NASB
25. see John 8:3–11
26. John 9:5b
27. see John 8:32
28. John 8:39 TLB
29. John 9:21b TLB
30. see John 9:25
31. John 9:34 TLB
32. see John 9:35–38
33. John 10:11, 14, 17–18b TLB

34. John 10:24b TLB
35. John 10:30 TLB
36. John 10:37–38 TLB
37. John 11:27b TLB
38. John 11:32b NIV
39. see John 11:36–38
40. John 11:43b
41. Psalm 118:24a TLB
42. Zechariah 9:9b NIV
43. John 12:13 NIV; cf. Psalm 118:26a
44. John 12:13b NIV
45. see John 1:46
46. see Psalm 24:3–4, 7–9
47. Psalm 24:10
48. see Isaiah 52:14
49. Mark 11:17 NIV
50. Matthew 21:16b NIV
51. Matthew 22:21
52. see Matthew 23
53. John 12:28 TLB
54. John 12:19b TLB
55. see John 13:24–25
56. Psalm 41:9 NIV
57. Matthew 5:9a
58. see Matthew 19:30
59. see Zechariah 11:13
60. John 13:33a NIV
61. John 14:1–2
62. Matthew 26:31–35
63. see John 13:8b–10
64. Matthew 16:16 NIV
65. John 13:33c NIV
66. John 14:2b–3 NIV
67. John 14:2a NIV
68. John 14:9b NIV

69. John 14:6 NIV
70. John 17:22 NIV
71. John 16:6–7, 13a, 15 NIV
72. John 14:13–14 NIV
73. John 15:16b NIV
74. John 15:16a NIV
75. John 14:12 NIV
76. John 14:27 NIV
77. Psalm 45:7 NIV
78. John 16:24b NIV
79. John 15:13 NIV
80. John 15:9a NIV
81. John 17:22 NIV
82. John 14:20 NIV
83. John 13:34 NIV
84. John 15:10 NIV
85. John 15:18–20b NIV
86. Psalm 69:4a–b NIV
87. John 16:33 NIV
88. John 14:13
89. see Colossians 3:23–24
90. John 13:33a NIV
91. John 14:2c NIV
92. John 13:34a NIV
93. John 14:6a NIV
94. John 14:27a NIV
95. John 15:5a NIV
96. John 14:9b NIV
97. see Hebrews 12:2
98. Jeremiah 31:33b NIV

CHAPTER FIVE

CRUCIFIXION AND RESURRECTION

On the Way to the Garden

You were so confident that you would conquer the cross that you could promise your men everything ahead of time. A few days before your persecution, you made a bold proclamation that you had come to drive out the prince of this world. Yet privately, in the garden, just before you were betrayed, there were some anxious moments. Were you frightened of the possibility of denying your mission?

I was ready. I knew my father. I knew his ability to prepare me, and I knew his strength. I was one with him. Of that I was certain. I knew his word was never wrong, and I had all my trust in it. When the end came, I was determined. There was never a better-prepared man on the eve of a battle. Nobody ever before had God's promise that they would win. That's how confident I was. That was one side of me.

As the Scriptures make clear, however, I had a real battle. There was always my humanity, with its emotions and senses. I had to overcome that side again the last day of my life, just as I had every day of my life. After the meal, the challenge I had waited for all my life was imminent, and I knew from experience that I needed to be alone to finish preparing myself. I was to play the role another Old Testament character had played—Job.

If I remember the test correctly, Satan told God that Job, a righteous man, would deny God if he had to suffer. God said that he would not, and allowed Satan to bring all manner of suffering on Job to see if he would "curse God, and die."[1] Job's suffering led him to great doubts, but he never denied God.

He never did, but he was tempted. So, to answer your earlier question, "Was I tempted to deny my mission?" I was tempted in all ways as you are.

God prepared me even for that. My temptation was no surprise intellectually. God had told me to expect it, particularly the doubt. I knew my instructions but I also knew how much was being asked of me, and I knew that Satan would do everything in his power to defeat me, just as he had with Job. I had an idea that, like Job, I would come to a moment when I would have to depend totally on my faith, not on my senses.

That challenge appealed to me. Could I obey and trust my father when everyone and everything around me, including my own senses, was telling me to give up, that it wasn't worth it? In a strange way, I welcomed the battle. I knew the temptation would be great. I didn't know at the time how great it would be. Preparation helps tremendously, but there are certain things you never appreciate until you go through them. I knew there would be a moment when I would be on my own, and God would have to judge me. I figured Satan was hoping to break me at that precise moment.

I've always appreciated the book of Job, but at the same time I've wondered why the suffering went on so long—forty chapters, and on and on about suffering—with Job's having to go through such strange tests. Now I understand why God put all that in the book. It was, perhaps, more for you than for anybody else.

One difference between Job and myself that made it more difficult on me was that Job had no choice. I did.

I never thought of it before, but I can't think of one sane man in history who would choose to die willingly when he could have avoided it, and no one else in history who knew for years before the event happened exactly how he would die, down to the last detail.

My father is an interesting director. The first major human event which affected all of history and which placed a curse on the human race involved a battle with Satan in the garden when Adam and Eve were deceived. Now a second great event was taking place, also in a garden, which was to undo the damage of the first event. As it had begun, it was ending.

So you headed for the Garden of Gethsemane, a familiar place to you and to your men.

My time with my men was over, and I went to the garden to wait alone with my father. Immediately I had the wish to leave. I had taken Peter, James, and John with me, and left them in another part of the garden. I had told them how sorrowful I was, and had asked them to stay awake and to pray for me and for themselves. Waiting for your torturers puts unbelievable pressure on you.

My mind began to play out the next scene over and over again. I was to taste hell for all of them. It was to be hell in its subtle forms, such as regret, and hell in one of its more direct forms, such as physical pain. I knew I would have to suffer at the hands of others and be willing to be totally at their mercy. Not knowing exactly what torture would follow increased my anxiety.

It would be the most vicious abuse in history, for all the forces of evil would be despising me, trying to crush me. I would be judged for all their sins. They would tell me that I was the evil one—not them—just as it will be in hell. I was literally to take on the sins of the world at the moment they were giving them to me, and it would be a heavy load. I was to feel the shame, the curse. I would be tempted to act as they did, particularly since I would be tired and in pain.

I had to hold it inside. I could sense that everything inside me would naturally want to escape from that situation. I had to be on constant guard lest at any minute I would choose the option of escape. Grief became pronounced when I thought of my own father joining them in the abuse. He had to judge me.

He said those words very slowly, and even in the retelling, the grief was palpable.

I can't describe the utter darkness I experienced at that moment. My own father, my great father, would be cursing me. You would have to be as close to him as I was to understand how it hurt. It would be as if you were a child with the kindest, most loving mother in the world, who one day tied you up and then very slowly began to torture you to death. You would look up at her with your trusting eyes, but all you could see would be the fury that she would be taking out on you. Only in this case I knew that God was punishing me to save others who deserved the punishment.

I most dreaded the moment when my father would see me as the most evil sinner in the history of the world. He had to see me that way if I were to take their places. I feared his judgment because I knew how great his power was. His wrath had been stored up for centuries. All of his righteous indignation was to be directed at me. This was going to be more than simply a sadistic crucifixion. God would be laying on me all the sins of the world. All the evil imaginable would be condensed into that one experience that day, and it would be mine. I would feel darkness such as none will ever know outside of hell.

I knew God was right. I saw people just as he did. I would experience hell for them, not only in its physical pain, but also in the complete, utter abandonment by God. Having nothing good, nothing kind, nothing comforting around you, nothing but utter blackness where there is no God and where God lets the whole world turn its fury loose. It was as it will be when hell is a final devastating reality: "Cursed is everyone who hangs on a tree."[2]

I knew his plan, and I was already feeling the shame. In feeling so despised, so hated, I knew the emotional pain would be worse than the physical. During that experience all I would have to tell me I was good would be my faith. As holy as I was, I knew the shame of the crucifixion would take me to the edge of my faith—and even then nothing could totally prepare me for its totality. I was to take on all of the shame that will permeate hell for eternity as everyone blames his neighbor for being there.

I knew how they were going to give me their shame. To convince me I was despised, they planned to beat me unmercifully. They would spit on me, laugh at me, ridicule me, beat me again, and starve me. They would put nails in my hands and feet, strip me naked and abuse me continuously in front of my enemies and my friends and family.

The thing we all dread the most as human beings, at least initially, is physical pain. I faced the most intense period of physical and emotional pain ever experienced. I knew how pain humbles anyone. I knew how it could break you, how worthless it makes you feel, how you can doubt yourself. I was aware how much more vulnerable it makes you to verbal insult of any kind, how you will want to do anything to stop it.

I had my instructions: "Take it, and say nothing; accept the pain, the shame."

Is that what hell will really be like?

Everyone will despise everyone else. Everyone will attempt to destroy his neighbor. Everyone will distrust his neighbor because no one can be trusted. Hell will be ruled by one commandment. Hate your neighbor as you hate yourself.

None of this, "I want to go to hell because that's where all my friends will be"?

There will be no friends in hell, not one. There will be no camaraderie, no laughter, no sunlight. There will be only ever-present darkness, condensed evil. There will be nothing likable about anyone. Hatred, suffering, and violence will abound. People there will understand as never before what it's like to be in an environment where no hope for justice exists. Every waking moment, and there will be no sleep for escaping, will be filled with fear and regret. They will regret that they never took God seriously, regret that they underestimated his presence in the previous world where there was some sense of or hope for justice. They will miss God in ways they never thought possible. Every person's pain will be accentuated because of the constant, inescapable reality that a different choice could have been made. However, it will be too late. God will be gone forever.

Suffering and hell are unpopular subjects with everyone, including my father and me. This is why we went to such great lengths to help the people who choose to avoid it.

Your father's judgment still seems harsh in a way. Your teaching is that all men deserve death, yet to take someone's life who has never killed another seems unfair.

Everyone has been killing for years, both others and themselves. The world is engulfed with hostility—overt or hidden but ever-present, even in the homes of the nicest people in town. Do you think hostility, however subtle, doesn't take its toll? Just because it is a slow death doesn't mean it isn't a type of murder.

Do you think everyone knows this?

Unconsciously they do, in one of those big closets of the mind that most people aren't aware they have.

Such physical punishment as the crucifixion still seems cruel.

Death is cruel, and sin that caused it is unbelievably cruel. When Adam and Eve cruelly destroyed the boundaries of paradise, cruelty and destruction entered the human race. People have been secretly and overtly crucifying themselves and others ever since because they demand justice.

So another definition of sin is cruelty.

Precisely, and no one wants to think they're a real sinner so they deny it, bury it deep in their minds, but it's there. My crucifixion was to put an end to cruelty—to be the final act of cruelty, to be the last crucifixion as I restored man to paradise—for those who would have it. For those who don't want to be freed of their guilt, we designed another world called hell where people are left to their own desires. Heaven was to remain uncontaminated and perfect forever. Doubt not that the deepest human need is for the crucifixion. On the judgment Day, no one will disagree with that need. The real problem, as Paul said, is that "now we see through a glass dimly." People will not own up to their own destructiveness.

Alone in the Garden

Let's get back to the garden. What went through your mind there?

What kept going through my mind were these graphic images of a man dying on the cross. I had witnessed it before, and the Scriptures defined precisely what I would go through. The Scriptures were not fantasy. This was really about to happen, and I had seen men before hung on a cross with their backs raw from the beatings. Every time they had to take a breath, their faces would show the tremendous pain of putting pressure on their feet and hands to draw up to breathe. I had seen the scraping of their raw backs on the wood of the cross, collecting splinters in the wounds each time they breathed. I'd seen them scream. I'd seen the crowds gawking.

My father had made it very clear what he expected of me. I kept trying to think of who I was, "the Lamb of God which taketh away the sin of the world"; of verses that taught me what I was to do, "He was oppressed and He was afflicted, yet He did not open His mouth."[3]

I would tell myself, "You are the sacrificial lamb; that is why you came into the world. It is your mission; you can do it." I had his word that I could. I was the Messiah. I knew my father as no one else did, and as I was about to come face-to-face with his anger, it caused me to ask all over again every question I had ever asked about suffering. They were questions such as, "How can a merciful God allow suffering?" They were questions I had answered years ago.

I suppose you would have a word to say to the intellectuals who have pondered the question for years. Why does evil exist? How could God allow it?

That's a tremendously important question. Everything they ever thought about asking, I asked with great emotion. There was nothing theoretical about it at that point. I had thoughts like, "Why can't he just forgive them? Couldn't it be done another way? Can't I just take a few men and improve the human race that way? I could take my men and slip away. Nothing could stop us. I have the power. If I were cornered I could walk right through them."

Every possibility occurred to me all over again that night, all of which I knew weren't real possibilities. For just a second, every alternative seemed more possible. Thoughts about how unfair this was came to me. I had done nothing—nothing but cure the sick, make the blind see and the lame walk, feed the hungry, and teach people the truth. What I got in return was torture and death. Even among my own followers, one had betrayed me, and the rest were insensitive men who would run when they got scared.

The temptation for me to run was strong. I could feel one of my greatest battles beginning. I wanted to retaliate, but I couldn't. I had to take the evil of the world—death itself in all its forms including my father's judgment—and not give it back. I had to take it to the grave. I knew horrible destruction was mine if I accepted it, and fear engulfed me.

The next day was already so real to me that my sorrow and grief were too much. It was literally killing me. Once, when I opened my eyes, I looked down at the ground where I was kneeling and saw a pool of blood. As I wiped the sweat pouring from my forehead, I realized I was in so much agony that I was sweating drops of blood. I pleaded with him, "Abba! Father! All things are possible for You; remove this cup from Me."[4] I reminded myself that I had been waiting for this moment since before the foundation of the world, but the grief and the suffering wouldn't let up.

I arose to walk around for a minute, and went to where my men were just to be with someone, just to break that agitating, depressing anxiety for a minute. There they were, asleep. All I'd asked them to do was to comfort me by praying for me and for themselves. Peter, James, and John—how much I had loved them. I had spent so much time with these three in particular, pouring my life into theirs. How boldly they had talked. How loyal their words were. I woke them up and asked them if they couldn't please stay awake for just an hour. I wondered aloud if that was asking too much.

You also told them, "Pray that you may not enter into temptation."[5] Were you also thinking of yourself when you said that?

That's what the whole evening was about. They needed to be prepared for what was about to happen, just as I was trying to be. They were in the middle of a battle, and they didn't even know the war was on.

When I went back where I'd been praying in the garden alone, still nothing seemed right. I prayed more earnestly than I'd ever prayed in my life, but the pain only got worse. After about an hour I came back to my disciples the second time for comfort, and when I needed them most, once more they were asleep. At that point, I didn't think I could go on. Wherever I turned, I was surrounded by sin, pain, and apparent indifference.

The image of the cross overwhelmed me. My father's rage kept coming to mind. Death was everywhere, and death always brings its companions of fear, self-pity, retaliation, and cowardice. Death was trying to produce death in me, and it almost succeeded. There seemed to be no escape. I wanted to say, "Thy will be done" and mean it, but it was almost too much hostility to contain.

The grief was literally killing me. I was sweating more blood. I remember wondering what would happen if I died before I had a chance to atone. It occurred to me that it might happen, but I remembered he had promised I would complete my mission. Yet I was having a difficult time hanging on to those words. It kept coming back to me that at the time I needed him most, he would be turning all his fury on me. At that moment, I really thought I was going to die.

Then Psalm 6 came to my mind, and I fell on my face in tears and began praying it.

> Pity me, O Lord, for I am weak. Heal me, for my body is sick, and I am upset and disturbed. My mind is filled with apprehension and with gloom. Oh, restore me soon.
>
> Come, O Lord, and make me well. In your kindness save me. For if I die I cannot give you glory by praising you before my friends.[6]

My deed on the cross was to be a statement of praise for my father. As I hung there, hour after hour, I would, in effect, be saying: "He is righteous." I continued repeating Psalms 6 and 116, which also told me he had been waiting to hear this particular prayer of mine for centuries: "Death stared me in the face—I was frightened and sad. Then I cried, 'Lord, save me!'"[7]

I cried out to my father. "You said you would make me well. You said you would save me. You told me to ask you to visit me. Come, O Lord, and make me well. Lord, I'm asking you, deliver me from this hour of grief. I know you still want me to go through with the cross, father, but deliver me from this hour. Come, O Lord."

Suddenly there was someone with me in a shining white robe standing very calmly before me. My father had sent an angel! He just looked at me for a moment before he said, "Lord, all of heaven exalts you and is praying for you at this moment. Heaven anxiously awaits your return to your glory. The preparation that everyone is making for your return is all encompassing. The music alone that they have written for the celebration of your arrival would make what you're going through almost worth it. We all wait to praise you for your mighty deed, for we know you will do it. You are his only begotten son." I knew this was his angel. There was none of this, "If you are the son of God," I had heard from Satan.

I prayed to my father again and rehearsed everything. The visit from the angel had brought to me some sense of perspective.

Yet nothing could make that image of the man on the cross go away.

He would gasp for breath, with nails in his hands and feet with all his weight on them. Death would come because he couldn't get enough oxygen when his muscles gave out. He would be dying, with a look of horror on his face and panic in his eyes. He would experience total helplessness, with everyone's eyes fixed on his torment. I was going to let them do that to me. That man would be in the hands of an angry God. It was my duty, and my duty to do it his way, without uttering a word: "He was oppressed and He was afflicted, yet He did not open His mouth."[8] Except for those forlorn words of desperate abandonment, "My God, my God, why hast thou forsaken me?"[9]

All my life I had feared those words. I couldn't imagine myself ever experiencing that, and yet I had known Psalm 22 all my life. With my father's help, I could endure the cross. For him to forsake me, however, and not only forsake me but to judge me, was a bitter pain. My father would really judge the people of this world through my torment. There would come a time when he really hated me and what I represented. He had to!

I could already feel the torture of crucifixion and hear him saying to the people of this world as I stood in their place, "For all the physical pain that you have brought to others, first I bring you physical pain. For all the lives you have taken, I take yours, but not before I let them torture you just as you have tortured others. You have stripped them naked and humiliated them. I will shame and humiliate you. You have made their families and friends watch them writhe in pain. I will do the same to your family and friends. It will be a slow death so you can experience it likewise.

For all of you who think you have never hurt anyone, I will show you all the ways you murdered and tortured your fellow man. There are many ways to kill. For all the names you have called others at moments they least needed it, I call you names. For all the mocking you have done, I mock you. For all the times you have hated and encouraged others to hate, I hate you and cause the people to despise you. For all the people you have judged to be despicable, I judge you in the same way to be one of them. For all the times you took advantage of your brother when he was defeated, I trample you even when you are down.

"For the various ways you've made others your victims, manipulated them with your power, insulted them without thinking or caring, I do the same to you. All the helplessness you created I give back to you. For all the pride you demonstrated at others' expense, lording over them, and for all the times you secretly tried to take away your brother's self-esteem while pretending to be righteous, I surround you with 'righteous' men who will strip away your dignity. For all the poor suffering people who surrounded you for whom you had no time, in their name I neglect you in passing. For all the times that your pride made you certain you were right, I surround you with proud people who are certain you are evil."

He was deliberately going to judge them through me. That was what I feared most.

The Scriptures say, "Our God is a consuming fire."[10] You were to feel the heat of his flame.

I knew that, and by my silence I would be saying that I agreed with the punishment. I did. I was not sure I had the strength to withstand it.

The helpless panic was beginning to overwhelm me, and there was no break in the tension. I was praying as earnestly as I could, "Lord, help me to do it, to accept it. Give me the strength. Everything is at stake here. I knew it would be hard, father, but I never knew it would be this unbearable." The pressure didn't decrease, even after I prayed long and intensely, even after the angel had been there. I remember thinking, "Father, I don't know how you would do it, but please get me out of this if it is your will. All things are possible with you; please let this cup pass from me." Drops of blood were still pouring from my head.

I had spent three hours trying to overcome this, but I could not. I was tempted to doubt myself. I wondered, "Would the son of God really be this frightened? Despite the confirmation all along, the Scriptures, and the miracles and the angel having been there, I began to ask myself: "Suppose all of this is phony? Suppose I am just some special kind of being, and a 'god' I don't even know about is running the universe and playing a terrible trick on me." Even after all my preparation, I was beginning to worry about death. I wondered, "Are you being a hypocrite? Would the son of God be this afraid?"

I was struggling not to lose perspective. Then I remembered what Elijah had said on the mount of transfiguration, "You will have doubts that will surprise even you, but remember his promise. You will do it." Recalling Elijah's visit at the transfiguration upheld me. It made me once again know my father and his constant faithfulness in preparing me. He had sent Elijah to warn me of this trial of confusion, which is often Satan's greatest weapon.

Something else Elijah had said moved me: "He has already let us into his kingdom because of what you will do." I thought of his words again, and how powerful his promises were. In the face of all my emotions, he was telling me that he knew I would face them and that despite their power, I would overcome them: I would do it.

He was so utterly benevolent. In all circumstances, even this one, if I looked for him and waited on him, he was there teaching me, strengthening me, guiding me, comforting me, living in me.

I thought of Abraham who trusted God to raise up Isaac even if he had to kill him. I thought of Job: "Though he slay me, yet will I trust in him."[11]

With that strength, I was able to say against all my pain and confusion, "Nevertheless not my will, but thine, be done."[12]

I gave him my life in a new way at that moment because he had given me his life in a new way. With a great struggle, everything was once again all his. I then could finally take in death itself, contain it, and not be destroyed by it nor become destructive because of it. I had overcome the world. I had overcome every evil emotion that destroys souls.

How easily we overlook the third most significant event in human history after the incarnation and resurrection. Suppose Jesus had put that cup down. How different history would have been. There would have been no salvation, no Christian church, no apostles, no martyrs, no New Testament, no Reformation, no Augustine, no Martin Luther, no John Calvin or John Wesley, no lasting democracy, no women's rights, no children's rights, no abolition of slavery, no civil rights, no hope, and no life. There would be only ultimate and final death for everyone.

Final Resolution

So God had to struggle. No matter how many times I read about you in the Garden of Gethsemane, it's hard to believe. But a major resolution took place in that garden.

In some ways the hardest battle had been fought. When I left the garden I knew that I could do it. I had done it in a real way, although the pain had just begun. When I finally resolved my accepting my assignment, I stood up. Not too far away I could see the lynching party coming across the Kidron Valley toward me with torches and lanterns.

For a moment, there was the peace before the storm as I watched the lights across the valley briefly penetrating the darkness. There is something beautiful about a light in the darkness, even more so a moving light. Once again the words came to me: "You are the light of the world." I thought to myself, "My light is so different. I leave no darkness behind."

As they got closer, I could hear the clanging of the soldiers' weapons as they slowly came into view. Suddenly I could make out the face of Judas as the light from their torches intermittently flashed on him. I'll never forget that moment. On the one hand, as Judas showed up right on my father's schedule, it gave me incredible confidence. On the other hand, part of me still couldn't believe Judas could betray me like this. I went to find my men, but they were asleep again. I told them to get up, for the time had come. I walked to meet the mob. I thought again of David's going to meet Goliath. Neither of us had been crowned king when we went into our biggest battles, but we both went in as kings—advancing.

The temple guards brought many soldiers with lanterns, thinking I would run or hide from them in a cave. They thought they would have to search for me. I surprised them.

When the soldiers came near I stepped out from behind some olive trees and said, "Whom are you looking for?"

They told me, "Jesus of Nazareth."

I said, "I am he."

Suddenly, they fell backward to the ground. While they were on the ground, I asked them again, "Whom are you searching for?"

As they stood up, stunned, the leader of the guard said, "Jesus of Nazareth."

I said to them, "I told you I am he—let these others go."

They did. It had been prophesied that none of my men would be lost and that prophecy was fulfilled.[13]

Then Judas, who had obviously brought the guards, walked over to me and with feigned affection said, "Master."

He then embraced me and kissed me on the cheek. I looked at him and asked him, "Judas, how can you do this—betray the Messiah with a kiss?"[14]

The kiss was to indicate to the soldiers my identity.[15]

Judas had wanted to make his encounter with me as brief as possible, but he found himself unable to move. He stood in front of me, unable to break his gaze. The word *friend* confronted him with the guilt he was trying so desperately to hide. He had already gone this far, but now he was uncertain. Judas was in the same situation as Herod when he had a chance to either betray John the Baptist or stand up for him.

Judas had one last chance. He could have freed himself from this situation, but he didn't. Judas made the same choice as Herod, the same choice of every person who decides for hell. The look in his eyes changed from one of hurt to one of determination. When I saw that, I told him, "Go ahead and do what you have come for."[16]

The look I never saw on Judas's face was of repentance or true sorrow, and without that, no one can attain heaven. Although I had known what was going to happen, I'll never forget the feeling I had looking into Judas's eyes for the last time. We had been such close friends.

When they started to take me away, Peter, who had just awakened from a deep sleep, stormed in and pushed two guards aside and quickly seized me. He drew his sword swiftly and cut off the ear of one of the guards. That's like Peter, isn't it? Immediately I cried to him to stop and to sheath his sword. I said to him, "Don't you think that my father would send forty thousand angels here this minute if I asked him?"[17] I picked up the guard's ear, put it back in place, and healed it.

The mob had quieted, and I looked at the host of guards with all their weapons, spears, and swords. I asked them, "Am I some dangerous criminal that you had to come arrest me armed for battle? Why didn't you arrest me when I was in the temple? I was there every day." I reminded them, "Nevertheless, this is happening just as the Scriptures said it would."

You never quit pointing toward the Scriptures.

Anyone who reads the Scriptures will understand the plan and purpose of my death and resurrection.

Why was it judgment, if God is a God of love? Wasn't there another way?

At the very center of God's being is the desire to express love continually. That desire is the driving force behind his personality, and that by necessity includes the protection of love. Perfect love cannot exist without justice. Therefore hell exists to protect love, and it will be an eternal testimony to how great God's love is. You cannot understand the need for hell entirely yet, but God's determination to establish it gives you just a hint of how passionate his love is.

When justice is served, the scales within us and within the world are once again balanced in order to allow love to operate. In this way, justice creates love. Listen to Proverbs:

> Punishment that hurts chases evil from the heart.[18]
> Foolishness is bound in the heart of a child; but the rod of correction shall drive it far from him.[19]

Justice received is meant to work inside you to create a different person. Actually, the desire for love inside each of us demands justice from ourselves because we are made in the image of God. That's why God couldn't "just forgive" us. Forgiveness has its limits. We would not yet be balanced inside and at peace. The lovely, impartial lady of justice inside each one of us would be unsatisfied. We would still continue to punish ourselves as well as our neighbors. Every person cries out, "I can love only myself and others if I am a fair, just person." No one can balance that lady's scales except through me.

Why did God allow evil in the first place?

It was necessary. When the trinity planned the whole creation, we wanted to make men and women totally free to love us or reject us. We realized the high cost of making people free to choose. They would break the bond between us and try to succeed alone. Only one thing could restore the bond between people and God. One thing could create a stronger bond of unsurpassable love—my atonement. An inconceivable price was paid for the relationship at the exact moment the sacrifice was least deserved. From that moment on both people and God could have a more valuable relationship. The gift of life and being God's favorite creature had not forged a strong enough bond. Only the gift of ultimate sacrifice would do it.

That was one of the reasons evil existed. In relation to evil, we could create maximum love. Everything, including evil, ultimately testifies to the goodness of God. Certainly your evil testifies to your greatness. As C. S. Lewis pointed out, the higher up the scale of development one goes, the greater the capacity for evil. A cow can be only so bad, but a man can be really evil, and an angel like Lucifer even more so.

The Trials

I am impressed with your resilience. You had been through an emotionally draining experience in the garden, yet you were bantering with the mob, challenging them. This toughness characterized your trials with the Pharisees, Herod, and Pilate.

As I have told you, no one took my life from me; I gave it. As soon as they took me captive, I knew I would go before the high priest. These were his guards, and on the walk back to Jerusalem across the Kidron Valley from the Mount of Olives I wondered exactly who was going to beat my face in and spit in it as the Scriptures said would happen. As it turned out it was a total team effort on the part of the high priest's lackeys and the Romans.

Later that night and early the next morning, you had many "legal" trials, if I can call them that.

There were seven in all.

The first one was with the Jewish high priest.

It was the "religious court." The first thing the high priest did was to ask me what I'd been teaching my followers. I told him, "What I teach is widely known, for I have preached regularly in the synagogue and temple. I have been heard by all the Jewish leaders, and I teach nothing in private that I haven't said in public."

Then I asked him, "Why are you asking me this question? Ask those who heard me. You have some of them here."

Just then one of the soldiers standing around caught me unexpectedly with a huge fist. The pain had started and the blow knocked me to my knees. He reprimanded me, "Is that the way to answer the high priest?"

I told him, "If I lied, prove it. Should you hit a man for telling the truth?"[20]

The authorities tried to determine some way legally to find me guilty of a capital offense, but they couldn't. Their phony witnesses tried to make up or distort what I had said. For example, when I had told them, "Tear this temple down and in three days I will build it back," referring to my resurrection, one of the witnesses claimed that I said I was going to tear the temple building down. They couldn't get their stories straight, and it was almost amusing how they contradicted each other.

It became apparent that this court had no evidence. The high priest who was also the judge turned to me and asked, "What do you have to say?" I remained silent. I was thinking, "I have nothing to defend, and you know it." I was also amused, saying to myself, "These people are even botching my crucifixion. Am I going to have to bail myself out so I can get myself killed?" Sure enough, after an hour and a half, their witnesses had proven nothing.

Out of desperation the high priest decided to force me to answer the question and said, "Are you the Messiah, the Son of God?" To help him out of his dilemma, gladly I said, "I am." I added, "And one day you will see me at the right hand of God returning to earth."

I wanted to remind the high priest and everyone else that I was giving up my life willingly, but that later I would return, and they would have a chance to see me then, also.

Immediately this religious, pious man stood up and tore his robe. I understood the message. The only time the high priest could tear his beautifully decorated robe, specifically designed by God, was when God's holiness was debased. Later my father would tear the great curtain that separated the Holy of Holies from the people to answer the high priest, but at this time I said nothing.

What did they do with that answer?

The high priest and his associates vehemently attacked me, scream-ing at me. Repeatedly they told me that I was the most evil person who had ever lived. "Liar! Liar! Liar!" They made verbal attacks against my mother again. "No wonder I had turned out to be evil; look how I had begun life."

My anger grew as I had expected it would, but I said nothing, just as I was instructed. All along I kept talking silently to myself. I had planned to recall certain Scriptures at different moments, and Psalms 5 and 7 had been reserved for this moment for centuries. As these men battled my soul with their rage, I battled their rage with the word of God.

> O Lord, hear me praying; listen to my plea, O God my King. . . . Lord, lead me as you promised me you would; otherwise my enemies will conquer me. Tell me clearly what to do, which way to turn.[21]

Psalm 7 in particular described me in the midst of my enemies' plot.

> I am depending on you, O Lord my God, to save me from my persecutors. . . . It would be different, Lord, if I were doing evil things—if I were paying back evil for good. . . . God is my shield; he will defend me.[22]

I was still a man whose feelings could be hurt. I handled the anger that they stirred in me by turning it over to my father. My task was to forgive the people of this world, and that I intended to do, even if these men who were taunting me incessantly might never, under any circumstances, accept my forgiveness. I took great comfort in know-ing my father's justice would prevail with those people, who had no comprehension of my justice.

The Pharisees and the guards and the servants began spitting on me. They blindfolded me, and everyone began to hit me in the face with their fists saying, "Tell us, prophet, who hit you that time?" After the hearing, even the three bailiffs on the way out of the courtroom hit me in the face.

Not having enough evidence, they rushed me to a Roman trial with Pilate, the governor of the Roman territory. These being the Jewish holy days, my people couldn't be responsible for sentencing a person to death during that time. On the way to visit Pilate, I could feel my face starting to swell. Indeed the Scriptures were right. I felt exactly like a lamb being led to a slaughter.

What happened with Pilate?

The trial actually started outside on the steps in front of Pilate's palace. You see, the Jews couldn't go into a Gentile house because it was their religious holiday. What they didn't know was that this was happening to fulfill the prophecy of my crucifixion because only the Romans used crucifixion as a death penalty. For capital offenses, the Jews stoned people to death, but again, not during the Jewish Holy Days. When they brought me as a prisoner before Pilate, he came out on the steps. They told him I had caused much trouble, that I'd been telling the people, on the authority that I was their Messiah, not to pay taxes to the Roman government. Of course, I had not said that.

Pilate looked at me. I was dressed in an old robe, my face swollen from the beatings and stained with spittle. Surrounded by guards, to the onlookers I was a dangerous character. He asked me, "Are you the Messiah—their king?" I told him, "Yes, it is as you say." I wasn't there to plead my case.

The entire Jewish council and the crowd that came with them screamed at me, "Lucifer's child! You set yourself up as God and claim to be the special son! Vanity, vanity, all is vanity! Liar, son of the devil, you'll see God all right, looking up at him as he judges you for blaspheming his holy name!" Some of them started quoting Scripture, "Cut off your enemies, Lord," and similar verses.

I just looked at them and said nothing. Pilate was impressed. I wasn't pleading with him as prisoners typically did. He tried to stop the screaming, but they continued, telling him I'd been causing riots from Galilee, some forty miles away. When Pilate learned that I was a Galilean, he seemed relieved and sent me to Herod, the governor of Galilee who happened to be in Jerusalem at the time.

As they shuttled me to my various places of trial, first to the Sanhedrin, then to Pilate, and now to Herod, I walked across the tremendous bridge high above the Tyropoeon Valley separating the temple from Herod's palace. One last time I looked out over Jerusalem as its rejected king.

As we continued walking over the bridge from the temple, we passed by the place where Satan had miraculously transported me and tempted me to jump down the four hundred fifty feet. When we reached that point, one of the temple guards said, "If you want to get out of this, you had better jump." I knew that voice by now. Satan was urging me again to jump. One more time I thought to myself, "I could do it." I kept walking toward Herod's palace, to the area on which the home of my royal ancestor David had stood. That palace reminded me of my real palace in heaven I would be visiting shortly and of the mansions there I had just promised my followers at the last supper. Once more I could see my father's encouragement, as he made sure that I visited all the palaces on the day of my death to remind me that I was the real king. My kingdom was around the corner. He had always sent me reminders of my royal identity, from the gold box at my birth to burial in a rich man's tomb. I hadn't seen it yet, but I knew that it was as good as done.

I met Herod. His father, Herod the Great, had murdered many Jewish infants trying to kill me. Here was the man who had ordered my cousin, John the Baptist, to be beheaded. When I got to his palace, Herod told me he had heard about me for many months. I'm sure he was particularly interested because his business manager's wife, Cuza, was one of my followers. Herod said he wanted to see a miracle. I said nothing. He then asked me many questions, but I refused to answer. He had said nothing to prevent John's death when he could have. I had nothing to say to him. He and his soldiers then began to mock me. Still I said nothing, but I thought: "You don't know what you're doing. One day I shall come into my kingdom in shining raiment indescribably greater than this." Even in persecution, in the mocking, I was reminded of who I was.

With all his bravado, Herod was frightened of me just as he was of John. Finally, finding nothing wrong with me, he sent me back to Pilate.

Round Two: The Flogging

What happened when you were returned to Pilate?

He had the guards bring me inside his palace to talk to me alone. The Jewish authorities had continued to tell him that I claimed I was king and that I was going to lead a riot. When we were in private, Pilate asked me again if I were the king of the Jews. I asked him if he meant "king" as the Jews meant it or as the Romans. He snapped at me, "Am I a Jew? Your own people and their chief priests brought you here. Why? What have you done?"[23]

I told him, "My kingdom is not of this world. If it were, my men would be fighting for me. But my kingdom is in another place."

Pilate asked me again, "You are a king, then?" I said, "I was born to be a king, and for that reason I came to bring truth to the world. All who love the truth are my followers."

He became sarcastic and said, "What is truth?"[24]

I didn't reply. He looked at me for a moment and returned outside.

Thinking of a way to escape the situation, he told my accusers that neither he nor Herod found me guilty of inciting riots against Rome and that I had done nothing warranting punishment. In an attempt to appease their wish to condemn me, he let them know that he considered me a prisoner. He suggested to the crowd of Jews that, since it was his custom to free one Jewish prisoner every year at Passover, he could free me, the "king of the Jews."

As Pilate was holding court and presenting this offer to the crowd, a messenger came with a message from Pilate's wife. Pilate became irritated and rumbled, "What does she want with me at a time like this?" The messenger said, "Sir, she is very worried."

He looked at me as soon as he read the message. His eyes told me that it had to do with me, and that whatever his wife said frightened him as well. Now, more than ever, it was obvious that he didn't want to go through with this. Later I learned that his wife had sent a message telling him to have nothing to do with me, that I was an innocent man and that the night before she had a vivid nightmare about me.

By now the Pharisees had the crowd in a frenzy, and, in response to Pilate's offer of releasing a prisoner, they screamed, "We want Barabbas—give us Barabbas." Barabbas was a convicted murderer who had led riots, and they were calling for him to be freed instead of me. How fickle they were!

Emotionally, I was caught off-guard, and suddenly I was almost ill as I thought, "That sadistic mob: they want Barabbas." I really hadn't been expecting the viciousness of the crowd at that time. I knew the Jewish priests would involve the Romans, but it now seemed as if the entire city was against me.

It was about eight o'clock in the morning. I'd been up all night. I hadn't eaten or drunk anything since supper the night before, and my face was throbbing. My father had prepared me for fickle crowds. Still, each rejection was fresh pain. The thought went through my mind, "Barabbas, the murderer, goes free, and the free man becomes the murderer. Now, more than ever, I can see who I'm dying for, whose place I'm taking. I'm dying for Barabbases of the world." As I told you, my father thought of everything.

When Pilate saw that he couldn't stand up to the crowd, he had another idea. He ordered the soldiers to flog me. As the Roman soldiers were taking me down to the stake in front of the Praetorium, the governor's palace, to be flogged, my mind immediately went to the Scriptures and to my role in Isaiah.

I gave My back to those who strike Me.[25]
He was wounded for our transgressions, he was bruised for our iniquities: the chastisement of our peace was upon him; and with his stripes we are healed.[26]

I kept telling myself, "The Lord is my strength; through him I shall triumph valiantly." I was preparing myself. All during my trials and tribulation that day I would find myself right in the middle of either Isaiah or Psalm 22, the two most extensive prophecies about the crucifixion. Often I could see what part of my script was coming next such as the unmerciful lashing I was about to suffer. It didn't make the pain any less but it strengthened my courage and confidence. I had won the first round when the Jews had beaten me at the first trial early that morning. Now would come the infamous Roman flogging, which was feared throughout the Empire.

They stripped off all my clothes and tied my hands to a half pillar so that my back, my buttocks, and my legs were fully exposed.

Then it started. The whip was a "cat-of-nine-tails" with lashes of thick leather and little iron balls on the end that dug into flesh and ripped it out with each blow.

The first lash came, and the pain was excruciating. By the third lash my entire back was on fire. I had never experienced pain like that. I never knew I had so many nerves. Before the pain could subside more than a second, the next blow came, worse than the one before. Every time he hit me—thirty-nine times in all—I didn't see how the pain could get any worse. But with each succeeding lash, the pain became more searing. Finally it reached a point that between lashes there was no subsiding of the pain whatsoever.

As I began to bleed, my blood stung the raw flesh. My back and legs were so sensitive by now that even the air current that came just before each blow of the whip hurt. Between blows I tried to think of my father's words to me: "Yea, though I walk through the valley of the shadow of death, I will fear no evil: for thou art with me."[27]

Then another blow would come, taking me to a new depth of pain. I tried to concentrate. "Though he slay me, yet will I trust in him."[28] "Weeping may endure for a night, but joy cometh in the morning."[29]

Several times I almost cried out, but I was determined not to. My father had promised me that I wouldn't: "He was oppressed, and he was afflicted, yet he opened not his mouth: he is brought as a lamb to the slaughter, and as a sheep before her shearers is dumb, so he openeth not his mouth."[30]

With every blow, I clung to the power of those words as the torturer ripped off more of my back. Most prisoners by this time would be screaming in agony, some reaching the point of hysteria, begging the man to stop. Although obviously I was in pain, I "opened not my mouth."

The man with the whip noticed my silence. You can imagine the type of soldier who would volunteer for the job. He began to mock me, "So we've got a tough one here." The contest was on. He was determined to make me beg for mercy. He was accustomed to having prisoners beg him for help, and I was determined that I would not. I begged my father all the way, but not him. Between blows, I talked to myself. I could think only for brief moments, and much of the time I just held onto the words, "He openeth not his mouth"—lash—"He openeth not his mouth." Other times I would think, "By his wounds we are healed"—lash—"by his wounds we are healed"—lash—"by his wounds we are healed"—lash. Or, "The chastisement of our peace was upon him"[31]—lash. "This one is for Matthew's peace"—lash. "This one is for Thomas's peace"—lash.

The soldier began to whip me more and more forcefully until he had lashed me with all his might, cursing me every time. "See how you like that one, teacher"—lash—"Did you know this would happen, prophet?"—lash. Still I hadn't said a thing.

I had taken over twenty-five lashes now in silence, and he was going to break me. Very quickly he went over and picked up a bucket of salt water and threw it on my raw back. It was like being on fire, and then all of a sudden the fire becoming twice as hot. He picked up the whip again, and the lashes continued. I thought I would explode.

All through this, I kept clinging to God so that I wouldn't give in. "I will praise you, Lord, for you have saved me from my enemies"—lash. "You refuse to let them triumph over me"[32]—lash. "Lord, I trust in you alone. Don't let my enemies defeat me"—lash. "You are my Rock and my fortress . . ."—lash. "Pull me from the trap my enemies have set for me"—lash. "You alone are strong enough"[33]—lash.

Toward the end of my flogging the man with the whip became very quiet, but started hitting me faster with less time for recovery between lashes. It was his last trick. Despite the pain, I could hold on to my father's words, though I thought I was going to faint: "They that wait upon the Lord"—lash—"shall renew their strength"—lash. "They shall mount up with wings like eagles"—lash. "They shall run and not be weary"—lash. "They shall walk and not faint."[34]

Finally it was over. I had won the second round. I had not uttered a word.

Every time another prophesy of pain was fulfilled, I would think to myself, "There's that one." Throughout my mission I kept telling myself, "Remember who you are—the lamb. 'The lamb of God that takes away the sins of the world'" as John the Baptist had told me in those magnificent words he had spoken in his deep resonant voice at my baptism. Many times during my suffering, remembering my role as the Passover lamb would take me back to that unforgettable baptism my father had made so special. John's words echoed in my mind— followed by the greatest words that had ever been spoken to me when I heard my own father's voice for the very first time "This is my beloved son in whom I am well pleased." He had spoken to me then on the heels of my solemn vow to accept my baptism, my death. Now that the real baptism was here, I thought back to my promise and to his instructions. Most of all, those words "my beloved son" sustained me. I had worked to please my father, and I never forgot how magnificent it was to hear him tell me I was exactly the kind of son he wanted. I never wanted to disappoint such a loving father. Over and over I had to remind myself, "You're the lamb that pleases him." Sometimes all I could think was "The lamb—The lamb."

At other moments in my journey of pain that day "lamb" would cause me to picture my baptism by John, and I would be ever so briefly comforted in an entirely new way, as though it had just happened. My father remained with me.

Round Three: The Mocking

The third round started very quickly. They cut me loose, and I fell in a bloody heap and lay there for a minute. Then they lifted me and dressed me in a purple robe, rubbing it into the weeping, bleeding wounds on my back to make sure the robe stuck and pulled every time I moved. The soldiers took me to a bigger room. One of them came up to me with a crown of thorns and jammed it down on my head until the thorns lacerated my scalp and forehead. Blood was running into my eyes, but I could not wipe the blood away because my hands were tied behind me.

Next they blindfolded me and began playing the game called "Circle of Eight." Eight Roman soldiers surrounded me, and as they walked around me, one of them would hit me in the face. Then they would take the blindfold off while each one continued to walk around me, and I was supposed to guess which one had hit me. If I didn't get it right, which of course no one ever did, they blindfolded me for another round. How they relished the cruel game.

The entire time they ridiculed me, particularly the man with the whip, who made sure that he was in the circle. "Tell us who hit you, prophet! Are you helpless, oh, great one? Where is your mighty father?" I was prepared not to retaliate, but to submit to this for the world's sake. The pain was almost overwhelming. I didn't know how much longer I could go on. My head ached, my face and the thorns in my scalp. My back was one great raw nerve. Now the taunting.

I didn't have long to think clearly because I was always between blows. As soon as my head stopped spinning from the last one, the blindfold would be off, and they would be walking around me very fast; screaming at me, taunting me, spitting on me, pulling my beard. I was losing concentration with all this movement and pain. It was so difficult to concentrate on what I was doing that I was tempted to strike out at them. I remember at one point, with my head still reeling, thinking that they had just broken my jaw. I had his promise that no bones would be broken, though. I persevered.

When they removed the blindfold, the man with the whip was standing there, shaking his fist in my face and screaming, "You think your father is greater than this?" I remember for just a second wanting to break my hands loose, and I could have done it anytime, and grab his fist, smash it in his face and then ask the others if they had any questions about my father.

I quickly put those thoughts out of my mind by thinking about who I was and what I was doing. I would tell myself, "You are the lamb of God that taketh away the sins of the world. Take it. Take it." Or, "He was wounded for our transgressions, he was bruised for our iniquities. It will be over soon. Do it for them."

I continually reminded myself, "not much longer. This time tomorrow it will be finished. This is only one day. I'm going to see the father." Then another blow, and I would have to search once more for his words. Of all my father's words that I recalled, I clung to those in the middle of chapter 50 of Isaiah. I knew them well because that was one way I had prepared myself for this moment.

> I gave My back to those who strike Me, and My cheeks to those who pluck out the beard; I did not cover My face from humiliation and spitting.... Therefore, I have set My face like flint, and I know that I will not be ashamed.[35]

I fixed my mind on those words, lived them out, and won the third round, even though I was wobbling like a drunkard. *(He started laughing here.)* I was the most beat-up champion you ever saw.

They brought me back to Pilate one more time, and I was a sight to see. Pilate immediately brought me out to the crowd that was still gathered and shouted to them, "Behold the man!"[36] I was barely recognizable. My face had swollen grotesquely, and one eye was almost shut.

Pilate was obviously saying to them, "Isn't this enough?" I'll never forget standing there above the crowd on that "stage," beaten and bleeding, with my body in infinite pain, and hearing them answer louder than ever: "Kill him! Kill him! Kill him!"

You can prepare for pain. Thank God for that, but it still hurt. As they were chanting, one man called out above the crowd, "He calls himself the son of God." You should have seen Pilate's eyes. He took me back inside and sat down on his chair as I stood there in front of him completely exhausted. I hadn't sat down in over twelve hours except for the moment I collapsed after they flogged me.

He asked me, "Where did you come from?" I didn't answer him, and he became furious. "Don't you realize I have the power to kill you or release you?" I told him, "You have no power but what my father gave you, but those who brought me to you have the greater sin."[37]

When I said that, letting him know who was in control, Pilate became even more agitated and tried to release me again. He reminded the Jewish leaders and the crowd that neither he nor Herod had found any wrongdoing on my part. The crowd kept screaming, "Crucify him! Crucify him!" He argued with them, "Why, what has he done?" Again from the mob came the reply: "Crucify him! Crucify him!"

The Pharisees standing there told Pilate that any rebel who claimed to be king was no friend of Caesar's. Pilate could see that the Pharisees were manipulating the crowd and manipulating him, but he was also afraid of a riot. In the end, immediate fear won out over eternal fear. Finally, Pilate had them bring him a bowl of water. Before the thousands of people, he symbolically washed his hands of the matter and said, "His blood be upon you." The out-of-control mob shouted back, "And upon our children!"[38]

Then Pilate turned me over to his soldiers to be crucified. I went in total justification before the Law. I had won another round.

The Road to the Cross

Any joy over that victory was short-lived. The soldiers immediately took me into the armory and called out the troops. The ones who wouldn't join in before now did so freely, because they were sure I was going to die. This time they put a scarlet robe on me and made a new crown for me from longer thorns and jammed it further down on my head. They then placed a stick in my right hand to symbolize a scepter, and all kneeled down and began to mock me, "We praise you, oh, king." Several of them came up and spat in my face. The saliva mixed with blood ran down my forehead, into my eyes.

They meant that to be a bad experience, but my father used it momentarily for good. As I looked upon them while they were kneeling on the ground and looked at the scarlet robe they had placed on me which was so different from the white robe that was mine, I thought of the verse, "Though your sins be scarlet, they shall be white as snow."[39] I was wearing the sin of the world, but the message from my father was clear even in their mocking. "You are a king, but not of this world."

The soldiers took my "scepter" from my hand and on the way out began to mock me and beat me over the head. Such bravado against the helpless!

Then you got your cross?

It was happening just as my father said it would. They had flogged me, spit on me, and pulled my beard. I knew what was coming next. My cross. It's strange what comforts you at a time like this. I took comfort knowing that they wouldn't break any of my bones and that I was to have a sign on that cross.

One of the most difficult things about the crucifixion was the constant temptation to rid myself of pain. I could have stopped it at any moment. I was prepared to submit for the world's sake, prepared not to retaliate. The pain, however, demanded relief. My head was bursting, and every step jammed the thorns further into my scalp. Several of my teeth were loose. My face was bleeding, also my back, which felt like hot coals. I grew weaker and weaker as the trials progressed. I still hadn't had a drink of water since supper, and now from the bleeding I reached a point where physically I expected to collapse. That's when I got my cross. That's usually when we get it. Paul wrote that the Lord never lays on us more than we can bear.[40] Sometimes you wonder if his scale and yours aren't vastly different. This was one of those times.

They gave me my cross to carry out of the city and up the big hill that now seemed like Mount Everest. It was unbelievably heavy. I had to drag it behind me, pulling it down the road on my shoulder. It helped that I had been a carpenter and knew some ways of dragging a big load, but still I had to use my back and my shoulders that were bleeding from the flogging. My robe stuck to the wounds, and now the cross rubbed against them. I couldn't take a step without making the pain worse.

I remember another thought that passed through my mind when I got my cross. "I have worked with wood all of my life, and here is the one piece I've been waiting for." Even though I had never seen it until that moment, I had been married to that cross my whole life—"bone of my bone, flesh of my flesh."

I used to think about the cross as I was working with wood. The wood was a symbol of me; once alive, now dead. I would think, "But one day you're going to live again." At the same time, wood, though dead, was incredibly strong—it gave strength in many ways to virtually every household, just as my being dead would do. As I went up the hill with my cross I couldn't think of anything for very long, but I tried to battle the pain all the way with my father's words.

The Lord is the strength of my life; of whom shall I be afraid?[41]
He is my defense; I shall not be moved.[42]
Weeping may endure for a night, but joy cometh in the morning.[43]

I was determined to hold on to those words, and also determined not to cry out: "He was oppressed, and he was afflicted, yet he opened not his mouth."[44] I kept telling myself, "This is why you came into the world. Think about tomorrow. Think about tomorrow and the father. You will see the father."

As the cross bore down on my back, getting heavier and heavier, I kept thinking of Isaiah's words, "He bare the sin of many, and made intercession for the transgressors."[45] I went over and over those words, trying to get my mind to focus on nothing but them: "Surely he hath borne our griefs, and carried our sorrows."[46]

I would think of that cross as carrying their sorrows. All the work I had spent in training my mind was helping despite the pain.

I would then take another step. I would stumble. The pain would so overwhelm me that I would think of nothing else. Concentration became more and more difficult. I kept fighting. Water would have made it easier. All the way up the hill, I kept holding on to why I was doing this, "I was bruised for Peter's iniquity, I was wounded for John's transgressions, my mother's chastisement was upon me, by my stripes my father Joseph was healed. Death will cease to exist."

I kept trying to think of all of the people I loved, for whom I was doing this. My disciples—this was for them. It was for my brothers and sisters. How innocent they seemed at first, and yet how they had gone their own way. This was for them.

To keep my mind focused I would vary my thoughts, and sometimes I would think of my past glories on earth. I would dwell on my discovery at twelve, the gold box, my baptism, the transfiguration, and my triumphal entry into Jerusalem. I would think too of my future glory. My mother kept coming to mind. I thought of all she had done for me, and all she had been through for me. All would live in peace because of me. Then I would stumble again, and the jolt would send another round of pain through my body. The thorns would dig deeper. My swollen head would throb. The cross would feel like a mountain of sandpaper on my raw back. It sometimes took me a minute to bring my mind back to my thoughts. "What was it? Peace . . . prince . . . prince of peace . . . ?" "Blessed are the peacemakers: for they shall be called the children of God."[47]

With every step pain would battle me, make me focus on my body. I would think how much this was really costing. If only they knew. There were other dark thoughts, "The worst hasn't even begun yet. There will be bones out of joint, hands and feet pierced. I will gasp for breath." Those thoughts were almost as bad as the physical pain. The task seemed impossible. I kept telling myself, "Take one step at a time. You made it this far. Soon it will be over. He is my strength."

I suffered the stares. The road up the hill was packed with people. I felt as if all the eyes of the world were on me, watching me stumble and writhe in pain, but nobody would look me in the face. Every time I looked up they were horrified and shook their heads, repulsed. I could hear the comments when they saw my face. Sometimes it was a child crying, "Look at his face!" Or again it would be a woman crying out, "Oh, no!" when she saw me. At times, just that one word, "Oh," came out uncontrollably when a person first saw me. My face was disfigured by now. It was so distorted that I didn't look like a human being, but like a hideous monster. I was so offensive that very few could bear to look at me for longer than a second.

Always there would be someone saying, "Look, look at his face." Of course, the Pharisees and "their boys" were just ahead, making sure that the crowd was at its ruthless best. It sounded like a sporting event all the way up the hill.

I was the enemy. The crowd particularly hated me, too, because I was a picture of their own vulnerability. I portrayed their own deaths as well as their consciences. They were looking in a mirror, even though they weren't aware of it. The reflections enraged them. I felt their jeers, and experienced their closing in on me as if I were a dying animal. The memories of ridicule that had almost overwhelmed me when I was a child in Nazareth came back. I was a spectacle.

(He paused here for a long time.)

Shame is hard to take. It must have been unbelievably difficult.

Shame is one of the worst feelings in the world. That was as difficult as the physical pain, but he had told me that it would be like this. I couldn't have made it unprepared. Listen to Psalm 109, "My knees are weak from fasting, and my flesh has grown lean, without fatness. I also have become a reproach to them; when they see me, they wag their head."[48]

Isaiah said about me, "He is despised and rejected of men; a man of sorrows, and acquainted with grief: and we hid as it were our faces from him; he was despised, and we esteemed him not."[49]

My father told me again through Isaiah that I would be disfigured: "His appearance was so disfigured beyond that of any man and his form marred beyond human likeness."[50]

The crowd had been described in Psalm 69: "Those who hate me without a cause are more than the hairs of my head."[51] I felt the eyes, the backs turned to me, the ridicule, the horror on their faces, and the women weeping.

You still had some fight left in you at this point when you talked to the women, and you told them, "Daughters of Jerusalem, weep not for me, but weep for yourselves, and for your children. For, behold, the days are coming, in which they shall say, Blessed are the barren. . . . Then they shall begin to say to the mountains, Fall on us, and to the hills, Cover us."[52]

Destruction was on the way to them. As much as I could when I was going through that horrible experience of being gawked at, I focused my mind on my future glory. I thought about another time my face had been changed—at the transfiguration. That's who I really was.

Carrying such tremendous pain your mind works in snatches, and I could get brief glimpses of the future. I remember thinking about the wonder in my disciples' eyes on the mountain. I kept telling myself it wouldn't be long until I received that again.

The crowd and the cross kept distracting my attention. Five days ago, crowds had cheered me, and perhaps some of the same people now ridiculed me or wouldn't look at me. The contrast made the ridicule stronger, as we went out the same gate I had come through five days before. That's where all the people had gathered on what is now known as Palm Sunday shouting with one voice, his voice, "Hosanna, Hosanna." I focused on that day as long as I could. The glory that had lifted me up would be mine again soon. I would return through those gates one day.

There's still a gate waiting for you. *

Yes, it will be until I return. I fought to look at that crowd through the screen of the future, the screen of the father, the screen of the past.

---

* The East Gate to the city of Jerusalem has been closed for years. The prophet Zechariah predicted that it would remain closed until Christ walks through it when he returns. Several people have attempted to destroy the gate and that prophecy, but their efforts have failed. The gate still stands.

I thought often of my baptism. I could still hear those words beyond belief, "This is my beloved son." My beloved son. I thought how the voices of the angels after the temptation were so different from those around me now. Then my mind would grasp for the transfiguration again—for the robe so bright, for Moses and Elijah and the voice. I recalled the other walk home with my parents from Passover at age twelve, the time "I met the Magi" and received that gold box.

I had a treasure full of memories. My father had made sure of that. Yet they were nothing compared to my forthcoming glory. I already had a glimpse of it, but I couldn't see any of those memories for very long.

Final Steps

The further I went, the heavier the cross became and the more difficult it became even to think. Sometimes all I could do was react. At several of those moments, I would just pray, almost beg, for a friendly face who would look at me. Usually I would find one. There would be someone who would hold my gaze even though it was obviously painful for them, or someone who would say simply, "Lord." Once I looked at a lady who said everything through the tears of compassion rolling down her cheeks. She made no effort to wipe them away. She just looked at me with love. I knew that I would meet some in that crowd in heaven.

Then I would stumble again or the pain would grab me or the soldiers would push me or someone would insult me. My legs were weak, and my rational senses were going. Reflexively I was hanging on to my father's words to me, "With his stripes we are healed"[53] and "The Lamb of God that taketh away the sin of the world."[54]

I would cling to a brief thought: "I am the Lamb of God—the Lamb of God." When I would reach those points, the few words that meant the most to me were, "My beloved son." I was hoping that some of their reality could penetrate the fog of the moment. "Remember who you are; remember you can do it." If my father hadn't prepared me, I couldn't have done it.

In a way he had to leave me, but in another way his words were there moment by moment. At the same time he saw me as the most despicable person in history and judged me, he also saw me as performing the greatest deed in history. Imagine the mystery of how God could react so passionately both ways at the same time. I kept telling myself, "Don't take it personally. This is your job. That's why you're on this planet." Every time I would think I couldn't take it, I took it.

By now I was staggering with every step. I didn't have enough strength even to lift my head occasionally. My eyes were almost closed from the swelling. It seemed as though I had been walking under that load forever. I was so thirsty.

Finally, at one point my strength totally gave way, and I fell to the ground face down with the cross pinning me to the earth, knocking the breath out of me. I had dirt in my mouth, dirt covering my hair and my wounds. I was breathing dust into my mouth and nose, and I couldn't get up. Not even when one of the soldiers kicked me and hit me with his whip could I rise. I wanted to die right there, and at the same time I was afraid that I might.

The first thing I heard when I came to my senses was a man with the most evil laugh I've ever heard sarcastically saying, "So, you're going to raise yourself from the dead, and you can't even get off the ground." He laughed that laugh again and said, "Your father is so powerful." What a temptation it was. I wanted to use my power, to show him my father's strength. All I had to do was say the word, and I would be off that ground, and that man would be dead. But I didn't retaliate. While on the ground a verse from Isaiah came to me, "I the Lord thy God will hold thy right hand, saying unto thee, Fear not; I will help thee."[55]

God gave me different passages of Scripture at different times. I had prepared my mind for that journey, and my mind, living on his words, didn't let me down. I didn't give in to the scorner. I accepted my helplessness. I had won another round.

One of the soldiers conscripted a man named Simon of Cyrene to help me carry my cross. From that moment, one of my burdens was gone. My cross was no longer heavy. Simon scarcely said a word to me.

He could have let me bear most of the weight of the cross, but he didn't. He took it from me. That encouraged me. At that moment Simon was a symbol of my father.

By the time we got to the top of the hill, to the place they called Golgotha, I had almost reached the point at which I had been in pain so long that I was beginning to feel numb. They ripped off my robe that had been stuck to my back, and renewed the pain as if searing me with a flame. They cut off my undergarments, and I was totally nude.

I could see there were three crosses. The vertical parts of the crosses were already up, and they took the crossbar I had been carrying on my back and placed it behind me on the ground to nail both my wrists to the crossbar before lifting me up and nailing my feet to the center cross. While I was still on the ground some Roman soldiers continued the mocking, "Hey, king of the Jews" and then stuck a sign in my face which read "Jesus of Nazareth, King of the Jews" and was written in Greek, Hebrew, and Latin. They told me, "See what's going over your unfortunate head. Now the Jews can see their real king," as they erupted into further laughter. There it was, "King of the Jews," for all the world to see. I knew that sign was from my father, as if he were telling me, "Remember you are the king. I, the Lord God, am putting a sign on this cross that no one will ever take down." Even though my father had to leave me in a real way to judge me, he made sure I was comforted.

When the Pharisees saw the sign they were enraged and demanded that Pilate change the sign to read, "He says he's the King of the Jews." For once Pilate stood up like a man and said that the sign should stay just the way it was—but I knew their request would fall on deaf ears.

The Hanging

Two soldiers held my feet and my arms while two others prepared to hammer iron spikes through my wrists and my feet. "Finally," I thought, "here comes Psalm 22 again—that vivid picture of me on the cross. I knew this was coming too. I knew it. Go ahead. You just think you're in charge, but I'm the lamb." Then came the blows I had been waiting on.

The pain was incredible. I couldn't believe how sensitive my hands and feet were. I became weaker and then finally nauseous. Sweat broke out on my forehead because of the pain. That was nothing compared to the moment when they stood the cross upright and all my body weight rested solely on the nails in my hands and feet. It was as if thousands of volts of electricity were surging through me, pain. I had to shift my weight up and down to get breath. With every breath, there was a fresh dose of pain.

Eventually the overwhelming pain subsided just enough to allow me to look around, and I could see that the Romans were crucifying two other men with me. Just like my father had said would happen— "He was counted as a sinner"—another prophecy out of chapter 53 of Isaiah was fulfilled.[56] Inside I was shouting, "My father is still in charge" and outside I was preaching with my actions.

As I looked down on the two men in agony, I watched them drive the nails in the wrists of the man to my left, and heard him scream as they put him up on the cross. I hadn't screamed because I had my instructions not to, again out of Isaiah 53, "He was oppressed and He was afflicted, yet He did not open His mouth; like a lamb that is led to the slaughter, and like a sheep that is silent before its shearers, so He did not open His mouth."[57] With his help, I hadn't. As I looked down on what they were doing to this man, I could see from another angle just how cruel the Romans were and just how much suffering there was in the world in general. I kept telling myself, "This is why I'm doing this so that people won't have to suffer anymore—so they can quit punishing their neighbor and equally so themselves. I am doing this so that suffering will be finished. It's not going to be the same."

The man on my left was lifted up on his cross, and after a few minutes, between breaths, he started muttering to himself, cursing his persecutors below. The second man followed him up on my right, screaming in pain too, but not as belligerent.

The crowd stared at my nakedness and agony. As they did, I thought of the snake Moses held up for everyone to look at so they would be healed: "But I, when I am lifted up from the earth, will draw all men to myself."[58]

With each wave of pain I would lose my train of thought. It was getting more difficult to concentrate on anything but the pain and ridicule. Between breaths I tried to keep my thoughts brief so that I could remember where I was. And I was so thirsty.

The temptation to come down from the cross was so strong at first. I kept repeating my father's words to me,

> He is my defense; I shall not be moved.[59]
> With his stripes we are healed.[60]
> The Lord is my light and my salvation.[61]

The pain was all encompassing, and I was doing everything I could to combat it. I tried thinking of the future: "Thy throne, O God, is for ever and ever."[62]

Pain makes the hearing more sensitive to noise, and I could distinctly hear even the priests calling me names, daring me to come down, screaming blasphemies at me. To counteract them, I kept going back to the words at my baptism, "This is my beloved son, in whom I am well pleased"—my beloved son. Those were the words I had lived on in the wilderness for forty days. Those words were so powerful that I never failed to remember them. I recalled all the beautiful names that my father had called me in the first part of Isaiah, and I repeated those names over and over to myself.

> For unto us a child is born, unto us a son is given: and the government shall be upon his shoulder: and his name shall be called Wonderful, Counselor, The mighty God, The everlasting Father, The Prince of Peace.[63]

I would get through those words and then start again. Other times I would quote to myself complete psalms from memory, one after the other. I did anything I could to combat the pain. I had won another round.

You were prepared.

I became more aware of what a spectacle I was. This got worse later. I had never been nude in front of a crowd. As I looked down at them, particularly at the people I knew, I was shamefully embarrassed. When I wasn't completely overwhelmed by the physical pain, I was painfully self-conscious.

I saw my mother with my aunt on one side of her and my disciple John on the other. Next to them was John's mother and Mary Magdalene, out of whom I had cast seven demons. I looked at each one of their faces and began to tell myself, "This is part of why you're doing it; for them, for the people you love." My mind was fading in and out, and on one occasion for several minutes all I could do to comfort myself was just to look at those five people who loved me and for whom I was doing this.

The Pharisees and others continued to berate me. I felt like a criminal. Here I was surrounded by two criminals, hanging on a cross like a guilty man, being ridiculed by a mob. It's impossible not to feel it when people degrade you, even if it isn't true. Once I thought of other people who had treated John the Baptist unjustly, and of Joseph who was betrayed by his brothers, unjustly accused by his boss's wife, and thrown in jail to rot. Isaiah was sawn in two for telling the truth. David was chased by Saul for years and was continually accused of being a traitor.

At the moment when I was thinking about those heroes, I looked down and could see a group of Roman soldiers laughing, gambling among themselves for my robe. Once more I was looking right at Psalm 22, which had predicted precisely this moment, "They divide my garments among them, and for my clothing they cast lots."[64] Once more I knew my father was with me still. I thought of how Joseph lost his own cloak, and I went over David's words in various psalms. These two men had suffered when they were young and were a source of strength. Joseph and David were with me on that cross. They had comforted me all my life.

The scoffers continued. These people were telling me in hundreds

of ways, "You are evil. You are vicious. You are deceitful. You are egotistical. You are blasphemous, violent, and criminal for misleading the
people." It was impossible not to feel the degradation when, hour after hour, people were placing all their evil on me. Truly I became sin
for the world, and it was terrible. Everything about sin was offensive
to me. I hated all the evil that they were giving me.

Psalm 69 had told me I would feel like this:

> I am come into deep waters, where the floods overflow me. I
> am weary of my crying: my throat is dried: . . . They that hate
> me without a cause are more than the hairs of mine head: . . .
> Because for thy sake I have borne reproach; shame hath cov-
> ered my face.[65]

Just as Psalm 69 said, I was up here on the cross taking all this evil
for one reason—because I loved my father and his truth, and I had
told the truth to the people: "For the zeal of thine house hath eaten
me up; and the reproaches of them that reproached thee are fallen
upon me."[66]

I was up here because of zeal for my father, because of loving God.
Resentment was trying to creep into my mind, but I kept looking at
my friends and going over my father's words. I would tell myself, "You
have to get through this for them or they are lost." I would think, "Give
me your evil. Give it to me. I've got to take it away." I had to prove that
good and love were stronger than evil. I had to show that love did not
retaliate. I absorbed evil, as Isaiah had prophesied, "He will swallow
up death forever. The Lord God will wipe away all tears and take away
forever all insults and mockery against his land and people."[67]

I was able to see that evil is absolutely blind, and I am the world's
only hope. Only I could swallow death and live. I kept telling myself,
"This is your glory. This is why you came into the world. You are the
lamb."

I also thought of all the Old Testament people I loved—Adam,
Moses, Abraham, Jacob, Joseph, Samson, Ruth, Esther, David, Samuel.
Daniel, Solomon, Jeremiah, and Isaiah. I thought of others who would

come, people such as Paul, Barnabas, Luke the physician, Timothy, Augustine, and many others.

None of these could be reconciled to my father without me. All had that terrible evil disease—sin. I knew that any one of them under the right circumstances could be in the crowd below me expressing the evil side of his nature. People exactly like them were in that crowd. People like Paul wouldn't realize what they were doing to me, yet they one day would be great followers.

"They're all dead, spiritually dead, and I'm going to take that away from them. I'm taking death with me to the grave, and I'm coming back to life and bringing eternal life." The people couldn't really take in what was happening on that cross. They couldn't see who I was and who my father was. The ultimate curse for spiritual blindness was, of course, physical death. Death was all around me.

Last Words

As these thoughts were passing through my mind, I listened to the prisoner on my right direct a string of profanities at the Romans. What else could they do to him? He figured he might as well get in his licks.

I looked at him and thought that he needed to be rescued from his anger, too. All these people could be reconciled with my father entirely and spend eternity with us if I would take away their evil from them. I thought back to that last supper and to my disciples. God knew how much I loved them. If it was my task to bring about reconciliation, I was going to do it like a champion.

Even during those horrible moments on the cross I was filled with the most indescribable love for my people. I wanted to bring them and my father together. I would do anything to bring about that oneness. This was my glory—to accomplish that reconciliation. That was when I looked down upon the crowd and prayed, "Father, forgive them; for they know not what they do."[68]

That was the first thing you said to the crowd from the cross. It was one of seven brief statements you made while you hung there.

I would think, "Father, punish me for their sins. Accept my suffering in place of theirs." My father took that opportunity fully to judge me. He did it in such a way that he was the one who put the nails in my hands and my feet, and he was the one who beat me. I became the most evil person in history. I was the chief of sinners.*

I was more determined than ever to go through with it even though I was still barely hanging on. My weakness increased the thirst. My tongue was so dry it was literally sticking to the roof of my mouth. I felt less and less able to cope, and the taunts hadn't let up.

All this had been going on for a long time then. It was past two in the afternoon.

Most of my bones were out of joint because of the continual weight I was putting on them. Every time I thought it was impossible for one man to suffer more pain, something else would happen. Whenever I moved, not only did the muscles in my back and legs hurt, but there was the most excruciating pain imaginable in my joints, particularly in my shoulders. I kept saying to myself, "It will not be much longer; not much longer. Most of the prophecies have been fulfilled. There aren't many left." The only thing that made me move was my shortness of breath, but I didn't know how long I would last. The Scriptures had been of some comfort, saying, "I the Lord thy God will hold thy right hand, saying unto thee, Fear not; I will help thee[69] and "weeping may endure for a night, but joy cometh in the morning."[70]

That verse particularly came to mind when the sky gradually turned as dark as night—something else my father did for me that day. About noon, with the sun beating down on me, the day grew dark, with a thick cloud cover overhead. I was in tremendous pain, with a mouth so dry I had no saliva, and all I could taste was dirt. Suddenly I could feel the coolness and see the black sky to match the dead skull. The breeze was like a cool washcloth to my face. With the black sky, God was saying, "I don't like one bit what you're doing to my son"—even though he knew the atonement was necessary. Silently, I thanked him, "Father, I know you are still with me." Between the unbelievable pain

---

* In 1 Timothy 1:16, Paul takes this title.

and the confidence that came from my father's comfort including living out prophecy, my emotions were swinging as far as you could imagine at any one time.

The darkness held another message: "I sent you the light of the world, and that light is going out now—pay attention." It was a warning that without me everything would be dark forever. Hell will be darker than you can imagine. I felt as if I were in it. The darkness seemed to go on and on.

I kept fighting to keep my head above the pain, but I was so exhausted I kept sinking deeper and deeper. Finally, I reached the point almost of irresponsibility. All I could hear was the ridiculing, and all I could feel was the pain. I couldn't hear my own voice. I couldn't speak.

Suddenly, the man on the cross to my left cursed me, "So you are the son of God. You can't even save yourself. Prove you're the Messiah. Save yourself, and us, too. Prove it. Prove it if you can." It was too much, the last thing I had expected. I had known that the crowd, and the Pharisees, and the Romans would ridicule me. I had known that my disciples would leave me, but ridicule from a criminal who was guilty was almost unbearable! The criminal on my right defended me: "Don't you even fear God when you are dying? We deserve to die for our evil deeds, but this man hasn't done one thing wrong." Then he looked at me and said, "Jesus, remember me when you come into your Kingdom."[71]

I looked at him briefly as we were both getting a breath, wincing in pain. You can't imagine what that man did to pick me up. He had given me strength. He had carried me on, and it thrilled me to say to him: "This day you will be with me in Paradise." Even on a cross between two criminals, my father had found a way to comfort me.

Satan had gotten his man into that drama. He was trying to get me to step outside my father's will, to "jump down," as he had tempted me to do on another occasion. Once again, he had used the subtle word "if." But in the unfolding drama, my father had also gotten his man next to me. This "useless" criminal had given me new strength. I was again reminded that it was worth it. Heaven would be full of people who stood up for me.

I looked at John standing there with my mother, and I told him, "Behold, your mother!"[72] I wanted him to take care of her.

By now my thirst was so great that finally I said aloud, "I thirst."[73]

They offered me some wine to kill the pain, and I refused. As much as I wanted relief, I refused because I was God, and I was accomplishing salvation not by numbing the pain but by accepting the pain.

My chest was heaving. The pain was now wearing me down more than ever. I was constantly short of breath and so thirsty.

It was extremely dark. It was past three in the afternoon by then, and I had been on that cross for more than six hours. Everywhere I turned, there was no relief. There was no relief even in thinking about all the memories—the last supper, the transfiguration, the miracles, or even my baptism. I could no longer hear those words "My beloved Son." They all seemed too far away, as if they had never happened. It was so hard to concentrate. Thinking about my future glory seemed too far away. I felt suspended in time, as if I had been there and would be there forever. The pain was unbelievable. The staring and mocking never let up. "So you trust the Lord. Why? Is he really looking after you? Healer, heal yourself." "Why don't you come on down, prophet?"

I was defenseless. My mother and John my friend were too far away to comfort me. I looked at the man on my right, and at that point he wasn't any help. He was in as much pain as I was. It was like looking in a mirror. Frighteningly, my father's words had no comfort for me now. "The Lord is my strength." I had no strength. His words seemed as dry as my mouth. That had never happened before, and I felt a terrible panic. I waited a minute and went back over his words, but it was only worse.

It became blacker and blacker for me. I was squirming like a worm on the end of a hook with all of my enemies watching me squirm and enjoying it. I was totally alone. Now my father was gone, too. I was dangling there, disfigured, gasping for air, writhing in pain. I was totally helpless. I wondered how much longer this would go on. Would it be forever? Time was standing still. The oppression was horrible. It seemed impossible that there could be this much pain. Every time I would try to get back up that mountain, "Think of your glory, think of why you are doing it, the Lord is my strength." Nothing—I would just fall back again. No comfort from his words. I wanted to run, to get down—but he was still my father—but now he was gone. My head was pounding, blood and sweat were in my eyes, my back and legs were rubbed raw, my hands and feet were on fire, my joints were throbbing, all out of place; I was constantly short of breath, and I was suffering incredible thirst. I couldn't take it any more. Suddenly I screamed: "My God, my God, why have you forsaken me?"[74]

When that came out of me something happened. I was back at the beginning of Psalm 22, and almost reflexively, I began to quote it from memory. Now I was back home. First that psalm went through all my experiences on the cross. My strength poured out like water, my bones out of joint. My dry mouth, the mockery, and the gambling for my robe were all part of it. Then the psalm comes to that great part, "I will declare your name to my brothers."[75]

There they were. I could see some of them. My spirit began to lift, and then came the next part of the psalm as though he were reading my mind: "For he has not despised or disdained the suffering of the afflicted one; he has not hidden his face from him but has listened to his cry for help."[76]

My father had heard me, and his voice was getting louder,

> All the ends of the earth
>   will remember and turn to the Lord,
> and all the families of the nations
>   will bow down before him,
> for dominion belongs to the Lord
>   and he rules over the nations. . . .
> Posterity will serve him;
>   future generations will be told about the Lord.
> They will proclaim his righteousness
>   to a people yet unborn—
> for he has done it.[77]

He was telling me that I had done it. When I got to that place, I began to feel an ecstasy. Good was greater than evil. I had done it. I had accomplished my task. I had given every last ounce of strength, and the fight was over. The son of God was the winner, to reign forever.

I looked out on the crowd. I knew I'd taken their evil away from them and not given it back. Justice had been done. I had conquered fear. I had conquered hatred. I had overcome all evil. I had defeated the cross.

The fight was over. I was still very thirsty, but I could wait for a drink because I was leaving, and where I was going I could have anything I wanted. In fulfillment of prophecy, someone offered to quench my thirst. Typical of the world, all they could ever offer me was bitterness. I drank sour wine, vinegar. They passed the vinegar up to me on a sponge, and I drank it. It was one final way of saying, "I take into me your bitterness."

Appropriately, that prophecy was from Psalm 69. That bitter psalm that had haunted me all my life, the psalm that had told me that I was to suffer unmercifully as a child and even more unmercifully as an adult on a Roman cross, that psalm whose every painful word I knew completely and had carried with me for years, now I could finally lay to rest. By drinking that cup, I was also saying one more time for everyone to hear, "Thy will be done. In the face of all the world's bitterness, to God be the glory."

Then I looked at the crowd and said, "It is finished."[78]

I suffered not one second longer. With the power of the son of God, I showed them that I gave my life, and nobody took it from me. I chose the moment of my death. For a few seconds, I intentionally paused and held my head particularly high as I looked out over the crowd to let them know I had conquered their shame. Finally, I looked up toward my father in heaven, took as deep a breath as I could, and shouted that glorious verse from Psalm 31 that I had waited for all my life, "Into Your hand I commit my spirit."[79] I left with my head up. It was over.

Burial

After you died, a Roman centurion who had witnessed the entire event spoke for all of us. He had watched how you had reacted the whole way from the flogging through the cross when the world had thrown everything at you. He observed that you handled it all like a king. The Roman soldier proclaimed for the whole world to hear, "Surely he was the Son of God!"[80]

I really did conquer the Romans as my people wanted me to do. I just did it in a way they didn't expect. My father and I didn't have to overcome the Romans. Those we wanted came to us.

What happened next?

After it was over, all the other events happened just as the prophets said they would, even down to the fact that the other two prisoners' legs were broken to hasten death, but mine were not broken.* Scripture had to be fulfilled. After I died, Joseph of Arimathea, one of the few Pharisees who had been a secret disciple of mine, came forward in a great act of courage to ask Pilate for my body so that he might bury it.

Pilate was shocked that you had died so quickly.

Pilate knew something was happening, but he couldn't quite figure it out. He couldn't control me *(laughingly)*. It was so obvious that I was God, and he wasn't. I chose when to die, and my father picked the circumstances. Pilate checked with his soldiers, and they confirmed that I had died, so he gave Joseph my body.

---

* Often a prisoner's legs were broken to hasten death, because the crucifixion was a long-drawn-out cruel torture. In this case, the Sabbath was rapidly approaching, and the Jews did not want men exposed on this day. Broken legs prevented a person from pushing up or breathing. Both men who were crucified with Jesus had their legs broken and thereby suffocated.

So two men named Joseph took care of you from the time you were born until the time you died.

Joseph of Arimathea, who was not a big man physically, got a ladder and with his big, beautiful robe on, in front of all of the people, including his peers, went up that ladder, got my body, and brought it down over his shoulder with my blood and dirt staining his clothing. Nicodemus, another Pharisee who believed in me and who had once sneaked out in the middle of the night to see me so that no one would know, now made his own courageous stand as well.

That's what my crucifixion will do for you when you understand it. Nicodemus started out being afraid to let people even know that he was interested in me. He kept listening to me and believing me, though, until one day I was his Lord, and he could say so in front of the whole world. He came with Joseph to the cross and brought embalming ointment made from myrrh and aloes. Together, in front of all of those people, they carried my body to the tomb and wrapped it in a long linen cloth and saturated it with those spices. Once again I was being wrapped in swaddling cloth.

The uniformity of the Scriptures never ceases to amaze me. You came into the world wrapped and went out wrapped. Through all his different coauthors, God continually puts down markers as if to say, "See how it all fits together."

The body that they were wrapping had no broken bones. One more time my father was saying the same thing he said in the third chapter of Genesis, "You can bruise my son, but you can't break him." He was also telling everyone that his framework will prevail. You can't break it. He's too strong. That was the message.

It was almost sundown, and the Sabbath was just beginning.* As Mary Magdalene and Mary the mother of James and Joseph watched, my body was taken to Joseph of Arimathea's personal tomb, which

---

* The Sabbath lasts from sundown Friday until sundown Saturday, and the Jews were not to do any work on that day.

was nearby. Joseph, who was a rich man, had a large tomb. That fulfilled the Scripture "And he made his grave with the wicked, and with the rich in his death; because he had done no violence, neither was any deceit in his mouth."[81]

I was taking another man's tomb, as I had taken his place on the cross. I died with the poor on the cross and was buried with the rich. I died for every man.

The Pharisees, in their usual manner, were going to stop God; so they got the Romans to put a seal on the stone that closed off the entrance to the tomb.

Some theologians have said that it was not your physical death that was important. The source of the atonement was your spiritual death, when God separated himself from you spiritually and, in some way laid on you the sins of the world. That was the point when you were the most troubled on the cross because you, being perfect, were so offended by this stench of sin.

In a real way he laid the sins of the world on me through my humanity. These people separate my spiritual nature from my human nature as if I were not one person. My human experience was in a significant way the means he would use to judge the world.

I told you what went through my mind in Gethsemane. He was judging me in every way human beings can be judged for every crime they have committed. By having those crimes committed against me, I felt every one of them. That was the offense. None of those crimes was who I was, and none of them did I deserve. It was a tremendous offense to me physically, emotionally, and spiritually. It violated my integrity in every way.

These people who say my human suffering was not important don't have a high enough estimation of humanity. They think my taking human punishment was not really important because they don't think being a human being is really important. They don't understand the incarnation.

How would you summarize what happened on the cross?

All your sins were destroyed on that cross. I acquired certainty for you. No one had ever conquered death before, even though I had prolonged the lives of a few people for a few more years. You now have someone who had made it through. It was my purpose to get there. I had to prove that love was greater than evil.

During your trial and persecution, even though you were being judged by your father, yet his words were with you. He was with you, as you attested when you gave your life.

Not for one second did he quit empathizing with me. In the midst of my pain, he felt every blow. At the same time, he judged me. His ability to do that made salvation possible. Without that greatness, everyone would be damned. It's amazing that a personality can be that dichotomous, can feel two powerful emotions at the same time and be fully conscious of both. He was pouring all that rage out on me, and yet, every second, he felt it with me.

As he judged me, he thought of every person in the world. When he had me called names, he thought of everybody who had ever called anyone a name, anyone who had ever gossiped. When he had me physically abused, beaten up, he thought of everyone who had ever been abused physically or ever thought about abusing. When he had them persecute me and kill me, he thought about all the dictators who had ever persecuted people. He thought of all of the parents who have abused their children and all the neighbors who have abused each other. Whoever you are, he judged you when he judged me. I can testify that you were judged. It was a tremendous judgment. It was so much that his sense of justice was satisfied forever.

My father is so much greater than you know even now. You will be shocked when you get to heaven, because of the wonders to be revealed. You are given glimpses of him here. Imagine a personality so patient that he can wait thousands of years to carry out his plan. Before he started on "this project," he knew exactly how long it would take, down to the last second. He is omniscient.

There is something tough about your father. He insisted that you pay the price for justice in full. Also, as you read the Old Testament, he repeatedly says, "Don't ignore me. If you do, you will pay an extreme price."

He's stern but intrinsically fair. Don't think that you can ever take advantage of him. Don't think that not everything counts with him. He's too important, and, in his image, he made you important, too. God will have you be who he made you to be, or he will turn you over to yourself. Then you can be your own god. Never think that you can take advantage of God.

After one full day, your body was resurrected. What happened? How did you feel, coming back from the dead?

Early Sunday morning Mary Magdalene came by herself to visit my grave. She had been unable to sleep that night because she was so grieved. Since she was lying awake, at the hint of daybreak after the Sabbath was over, she thought she would go out and visit my tomb. Later that morning she planned to return with several other women, including Salome and my Aunt Mary, my mother's sister. Caring not for her own life, and thinking only of me, Mary walked all the way to my grave alone in darkness.

Just before she got there, an angel suddenly appeared at my tomb. There was a great earthquake. Then the angel rolled back the stone from the tomb and sat on top of it. With his face brightly shining and his robe a brilliant white, he stared down at the Roman guards. They were so terrified that they fainted.

When they recovered and saw the huge rock still rolled aside and that the tomb was empty, they decided that their true friend was the chief priest, and not their superiors. They ran to the temple and told the priest what had happened. The priest paid them secret bribes to say that my disciples had come in the middle of the night and stolen my body while the guards were asleep. The priests promised these guards that if the story got back to the governor, they would take care of it, and the guards would not get into any trouble.

By the time Mary Magdalene got there the first time, all she saw was an empty tomb and my grave clothes. She ran to get Peter and John, and didn't yet comprehend that I was alive.

Immediately Peter and John ran to my grave. John got there first, but he wouldn't go inside. As usual, when Peter got there, he didn't hesitate. Unafraid, he walked inside the tomb. There he found the linens from around me unwrapped and left lying in a neat bundle. A napkin that had been around my head was lying to one side by itself. The angel had done that to let everyone know I was completely unwrapped. I was free of the tomb.

Did you see your father after that?

I did. You should have seen it when I first walked into heaven lined with angels shouting for joy and my father in his glory as I walked to him dripping in blood. That moment was preserved forever, and one day you will get to see it. That's all I can tell you. Read the book of Revelation if you want to know more.

The women who had seen me on that resurrection Sunday found the eleven disciples as soon as they got to Jerusalem and told them what they had witnessed. As usual, these men, destined to be world-famous apostles, didn't believe them. Not even Peter and John believed, and they had already seen that the stone was rolled back, and the grave was empty. Some of them ran out to the tomb again, but they still didn't believe that these women had seen an angel. After all, they reasoned, if an angel appeared, he would certainly visit the apostles first and not "just" women. Besides, who could really believe that Jesus was alive?

The disciples ignored my instructions to go to Galilee, and they remained in that room, filled with fear, as their once-dead leader roamed the world. Peter, however, being the man that he was, had a bit more courage because of the light that had been given to him at this point in the day. In daylight, with his life in greater jeopardy because of what he believed the Pharisees would do to him if he were caught, he returned once more to the grave alone. You don't think I would miss a chance to honor that kind of faith, do you?

Peter was the fourth person to see you that day.

After I appeared to Peter, I met two followers of mine. One was Cleopas, an uncle by marriage. His wife was my Aunt Mary, who had already seen me. These two men were walking to the village of Emmaus, about seven miles from Jerusalem. They were talking about my death as I came up beside them on their walk, disguised as a traveler. They were obviously distraught, and I asked them why they were so sad.

They couldn't believe that I hadn't heard about the death of Jesus whom they had thought was the Messiah before he was killed. These two men told me they had talked to Jesus' disciples that morning and had heard the women's story that Jesus had appeared, that he was risen from the dead. The disciples themselves had substantiated that the tomb was empty, but who could believe it? Who could believe hysterical women, even if one of them did happen to be Cleopas's own wife?

I told them they were very foolish. I wondered why it was so hard to believe what the prophets had written. What the women said had all been predicted in the Scriptures. I began at the book of Genesis and went through the Scriptures, quoting passage after passage from the prophets and explaining what they meant. By the time we got to Emmaus, they had learned much and were tremendously encouraged by the Scriptures. They begged me to go home with them.

You must have been an extremely comforting resurrected man. Even when you rebuked them, they still wanted you to come home with them.

As we sat down to eat, I asked God's blessing on our food. I took a small loaf of bread and broke it and began passing it to them. That was when they recognized who I was. As soon as they did, I disappeared.

Why did you appear to those two followers, who weren't any more spiritual than the eleven disciples? Why did you come to two men who weren't in your "inner circle"? We don't even know the name of one of them.

They weren't unknown to me. I knew both of them. I came to the whole world.

You appeared to your followers five times that day alone, not counting your journey to heaven. As I read the story, it's as though you are saying to the world in your typically subtle way, "See what I've done? I died for you—all of you."

The resurrection is the heart of it all.

Your fifth and last appearance of the day was to your disciples that night in Jerusalem.

It was Sunday night, and they continued to be frightened, in shock, still hiding out in that room. Peter and the two men I had walked with to Emmaus, as well as Mary Magdalene and the other women, had told them that they had seen me, but the disciples couldn't believe it yet. They had had one shock after another. Judas had betrayed me. I had been publicly declared a criminal and killed, and Judas had committed suicide. Then they had heard that my tomb was empty, and that I had appeared. They had visited the tomb and had seen nothing, and they were still too afraid and confused to believe.

Suddenly I walked through the walls and appeared in their midst. As I looked around the room, I was instantly reminded of our last meal together. It was so good to be back with them, and this time I was free. They didn't share my joy immediately. If you've ever been the ghost ten men think they're looking at, you'll know how I felt. I had seen it two other times before. So I said to them, "Peace be unto you."[82]

That just frightened them more. The ghost could talk. Then I said to them, "Why are you frightened? Why do you doubt that it is really I? Look at my hands! Look at my feet! . . . Touch me and make sure that I am not a ghost! For ghosts don't have bodies, as you see that I do."[83]

I held out my hands, and not one of them would touch me. They were so different from the two women I met on the road who wouldn't let go of me. The disciples just stood there paralyzed, half full of joy and half full of fear.

Finally I asked them if they had anything to eat. With his hands trembling, Nathaniel handed me a piece of broiled fish, and all ten of them watched me eat it, uttering not a word. At this point, my disciples were just beginning to believe. Joy was starting to win out, but they still didn't know what to say or do. I reminded them, "Don't you remember my telling you that everything written about me by Moses and the prophets and in the Psalms must all come true?"[84]

I looked around, and I could see that finally I had reached them. I continued, "Long ago it was written that the Messiah must suffer and die, and on the third day rise again from the dead. Then this message of salvation was to be taken from Jerusalem to all the nations of the world. There is forgiveness of sins for everyone who turns to me. You, my friends, have seen these prophecies come true. You are eye witnesses. Now, just as my father promised, I will send the Holy Spirit upon you."[85]

I told them not to leave Jerusalem yet. They would know when they had all their power from the father. I looked around the room again and said to them, "Peace be unto you: as my Father hath sent me, even so send I you."[86]

I then breathed on each of them, and gave them their authority, "Receive the Holy Spirit. If you forgive anyone's sins, they are forgiven. If you refuse to forgive them, they are unforgiven."[87]

The look on their faces was impossible to describe. One day you'll see a most beautiful painting that captured that moment exactly, and that piece of art will hang in heaven forever. The first supper with my men on this side was no different than the last supper on that side. I no longer had to walk by faith. The anxiety, the uncertainty that faith demands, was over. I had done it, and I knew they would also. Nothing could stop my church now.

As I walked through the wall and left them that night, I remember thinking: "One day they will have a body like this, too."

Fishing and Forgiveness

After your second appearance to your disciples in Jerusalem, your next appearance was not until several days later when your men were out in a boat fishing on the Sea of Galilee.

They had gone back to their trade temporarily to earn some money. Once again Peter and the rest had spent a long night fishing with nothing to show for their labor. I appeared as a man walking on the shore and called out to them to cast their nets on the other side. They did what I told them and, in just a few minutes, they had a superabundant catch. By this, I was telling them: "I meant what I said. I'm going to make you fishers of men." They caught one hundred and fifty-three large fish and the nets weren't broken, which again was my way of telling them my father and I had great plans for them and that they would be successful. Nothing would fail.

One of my favorite stories is what happened afterward when you had a talk with Peter.

When they all recognized who I was, who do you think dove out of the boat and swam as fast as he could to me? It was Peter. He came the same way he came the first time I called him from the shore when I was starting my ministry. Peter, the disciple who had every reason to fear because he had just failed me, swam to embrace me with his big heart. That encouraged the rest of the disciples. This time no one asked who I was. They knew.

I had a fire going and breakfast ready. Once again I served them bread and fish, which brought back all the memories of the times in the wilderness when I fed thousands of people the same meal. That made the disciples feel even more comfortable around me.

Then I went over and sat down by Peter, who, knowing himself about as well as a human being can, had assured me on the evening before my death that he would give up his life for me. Instead he denied me three times.

He had started out loyally after my arrest. He was one of only two disciples who followed my captors into the city. The trial was at the high priest's house, and the pressure became too great for Peter. All the religious power got to him. He was standing around the high priest's courtyard, and a servant girl asked him if he were one of my disciples. He replied, "Absolutely not." Eventually Peter was allowed inside the courtyard. As he was warming himself around the fire with some officials and servants, another servant girl pointed out Peter and said, "This man was with Jesus of Nazareth." Peter said forcefully, "I don't know the man," this time swearing as he denied me.

Another of the high priest's servants, a relative of the man whose ear Peter had cut off and who had seen Peter do it, came up to Peter, accompanied by several other servants and said, "I saw you in the olive grove. Your accent gives you away. You are from Galilee." Swearing loudly again, Peter replied, "I told you I have never known this man, Jesus." The third time he disavowed any connection with me whatsoever, the cock began to crow. Peter was devastated.[88]

For Peter to be afraid was a failure for him. This was a man you would want next to you if you were outnumbered in a fight. He had been the disciple who came to meet me on the water. He was not so awed when he saw me with Moses and Elijah that he couldn't help but offer to contribute his ideas.

He offered to build all three of you a temple.

He was a man of action. Like everyone else, he had to learn his limits.

He never thought that he had been afraid of another man in his life. Yet he acted as the worst sort of coward, denying the one person he loved the most. The way he did it bothered him almost as much. It was not just a casual "no." He had been vehement to the point of swearing. He couldn't stand up to three people's accusations that he knew me, and two of whom were servant girls.

It was a blow to think, "I, Peter, am a coward," but that's the end of the rope to which everyone must come. I knew that Peter was deeply ashamed, and that his shame haunted him. I knew that because I knew Peter.

When I sat down next to Peter the morning after my resurrection, I asked him, "Peter, do you love me?"

He looked at me, "Yes, Lord."

Then I asked him a second time, "Peter, do you love me?"

He looked at me and said with a puzzled and hurt look on his face, "Yes, Lord."

I waited just a few seconds and finally asked him a third time, "Peter, do you love me?"

He hadn't caught on yet, and he said, very humbly, without his usual forcefulness, "Lord, you know that I love you."

I looked at him and said to him, "Peter, feed my sheep."[89]

You gave him three more chances to answer the way he really wanted.

Later I gave him some real opportunities to feed my sheep.

Peter didn't know it then, but a great revival was coming soon, just as the book of Jonah indirectly predicted. In Jonah's day, an entire ruthless foreign nation turned to God when they saw a bleached white prophet wash up on shore after the huge fish spit him out. Now another prophet had come back from the dead. This time the prophet's disciples would be doing the preaching, and Peter was to be one of them.

The next thing I told Peter was that he was going to die for me. He would get his wish. I was going to enable him to die as a brave man, to look death in the face, and this time to stand up for me. As usual, Peter didn't hesitate to say what was on his mind. He wanted to know if John would be killed, too. I had to tell him that it was not his business to worry about John.

This incident with his disciples, and with Peter in particular, makes me realize how much our lives are like the widow's mite. None of us has very much to offer, but Jesus takes it and blesses it and it becomes a great deal. The idea predominates in Scripture. From the little boy Jesus took the small meal, and fed thousands. A woman took all her savings and bought a bottle of precious ointment and gave it to Jesus, pouring it over his head before his burial. Jesus accepted it and told her story around the world for centuries, thereby giving hope to millions of people who have only small gifts to give.

All the disciples, including Peter, had to learn the lesson that in ourselves we have little to offer God. Peter the braggart, the coward, the loudmouth, offered Jesus his "piddling" life. Jesus took it and blessed it and Peter became the dynamic preacher, the brave martyr, the rock of the church. This disciple who was once renowned for his cowardice would write the classic Christian text on suffering, the book of 1 Peter.

It was the same for all of them. Matthew, renowned for his greed, became a gospel writer. John, who wanted to call down fire to destroy a town and to be exalted above all the other disciples to sit on Jesus' right hand, became known as the apostle of love. These limited followers continue to bear fruit for Christ and to reveal how great Christ's promise of "success" to his men was despite their faults.

It was the same way in the Old Testament. Ten of the twelve heads of the tribes of Israel, men whose tribes bore their names, were traitors— Joseph's brothers. Christ chose to come out of the tribe of Judah, not out of one of the tribes of the favored Joseph or Benjamin. Indeed, Jesus intends to honor his people.

The Finale . . . The Commencement

Over the next forty days, another of those increments of forty, you appeared to your disciples only a few more times that we know about. You appeared to five

hundred of your followers at a special gathering. You also appeared to your
half-brother James on at least one occasion but the Scriptures don't tell us the
reason. Why was it James?

James was like Peter. He had failed me terribly. As a young boy, he
ridiculed me for "being illegitimate." He came with the rest of the family
to rebuke me as I made my public claim to be the Messiah, after he
had already witnessed my miracles.

I had grown up with James, and I knew how hard he would be on
himself for failing me. The same "strength" he showed in confronting
me would now be turned on himself. He had really called God himself a bastard, and he knew it. He was my brother, and I had to comfort him. I couldn't leave him with that on his conscience.

I knew that if I could channel his strong will, he would be quite a
leader of the church in Jerusalem at a crucial point in church history,
when the Jewish Christians were trying to ostracize Paul and the Gentile believers. Rather than taking sides and ridiculing the Gentiles as
he was being pressed to do, James counseled unity. That unity has
lasted to this day.

James had learned his lesson on humility well. He got the reputation for spending much time on his knees in prayer asking God for
the wisdom and power he didn't have. Other Christians called him
"old camel knees" for the calluses on his knees.

A few years later I made my last appearance on earth to Paul, the
future apostle. Like James, he had been my enemy. Unlike James, Paul
came to the point of persecuting and killing people for believing in
me. When he realized what he had done, he was filled with remorse.
For Paul to be the kind of leader I wanted, I had to appear to him to
reshape his strong will. I had to shape it away from the Law on the one
hand and self-condemnation on the other.

Paul did not have the Scriptures that emphasize grace and forgiveness to fall back on. I wanted a man who needed to understand grace
and forgiveness himself to write those encouraging texts. I had to have
a man who had a heart for sinners.

In choosing Paul and James to be leaders of the early church, along with Peter, John, and Matthew, God continues his pattern of selecting utter failures to carry his message of grace to a fallen world. As always, each messenger carries the message he himself had failed to hear at first. All had utterly failed their Lord initially. Obviously Jesus wanted forgiven people to deliver his message of forgiveness.

After your resurrection, the Scriptures always refer to your manifestations as appearances and not arrivals. It's as if they are saying that now you don't arrive anywhere, you are already there. You just appear.

At this point, I was manifesting omnipresence.

Several modern critics attack historic Christianity by saying that your disciples plotted to perpetuate the myth that you had risen.

The other thing these critics say is that somehow my disciples were fooled. They claim that my body was moved or simply misplaced. These are the two basic ways they attack my resurrection. The answer to both lies regarding my disciples is simple. Only certainty gives courage. The only way my disciples and other followers could have withstood the sword that came down upon them for the first three centuries that the church existed, a time of persecution beyond comprehension, was to have unwavering certainty that I was alive. Only that assurance gave them the courage they needed, just as the certainty that my father was alive gave me the courage I needed. Otherwise, as Blaise Pascal observed, my disciples, being the fickle creatures men are, would have crumbled in five minutes under the pressure.

There was no reason on this earth for them to perpetuate a lie. Only persecution lay ahead for those who said I was alive. Who would live a lie to be persecuted? However, the resurrection can't be contained. It has no capacity for secrets. My resurrection radiates power to anyone, even to a coward like Peter. That's why he was so different after my return.

If someone is having a difficult time standing up for you, would you say to them, "Look at my resurrection?"

If you look at my resurrection long enough, it will give you the same strength that brought me out of the grave.

The last speech you gave that we know anything about, you made to your eleven disciples on a mountain in Galilee. In it you gave them their task that has come to be known as "the great commission."

I told them to meet me at this particular mountain. After they had been there awhile, I appeared to them. Some of the disciples by then were getting accustomed to my new power and reacted ecstatically when I appeared. Others still doubted that it was really I. They still thought I was a ghost. The critics who paint my men as easily duped fools are far from the truth. My disciples came fighting the whole way.

As we were eating supper, I confronted them about their own belief. I talked about their stubborn refusal to believe me, the Scriptures, and the women who had seen the angels. They were just like modern men and women who can't believe in miracles. The prophets had told them what would happen, I had told them myself, and it had occurred exactly as we all had predicted. I wanted to know what it would take for them to trust me.

I let them think about that. We finished the meal in silence.

Finally, as they were looking around at that beautiful view from the mountain, I told them what I wanted them to do,

All power is given unto me in heaven and in earth.

Go ye therefore, and teach all nations, baptizing them in the name of the Father, and of the Son, and of the Holy Ghost: teaching them to observe all things whatsoever I have commanded you: and, lo, I am with you always, even unto the end of the world.[90]

John the Baptist had baptized only with water, but I would baptize with the Holy Spirit. As the father had sent me with a difficult task to perform and yet with great authority, so I was sending them. I had completed the first part of the mission. I had died for everyone. Now the second part was to be partly their responsibility. They were to let people know what I had done. Of course, I would help them with their mission, just as my father had helped me.

It was so like Jesus after he had sternly rebuked his men to give them a chance to redeem themselves with a great task. Again it was so like him to bless them undeservedly by giving them great powers just at the moment they had failed him. To the end, he remained their loving but demanding savior. Once again as he told this story, I felt an excitement that the disciples surely must have felt, too. As a believer, I was going to do things in the name of the Father and of the Son and of the Holy Spirit.

Apparently, following that talk you walked with your men back from Judea, near Jerusalem, to the Mount of Olives just outside Bethany, and there ascended to your father.

Just as I had had the advantage of talking with someone—the angels—before I began my mission, my disciples had the advantage of talking with me. They had many questions on that walk to Bethany. Many of them were the same ones I had had before. "When will we use our power? How will we know what to say? What should we do? Do you think we can handle that much power without abusing it? When will we see you again? When will you return?"

I told them what I had learned and said that their teacher, the spirit, who had been my teacher would show them the rest. They were not to know specifically when I would return. That was only for us to know, but I had given them the signs to look for. On that walk together, I could see their spirits picking up. I could see their boldness growing.

It became so strong that in the next few weeks after I left, they would all go back to the temple in Jerusalem, this time unafraid to declare publicly their faith in the living God.

When we arrived at Bethany, I gathered them around me, and, just like at the last supper, I told them I had to leave. I was going to the right hand of my father and would sit down at my place on his right hand. I promised them that one day I would return to the very spot on which they were now standing, the Mount of Olives.

I looked around one more time, touched each of them one last time, and blessed them. Then I began ascending into heaven. As I looked down at them, I knew what Elijah had felt when he left the prophet Elisha in the same way, and what the angels felt as they left me after my temptation. I knew certainty. I knew my men would do it. The gates of hell would not prevail against them, against my church. They were bold now, and they were one.

The disciples waited in Jerusalem as Jesus told them to do, and at Pentecost the promised Holy Spirit descended upon them with great power. It was a magnificent event. A sound like the roaring of a mighty wind filled the room in which the disciples were staying. A flame like tongues of fire was above each of their heads anointing them. They all began speaking in foreign languages they had never known before. That same day Peter preached and led three thousand Jewish people from all cultures to declare publicly their faith in Jesus the Christ. God gave Peter a thousand converts for each time Peter had denied his Lord.

Thus began the movement that within a few short years had so much impetus that, as Luke records, it turned the world upside down. The deeds which were to provide the power for this movement, whether for two thousand or two hundred thousand years, were the life, death, and resurrection of Jesus, the God-man.

Notes

1. see the words of Job's wife in Job 2:9
2. Galatians 3:13b NASB
3. Isaiah 53:7a NASB
4. Mark 14:36 NASB
5. Luke 22:40b NASB
6. Psalm 6:2–5 TLB
7. Psalm 116:3 TLB
8. Isaiah 53:7a NASB
9. Psalm 22:1
10. Hebrews 12:29
11. Job 13:15a
12. Luke 22:42b
13. see John 18:4–9 TLB
14. Luke 22:48 TLB
15. see Matthew 26:50
16. Matthew 26:50a TLB
17. see Matthew 26:53
18. Proverbs 20:30 TLB
19. Proverbs 22:15
20. John 18:23 TLB
21. Psalm 5:1a, 8 TLB
22. Psalm 7:1, 3–4a, 10a TLB
23. see John 18:35 TLB
24. see John 18:36–38a
25. Isaiah 50:6a NASB
26. Isaiah 53:5
27. Psalm 23:4a–b
28. Job 13:15a
29. Psalm 30:5c
30. Isaiah 53:7
31. Isaiah 53:5c
32. Psalm 30:1 TLB
33. Psalm 31:1a, 3–4 TLB

34. Isaiah 40:31
35. Isaiah 50:6–7 NASB
36. see John 19:5
37. see John 19:11
38. see Matthew 27:24–25
39. Isaiah 1:18b
40. see 1 Corinthians 10:13
41. Psalm 27:1b
42. Psalm 62:6b
43. Psalm 30:5b
44. Isaiah 53:7a
45. Isaiah 53:12d
46. Isaiah 53:4a
47. Matthew 5:9
48. Psalm 109:24–25 NASB
49. Isaiah 53:3
50. Isaiah 52:14b NIV
51. Psalm 69:4a NASB
52. Luke 23:28–30
53. Isaiah 53:5d
54. John 1:29
55. Isaiah 41:13
56. Isaiah 53:12c TLB
57. Isaiah 53:7 NASB
58. John 12:32 NIV
59. Psalm 62:6b
60. Isaiah 53:5d
61. Psalm 27:1a
62. Psalm 45:6a
63. Isaiah 9:6
64. Psalm 22:18 NASB
65. Psalm 69:2b–4a, 7
66. Psalm 69:9
67. Isaiah 25:8a–c TLB
68. Luke 23:34a

69. Isaiah 41:13
70. Psalm 30:5b
71. Luke 23:40–42 TLB
72. see John 19:27
73. see John 19:28
74. Psalm 22:1 NIV
75. Psalm 22:22a NIV
76. Psalm 22:24 NIV
77. Psalm 22:27–28, 30–31 NIV
78. see John 19:30
79. Psalm 31:5a NASB
80. Matthew 27:54b NIV
81. Isaiah 53:9
82. John 20:21a
83. Luke 24:38 TLB
84. Luke 24:44 TLB
85. see Luke 24:47–49
86. John 20:21
87. John 20:22b–23 TLB
88. see Luke 22:56–62
89. see John 21:15–17
90. Matthew 28:18b–20